US SUPREME COURT DOCTRINE IN THE STATE HIGH COURTS

US Supreme Court Doctrine in the State High Courts challenges theoretical and empirical accounts about how state high courts use US Supreme Court doctrine and precedent. Michael P. Fix and Benjamin J. Kassow argue that theories that do not account for the full range of ways in which state high courts can act are, by definition, incomplete. Examining three important precedents – *Atkins* v. *Virginia*, *Lemon* v. *Kurtzman*, and *District of Columbia* v. *Heller*/*McDonald* v. *Chicago* – Fix and Kassow find that state high courts commonly ignore Supreme Court precedent for reasons of political ideology, path dependence, and fact patterns in cases that may be of varying similarity to those found in relevant US Supreme Court doctrine. This work, which provides an important addition to the scholarly literature on the impact of Supreme Court decisions, should be read by anyone interested in law and politics or traditional approaches to the study of legal decision-making.

Michael P. Fix is Associate Professor in the Department of Political Science at Georgia State University. His research focuses on the evolution of law and policy over time. His work has appeared in numerous political science journals and law reviews including *Political Research Quarterly*, *Social Science Quarterly*, *Vanderbilt Law Review*, and *Justice System Journal*.

Benjamin J. Kassow is Assistant Professor in the Department of Political Science and Public Administration at the University of North Dakota. His research focuses on how judges formulate opinions and the impact of judicial decisions, broadly defined. He has published articles in a variety of journals, including *Political Research Quarterly*, *American Politics Research*, and the *Journal of Law and Courts*.

US Supreme Court Doctrine in the State High Courts

MICHAEL P. FIX
Georgia State University

BENJAMIN J. KASSOW
University of North Dakota

CAMBRIDGE
UNIVERSITY PRESS

CAMBRIDGE
UNIVERSITY PRESS

University Printing House, Cambridge CB2 8BS, United Kingdom

One Liberty Plaza, 20th Floor, New York, NY 10006, USA

477 Williamstown Road, Port Melbourne, VIC 3207, Australia

314–321, 3rd Floor, Plot 3, Splendor Forum, Jasola District Centre, New Delhi – 110025, India

79 Anson Road, #06–04/06, Singapore 079906

Cambridge University Press is part of the University of Cambridge.

It furthers the University's mission by disseminating knowledge in the pursuit of education, learning, and research at the highest international levels of excellence.

www.cambridge.org
Information on this title: www.cambridge.org/9781108835633
DOI: 10.1017/9781108891141

© Michael P. Fix and Benjamin J. Kassow 2020

First published 2020

A catalogue record for this publication is available from the British Library.

Library of Congress Cataloging-in-Publication Data
NAMES: Fix, Michael P, 1980– author. | Kassow, Benjamin, author.
TITLE: US Supreme Court doctrine in the state high courts / Michael P. Fix,
    Georgia State University; Benjamin J. Kassow, University of North Dakota
DESCRIPTION: New York : Cambridge University Press, 2020. | Includes bibliographical
    references and index.
IDENTIFIERS: LCCN 2020009495 (print) | LCCN 2020009496 (ebook) | ISBN 9781108835633
    (hardback) | ISBN 9781108812979 (paperback) | ISBN 9781108891141 (epub)
SUBJECTS: LCSH: Courts of last resort–United States–States. |
    Judicial process–United States–States.| United States. Supreme
    Court–Influence.| Federal government–United States. |
    Stare decisis–United States.
CLASSIFICATION: LCC KF8736 .F59 2020 (print) | LCC KF8736 (ebook) | DDC 347.73/365–dc23
LC record available at https://lccn.loc.gov/2020009495
LC ebook record available at https://lccn.loc.gov/2020009496

ISBN 978-1-108-83563-3 Hardback
ISBN 978-1-108-81297-9 Paperback

In memory of Hubert and Betty Smith

M. P. F.

For all of the South Carolina public law alums
(past, present, and future)

B. J. K.

Contents

Figures

Tables

Table of Cases

Acknowledgments

As is always the case with writing books, we could not have completed this one without the help of many other individuals as part of the process. We apologize in advance for any names we may have forgotten; of course, our aim is to acknowledge those who helped either directly with the book or in terms of inspiration and encouragement along the way. Whether this be family, work colleagues, graduate school colleagues, or others in our lives, acknowledging their importance to this effort is key.

We want to start by thanking the following individuals for reading portions of the book project, the prospectus, or some combination of both of these things. First, critical comments by Tom Clark, Susanne Schorpp, and Amy Steigerwalt on a previous working paper forced us to engage with questions that spawned the idea for this book. Next, we wish to give thanks to Wendy Martinek and Eric Segall for providing critically important comments on the initial book prospectus. As this is a first book for both of us, their experience and insights were valuable in helping us see the weaknesses in our initial idea and in understanding how to frame the full book in a more cohesive way. We thank the following individuals who read several chapters, either in book chapter form or in conference paper form: Mike Nelson read and provided substantial feedback on earlier versions of Chapters 5 and 7; Brian Frye provided helpful comments on Chapter 2; Anna Law and Tom Hansford read and commented on an early version of Chapter 5; and Brent Boyea read and commented on an early version of Chapter 6. Most crucially, we want to thank Todd Curry and Kirk Randazzo for providing feedback on the book in its entirety, before completion, with an ambitious turnaround time request. Your feedback has been integral to making the book a stronger one. We also want to thank the anonymous reviewers for providing very important feedback to the project, and, equally importantly, encouraging Cambridge University Press to give this book a chance.

Finally, we want to thank Matt Gallaway, our editor at Cambridge University Press, for providing us with tremendous amounts of publishing-related information and encouragement, and all the editorial staff who helped transform the book from a "long manuscript" into a finished product. Your patience, help, and belief in this project has been absolutely integral to helping us complete the book. Without your hard work, prompt answers to questions, and help navigating the editorial process, the completion of this book would certainly not have been possible.

Additional acknowledgments for Mike: As a first-generation college graduate, I have always felt like a bit of an outsider in academia. Having supportive mentors and colleagues throughout my time as an undergraduate, in graduate school, and as a faculty member have enabled any successes that I have had. Without Kirk Randazzo and Lee Walker seeing something in a poor kid with a thick Kentucky accent, I would never have considered going to graduate school or pursuing an academic career. I was then lucky enough to have both Kirk and Lee on my dissertation committee (along with Don Songer) at a different institution. Their continuous support throughout my career has always been a source of motivation for me.

I would also like to thank my colleagues at Georgia State University for their support. I am truly fortunate to be in an incredibly collegial department where everyone supports and encourages each other. Getting to go to work everyday and interact with intellectually inspiring colleagues and students makes me a better scholar. I would also like to offer my gratitude to some specific individuals. Countless conversations with public law colleagues Bob Howard, Susanne Schorpp, and Amy Steigerwalt have been valuable when I was fighting with various questions throughout this project. Additionally, Jelena Subotic, Jeff Lazarus, and others were extremely helpful when I had questions about the book publishing process.

Beyond my professional colleagues, the support of family has been essential both in general and for this book specifically. Anytime I felt the impostor syndrome that plagues many of us, my family has always believed in me. I especially thank Autumn and Savannah. In addition to their support, I appreciate their understanding when this book project led to me working lots of long nights and weekends when I would have normally been doing family activities. I also thank my mother and my grandparents for their constant support and encouragement. While my grandparents never completed high school, they were always some of my biggest cheerleaders (even if they did not understand exactly what I did). I wish they had lived to see the completion of this book, but I dedicate it to their memory.

Additional acknowledgments for Ben: Many have broadly inspired me along the way, including current and former colleagues. I want to personally thank all of my colleagues at the University of North Dakota's Department of Political Science and Public Administration for believing in the quality of my work. You have collectively been a great source of encouragement and help, from initial discussions about the book project to questions I have had about the publishing process. Special thanks are also due to my former public law colleagues at Georgia State's Department of Political Science. These include Mike Evans, Bob Howard, Susanne Schorpp, and Amy Steigerwalt. Thank you very much for providing me with help and encouragement regarding my career and research. Still other collaborators on other research projects have been especially helpful with guidance, mentoring, and support: these include Greg Goelzhauser, Matt Hitt, Ali Masood, Doug Rice, and Chuck Finocchiaro. I thank you all.

I also want to take a moment to thank my family, both close and extended, who have believed in me over my life. Your faith and interest over the course of my life and career have been critical. It would not have been possible to finish this book without your consistent encouragement and interest in my work. My mother deserves special thanks for her interest, enabling me to have research time when visiting so I could be as productive as possible, or encouraging me to take a needed break ... You should know that I appreciate these things greatly. Chris, Jenn, Matt, and Rick, you also deserve special recognition for your encouragement in my career and for lending helping hands and ears when I needed these things the most. It is impossible for me to repay this in kind, but for all of my family, both those specifically named and those unnamed, just know that I love you all.

Finally, I want to thank my former dissertation chair and mentor, Donald Songer. Unfortunately, while Don was not able to see the completion of this book, his encouragement for me to further develop my research agenda and his specific help on my first published article (in *Political Research Quarterly* in 2012), planted the seeds that germinated and led to this project. Don's steadfast support, and encouraging yet critical feedback, are tremendously missed by all of his former students, including me. Don, I thank you for providing me with the mindset and skills needed to be able to bring this project to completion, and for your constant encouragement and for prodding me to think about the implications of my theories. Without the support and prodding, I am sure that this book would not have seen the light of day.

1

Introduction

PRECEDENT, *n*. In Law, a previous decision, rule or practice which, in the absence of a definite statute, has whatever force and authority a Judge may choose to give it, thereby greatly simplifying his task of doing as he pleases. As there are precedents for everything, he only has to ignore those that make against his interest and accentuate those in the line of his desires.

Ambrose Bierce, *The Devil's Dictionary*

The role of precedent in the law is complicated. On the one hand, it forms the basis of common law. Adherence to precedent, a doctrine known as *stare decisis*, forms the foundation that allows for the fundamental principles of stability and uniformity in the law to be built. As the Supreme Court itself has stated, "*Stare decisis* is the preferred course because it promotes the evenhanded, predictable, and consistent development of legal principles, fosters reliance on judicial decisions, and contributes to the actual and perceived integrity of the judicial process."[1]

The alternative view, reflected in the above quote from twentieth-century satirist Ambrose Bierce, is closer to the view held by many modern legal scholars. Segal and Spaeth, for example, describe the formal legal rules found in opinions as "merely rationalizing decisions" (2002, 88). Similarly, Segall asserts that "the Justices [of the Supreme Court] employ the fancy but misleading jargon of constitutional law (text, history, and prior cases) to hide the personal value judgments that actually support their decisions" (2012, 3). Finally, and perhaps most closely reflecting the definition that opens this

---

[1] *Payne v. Tennessee*, 501 U.S. 808, 827 (1991).

book, Paulsen argues that "sensible notions of judicial integrity would seem to require acknowledgment that stare decisis is a doctrine of convenience, endlessly pliable, followed only when desired, and almost always invoked as a makeweight" (2007, 1209).

As with most things, the truth likely lies somewhere between these two absolutist views and varies greatly across time, space, and context. Formally, the US Supreme Court unquestionably has the last word on the meaning of federal law, and its decisions are binding precedents for all lower federal courts and state courts. Thus, it is possible that *stare decisis* is simultaneously treated by the US Supreme Court merely as an obstacle or a means to an ideological end when it comes to their own future decisions, but absolutely binding on lower federal courts and state courts (when the latter are deciding a federal question). The Supreme Court has made it quite clear that it views this as true with respect to both federal statutory and constitutional law.[2]

However, this leaves open two important questions. First, while the US Supreme Court views its precedents interpreting federal law as absolutely binding on state courts of last resort, do state high courts always share this view? Decades of research argues that the answer to this question is a resounding "no." This work shows that state high courts are motivated by a number of factors when determining how to react to a relevant US Supreme Court precedent such as precedent age, precedent vitality, ideological factors, and specific case facts (Canon 1973; Comparato and McClurg 2007; Fix, Kingsland, and Montgomery 2017; Hoekstra 2005; Kassow, Songer, and Fix 2012; Murphy 1959; Romans 1974).

Second, even if we were to ignore all of this research and assume that state courts of last resort *always* follow US Supreme Court precedents faithfully when deciding *purely federal questions*, how often do such cases actually come before these courts? The answer to this second question is that it is quite rare for state high courts to see cases where there are solely federal questions.

---

[2] See, e.g., *Martin v. Hunter's Lessee*, 14 U.S. 304, 348 (1816); *Provident Institute for Savings v. Massachusetts*, 73 U.S. 611, 628 (1867) ("the decisions of this court in cases involving Federal questions are conclusive authorities in the State courts"); *Sims v. Georgia*, 385 U.S. 538, 544 (1967) ("Such rule is, as we have said, a constitutional rule binding upon the States and, under the Supremacy Clause of Article VI of the Constitution, it must be obeyed"); *Rivers v. Roadway Express, Inc.*, 511 U.S. 298, 312 (1994) ("It is this Court's responsibility to say what a statute means, and once the Court has spoken, it is the duty of other courts to respect that understanding of the governing rule of law"); *James v. City of Boise, Idaho*, 136 S.Ct. 685, 686 (2016) (*per curiam*) ("The Idaho Supreme Court, like any other state or federal court, is bound by this Court's interpretation of federal law. The state court erred in concluding otherwise").

Most cases state high courts see involve issues of state law only or mixed federal and state issues. In cases involving a mix of federal and state questions, state high courts can use doctrines such as adequate and independent state grounds to avoid the federal issues and focus solely on the state ones. Thus, in many cases, state high courts are under no obligation to follow US Supreme Court precedent.

In this book, we bring a new theoretical perspective to enhance our understanding of how state courts of last resort use relevant US Supreme Court precedents. Our central argument is that while US Supreme Court precedent serves a vital role in shaping legal policy in the states, state courts of last resort retain the final word on the details. The ability of these courts to determine whether and how to use US Supreme Court precedents with minimal interference provides them with a high degree of independent control over state legal policy. One implication of this is that the decisions of the US Supreme Court do not directly impact citizens in their daily lives. Instead, the legal policy content of those decisions is filtered through state high courts where they can be followed, enhanced, altered, or even ignored altogether. Therefore, while the focus of this book is on the use of US Supreme Court precedent by state high courts, its implications go far beyond these fifty-two institutions to further our understanding of the development of legal policy in the United States more broadly.[3] How state high courts use US Supreme Court precedent is central to understanding many broader questions about American law such as how legal policy develops and evolves, the nature of *stare decisis* in a system of judicial federalism, and limitations on the impact of US Supreme Court decisions.

1.1 A TALE OF THREE STATE COURT DECISIONS

In *Greenwood* v. *California*,[4] the US Supreme Court first addressed the question of whether a warrantless search and seizure of garbage left outside of one's immediate property violated the Fourth Amendment. In addressing this question, the Court applied the two-part test from *Katz* v. *United States* asking whether the individual had a reasonable expectation of privacy and whether

---

3   There are fifty-two state high courts in the United States rather than fifty, as Texas and
    Oklahoma have two state high courts (Texas/Oklahoma Supreme Court for civil appeals and
    Texas/Oklahoma Court of Criminal Appeals for criminal appeals).

4   486 U.S. 35 (1988).

that expectation would be considered reasonable by society.[5] While the Court held that the first prong of the *Katz* test was likely met, the second part was not for three reasons. First, the Court noted that "[i]t is common knowledge that plastic garbage bags left on or at the side of a public street are readily accessible to animals, children, scavengers, snoops, and other members of the public."[6] Second, the Court noted that the fact the garbage was placed in its location "for the express purpose of having strangers take it" diminished any reasonable expectation of privacy.[7] Third, the Court held that police were not required "to avert their eyes from evidence of criminal activity that could have been observed by any member of the public."[8]

As is common following a major US Supreme Court criminal procedure decision, several state courts soon confronted cases with similar issues raising questions about how to deal with the new precedent. One of the first such cases came later that same year in *State v. Trahan*.[9] In *Trahan*, the Nebraska Supreme Court held that *Greenwood* applied to similar questions in Nebraska as its own "prior case law has been consistent with the *Greenwood* rationale."[10] Following Nebraska's lead, many other state high courts concluded that their state constitutions offered no greater protection over the privacy of one's trash than the Fourth Amendment did.[11]

Conversely, the New Jersey Supreme Court took a different approach in *State v. Hempele*.[12] The facts in *Hempele* were, in the words of the Court, "almost identical" to those in *Greenwood*,[13] as trash in a closed container left on the street for collection was seized by police without a warrant in the course of an investigation. Applying the recent *Greenwood* decision, the New Jersey Supreme Court found that the action did not violate the Fourth Amendment. However, the Court did not stop its analysis at that point. It then turned to a discussion of the search and seizure provision in the New Jersey Constitution. While noting that the relevant text of the Fourth Amendment and the New Jersey Constitution were similar, the Court emphasized that it was its role

---

[5] 389 U.S. 347 (1967).
[6] *Greenwood, supra* note 4, at 40 (internal citations omitted).
[7] Id. at 40–41.
[8] Id. at 41.
[9] 428 N.W.2d 619 (Neb. 1988).
[10] Id. at 623.
[11] See, e.g., *Rikard v. State*, 123 S.W.3d 114 (Ark. 2003); *People v. Hillman*, 834 P.2d 1271 (Colo. 1992); *State v. Donato*, 20 P.3d 5 (Idaho 2001); *State v. McMurray*, 860 N.W.2d 686 (Minn. 2015); *State v. Schwartz*, 689 N.W.2d 430 (S.D. 2004).
[12] 576 A.2d 793 (N.J. 1990).
[13] Id. at 798.

to make an independent assessment of the meaning of the state constitution nonetheless:[14]

> In interpreting the New Jersey Constitution, we look for direction to the United States Supreme Court, whose opinions can provide valuable sources of wisdom for us. But although that Court may be a polestar that guides us as we navigate the New Jersey Constitution, we bear ultimate responsibility for the safe passage of our ship. Our eyes must not be so fixed on that star that we risk the welfare of our passengers on the shoals of constitutional doctrine.[15]

In its analysis of the question under the state constitution, the New Jersey Supreme Court went through each of the three reasons given by the US Supreme Court in *Greenwood* to justify its holding that the Fourth Amendment did not protect garbage set aside for collection from warrantless searches. Additionally, it addressed two more arguments raised by the state but not addressed in *Greenwood*: "because [garbage] is pervasively regulated and because it is abandoned."[16] In each instance, the New Jersey high court held that the reasoning was not sufficient to overcome the reasonable expectation of privacy requirement of the state constitution, concluding that a warrantless search of garbage was a violation of the New Jersey Constitution. A minority of other state high courts have also found a state constitutional right in this area post-*Greenwood*.[17]

Finally, unlike either the Nebraska or the New Jersey high court, the Illinois Supreme Court avoided the larger constitutional question altogether in *People v. McNeal*.[18] Rather than wading into the debate over whether to apply *Greenwood* – like the high courts of many other states – when faced with a challenge to a warrantless search and seizure of evidence in a garbage can, the Illinois Supreme Court made no mention of *Greenwood*. Instead the Illinois Supreme Court ignored the *Greenwood* decision,[19] grounding its rationale for upholding the specific search in the case on exigent circumstances. In doing

---

[14] State high courts have the power to interpret constitutional rights under their state constitutions different from similarly – or even identically – worded protections in the federal constitution under the adequate and independent state ground doctrine. The adequate and independent state ground doctrine is discussed at length in Chapter 2, Section 2.3.1 of this book.

[15] *Hempele, supra* note 12, at 800 (internal citations omitted).

[16] Id. at 804.

[17] See *State v. Crane*, 329 P.3d 689 (N.M. 2014); *State v. Goss*, 834 A.2d 316 (N.H. 2003); *State v. Lien*, 441 P.3d 185 (Or. 2019); *State v. Morris*, 680 A.2d 90 (Vt. 1996); *State v. Boland*, 800 P.2d 1112 (Wash. 1990).

[18] 677 N.E.2d 841 (Ill. 1997).

[19] Interestingly, it also ignored one of its own pre-*Greenwood* precedents directly addressing this question in line with the *Greenwood* decision. See *People v. Collins*, 478 N.E.2d 267 (Ill. 1985).

so, it avoided any need to address the question of whether a privacy expectation in one's trash existed under the Illinois Constitution.

1.2 A NEW THEORETICAL APPROACH

The issue of whether someone has the right to be free from a warrantless search of their trash may seem like a relatively trivial legal question. At first glance, one may think that all we can learn from *Trahan*, *Hempele*, and *McNeal* is that such protections exist in New Jersey, but not in Nebraska, and probably not in Illinois. Yet, these cases illustrate a point that goes beyond these three cases or this single issue. In these cases we see a significant range of reactions that a state high court can have when faced with a relevant US Supreme Court precedent. Taken together, they illustrate some of the core issues with existing studies of state high court reactions to US Supreme Court precedent, thus providing a clear illustration of why the more comprehensive theory presented in this book is needed.

Much of the prior research on this topic has reduced state high court responses to a simple dichotomy: comply or not comply (see, e.g., Fix, Kingsland, and Montgomery 2017; Kassow, Songer, and Fix 2012). However, this represents an oversimplification of the process. True, one could consider the behavior of the New Jersey Supreme Court in *Hempele* as noncompliant, and one would not be wholly inaccurate. The New Jersey Court did not follow the relevant US Supreme Court precedent. This is the definition of noncompliance. The problem here is that questions of compliance alone are not theoretically sufficient for many of the questions legal scholars should be asking. Unlike lower federal courts, state high courts are not agents of the Supreme Court. They are bound to the Supreme Court's precedents only in matters of federal law. The New Jersey Supreme Court specifically recognized this, finding that "The Hempeles left their garbage at a location accessible to the public. They cannot escape the force of *Greenwood*. The garbage searches …were valid under the fourth amendment."[20] However, as noted above, the New Jersey Supreme Court also considered the separate protections afforded citizens of New Jersey under their state constitution, finding that the New Jersey Constitution offered greater protection than the federal constitution. To term this noncompliance – as many existing empirical studies would – would be conceptually inaccurate as it would ignore over a century of US Supreme Court doctrine holding that state courts are free to decide cases on adequate and independent state grounds.

[20] *Hempele, supra* note 12, at 799.

The Illinois Supreme Court decision in *McNeal* illustrates another issue with much of the existing research in this area. Most studies of state high court responses to US Supreme Court precedents derive the sample of cases studied from all state high court decisions that cite the precedent. Under such an approach, typical studies of state high court reactions to relevant US Supreme Court precedents would simply exclude the *McNeal* decision. This would not pose a problem were *McNeal* the rare example of a case where a state high court ignores a relevant US Supreme Court precedent. However, as we show throughout this book, such behavior is not rare at all. For example, in Chapter 5 we show that in nearly 11 percent of cases where *Atkins* v. *Virginia* (a Supreme Court opinion that banned the execution of intellectually disabled individuals) is a relevant precedent, state high courts fail to include even a single mention of the precedent. Even more remarkably, in Chapter 6 we show that state high courts ignore *Lemon* v. *Kurtzman* (a Supreme Court opinion that created a test to deal with Establishment Clause questions) in nearly half of all cases involving questions of religious establishment. Thus, while existing work has enhanced our knowledge of how state high courts react to relevant US Supreme Court precedent, it tells us nothing about why these courts simply ignore these precedents altogether in a nontrivial – and systematic – set of cases.

We depart from prior work in this area in a way that moves past these issues to help us understand *whether and how* state high courts use relevant US Supreme Court precedents. Drawing on extensive historical and doctrinal background, we develop a theoretical framework that recognizes the true complexity of the US Supreme Court–state high court relationship. While many view the relationship between the US Supreme Court and state high courts as either strictly top-down or top-down with competing pressures from other state actors (Benesh and Martinek 2002; Fix, Kingsland, and Montgomery 2017; Hansford, Spriggs, and Stenger 2013; Hoekstra 2005; Kassow, Songer, and Fix 2012), such a perspective is inconsistent with the US Supreme Court's definition of this relationship going back to some of its earliest case law. State high courts are only bound by the decisions of the US Supreme Court when two conditions are met. First, the state court must be deciding a purely federal question. Second, there must not be an alternative way to adequately address the question relying on state law alone (or the state must elect not to pursue such an approach).[21] Absent these conditions states are free to treat US

---

[21] There is one limitation on this approach. State high courts can use their state constitutions to expand individual rights, but not to reduce them. With respect to individual rights that are in both the federal and a state constitution, the US Supreme Court interpretation of individual

Supreme Court precedents in the same manner they do the decisions of other state courts: as authoritative but not binding. Moreover, in some contexts, the roles are fully reversed. The US Supreme Court has held that it must follow the interpretation of state high courts with respect to the meaning of their own state laws and constitutions when dealing with matters of purely state law.

While we start from a foundational understanding of the relationship between the US Supreme Court and state high courts, we also recognize that this interaction occurs in a complex political environment. State high court judges are not merely politicians in robes, but neither are they models of mechanical jurisprudence. As such, our theory of state high court responses to US Supreme Court precedent bridges our doctrinal foundation with a rich political science literature on decision-making on state high courts. Specifically, we recognize that, like all judges, judges on state high courts are driven by multiple goals, and chief among these goals is a desire to set legal policy in line with their preferences (Baum 1997). We further recognize that "judges do not judge in a vacuum" (Fix 2014, 134). Unlike their federal counterparts, the vast majority of state high court judges do not hold their jobs for life.[22] Instead these judges must either face the voters of their state in a bid for reelection/retention or depend upon reappointment by the political branches of their state government. As such, state high court judges operate within a political environment where their decisions could impact their professional future. Regardless of their method of retention/reappointment, state high court judges are cognizant of the potential backlash the political branches of their state's government can bring against them for unpopular decisions (Leonard 2016; Romano and Curry 2019).

The primary contribution of this book is to introduce a theory that recognizes the importance of the legal policy motivations of the judges on state high courts, the political environment in which they operate, and the legal foundation that defines the nature of the US Supreme Court–state high court relationship. We build from neo-institutionalist theories used to explain judicial decision-making on state high courts in other contexts (see, e.g., Brace and Hall 1995; 1997; Hall 1987; Hall and Brace 1992; Hoekstra 2005; Langer 2002). Consistent with this literature, our principal theoretical argument is

rights are in effect a floor below which rights protections cannot fall. However, state courts are free to interpret their state constitutions as providing enhanced protections of individual rights (Brennan Jr 1977), and they frequently do so.

[22] Only Massachusetts, New Hampshire, and Rhode Island give the judges on their highest court life tenure–although New Jersey does as well after surviving one reappointment term by the governor. However, in both Massachusetts and New Hampshire, this is somewhat limited as there is mandatory retirement after age seventy.

that the decision by a state high court regarding whether and how to deal with a relevant US Supreme Court precedent is affected by an array of legal, political, contextual, and institutional factors. While we explain the details of our theory in greater depth in Chapter 3, it is sufficient at this point to note that we view state high courts as having available to them a set of four possible choices each time they decide a case for which there exists a relevant US Supreme Court precedent. They can either follow the precedent by applying it to the case before them, cite the precedent in passing without providing any analysis, negatively treat the precedent by criticizing or distinguishing it based on the facts of the case, or simply ignore the precedent altogether by making no mention of it whatsoever in their decision (as the Illinois Supreme Court did in the *McNeal* case discussed early in the chapter). How they select among these choices will be a function of the degree of flexibility afforded them by the precedent itself, the applicability of other legal doctrines (such as adequate and independent state grounds), the facts of the specific case before them, their own past usage of the precedent, the institutional design of their state judiciary, and their state political environment.

1.3 A ROAD MAP FOR THE BOOK

The questions raised in this introduction are of significance both for our understanding of how legal policy develops in the United States, and also for larger, normative reasons. The average American knows very little about their state courts (McKenzie and Unger 2011), and media coverage of these institutions is relatively minimal compared to the US Supreme Court (Hughes 2020; Vining Jr and Wilhelm 2011).[23] Yet we argue in this book that these institutions possess significant power to shape the meaning of US Supreme Court precedents and sometimes to ignore them altogether. Thus, it may well be that uniformity of the law is but a myth. Rather than a single flavor of constitutional law in the United States, we may actually have fifty distinct versions. This suggests that legal scholars, the news media, and the mass public alike should give these institutions significantly more attention than they currently do. At the end of the day, an individual's rights may depend less on what the US Supreme Court says they are and more on how the highest court of that individual's state responds to the Supreme Court's decision defining those rights.

---

[23] Recent work by Curry and Fix (2019) suggests that in some cases, state high court judges themselves may be working to increase knowledge about their institutions through the use of social media platforms.

The remainder of this book will clarify our central argument and marshal empirical evidence to support our theoretical claims. Throughout the book, we focus on communicating complex technical or doctrinal points via intuitive explanations given as much as possible in plain English rather than relying on technical jargon. Specifically, we will proceed as follows.

Chapter 2 provides a historical overview of the evolution of *stare decisis*, or the idea that precedent should be binding on future court decisions, from its origins in medieval England to its modern form in the United States. This historical treatment provides context for the importance of our research question and shines light on some common misconceptions. Most importantly, the final section of this chapter provides a rich array of historical evidence to justify our departure from much of the prior literature that treats the US Supreme Court–state high court relationship as one where vertical *stare decisis* applies. Rather, using a thorough discussion of legal doctrines that (1) insulate state court decisions dealing solely with questions of state law from US Supreme Court review and (2) provide state courts the further ability to avoid US Supreme Court review even when federal and state law questions are mixed, we show that the US Supreme Court–state high court relationship is more akin to traditional notions of horizontal *stare decisis* in many instances. Our analysis of the history of legal doctrine in this area shows how these core legal principles facilitate a high level of state high court independence over legal policy even when faced with relevant US Supreme Court precedent. In addition to providing a basis for our departure from existing theoretical explanations of state high court reactions to US Supreme Court precedent, our examination of the history of doctrinal development in this area provides a foundation for some of the core assumptions underlying our theory.

Chapter 3 elucidates our theory of precedent usage by state high courts. We begin by providing a brief overview of the literature on state high court decision-making generally and on the use of precedent by state courts specifically. We then show how our new theoretical approach fits in with this existing literature, where it departs from these existing works, and the core assumptions on which it relies. We devote the bulk of the chapter to expanding on the core of our theory outlined above. Specifically, we discuss each of the factors that we argue determine state high court decisions on whether and how to use relevant US Supreme Court precedents, and how each of these factors should influence those decisions. Throughout this chapter, we make use of both anecdotal examples and analogies to help clarify our theoretical arguments.

Chapter 4 focuses on the data and measurement issues created by our new theoretical approach. This chapter begins by providing an overview as to existing approaches that have been used to examine how state high courts respond to US Supreme Court precedents. We continue with connecting key elements from our theory and explaining the empirical implications of the theory of precedent usage by state high courts that we create. We complete the chapter by presenting our new measure of precedent usage, which includes *all* possible ways that state high courts can respond to a US Supreme Court precedent.

Chapter 5 contains the first systematic application of our theory of precedent usage to a specific US Supreme Court precedent: *Atkins* v. *Virginia*.[24] We begin this chapter by providing some background on the importance of the *Atkins* decision and how it fits into the broader death penalty jurisprudence in the United States. We also provide a detailed discussion of how state high courts have dealt with (or avoided) the application of *Atkins* in their own cases where it was relevant. Following this in-depth examination of a few state court decisions, we then present our theoretical expectations as to whether and how we expect state courts to use this precedent in cases where it is relevant. Finally, using an original dataset of all state high court decisions where *Atkins* was relevant, we systematically test our theoretical expectations and discuss our findings.

Chapter 6 offers our second application of our theory, this time to state high court usage of the US Supreme Court's *Lemon* v. *Kurtzman* decision.[25] *Lemon* differs from *Atkins* on a number of important dimensions that make the two applications nice complements. In the case of *Atkins*, the US Supreme Court gave lower courts a relatively clear legal rule, but provided only a vague standard to guide the implementation of that rule. In *Lemon*, the Court created a three-part legal test for deciding Establishment Clause questions that was extremely vague, both in terms of the meaning of each of the prongs and when the test itself applied. Additionally, later decisions of the US Supreme Court generated questions among judges and legal academics as to whether *Lemon* remains good law. This makes *Lemon* an example of a precedent that provides maximum flexibility for state high courts in terms of how to apply it and whether they need to apply it at all, even when dealing with a federal question.

While the uncertain status of *Lemon* might raise questions about its usefulness as an application, it is important to note that it is not unique. It is far from the only precedent to be questioned in subsequent US Supreme Court decisions to the point of generating confusion regarding its continued value as precedent. While such precedents are rare, like *Lemon* they are often in areas

---

[24] 536 U.S. 304 (2002).
[25] 403 U.S. 602 (1971).

of law that are politically and legally salient. Structurally, the chapter mirrors Chapter 5. The results from Chapter 6 again provide evidence for our overall theoretical framework, especially as relates to the importance of legal factors in determining how state high courts respond to, and use, *Lemon* over time.

Chapter 7 provides our final empirical application. This application examines state high court usage of the US Supreme Court's recent Second Amendment decisions: *District of Columbia* v. *Heller*[26] and *McDonald* v. *City of Chicago*.[27] Like *Lemon*, *Heller* and *McDonald* articulate a highly ambiguous legal standard and are vague as to when the standard applies. Moreover, the Supreme Court has provided no additional guidance to state high courts following these decisions, meaning that state high courts effectively are able to discuss them in virtually any way that they please. However, in contrast to the uncertainty surrounding *Lemon*'s continued application in Establishment Clause cases, *Heller* and *McDonald* remain unquestionably applicable to cases involving Second Amendment rights. As *Heller* and *McDonald* were decided relatively recently compared to *Atkins* and *Lemon*, there have not been a sufficient number of state high court decisions where these precedents were relevant to undertake a systematic statistical analysis as in Chapters 5 and 6. Rather, we combine the use of descriptive statistics of overall trends in state court reactions to *Heller* and *McDonald* with an extensive analysis of the relevant decisions of three state high courts: Massachusetts, Illinois, and Louisiana.

Chapter 8 is the concluding chapter of the book. In this chapter, we focus on three goals. First, we summarize the overall findings and how they fit into our theory of how state high courts use US Supreme Court precedent. Second, we provide several interesting conclusions to help inform future studies in this area. We specifically note the importance of accounting for all possible options that lower courts may have when confronted with US Supreme Court precedent. We also note the utility of using a nominal measure of treatment types to examine how lower courts use US Supreme Court precedent. Next, we relax one of our primary assumptions to show that while the specific precedents we examine in Chapters 5–7 all involve highly salient issues, our theory is generalizable to state high court reactions of non-salient precedents as well. Finally, we discuss several future areas of research that naturally draw from – and extend – the theory and findings from our book to additional contexts.

---

[26] 554 U.S. 570 (2008).
[27] 561 U.S. 742 (2010).

2

The Role of Precedent

A *Brief History*

To place our work in context, it is important to provide a brief discourse on the role of precedent in American law. To do this it is necessary to understand how the modern concept of *stare decisis* – or the belief that courts should view the decisions of higher courts (and in some cases their own precedents) as binding authorities – developed. The view of *stare decisis* as a hard rule of judicial decision-making is not traceable to a single point in history. Rather, it evolved over hundreds of years of English jurisprudence. While there are records of judgments made in accordance with custom and tradition as far back as the sixth century (Lewis 1930a), it was not until the eighteenth or nineteenth century that modern notions of precedent as binding authority truly developed. Thus, our brief discourse on the role of precedent in American law requires that we first delve into the history of precedent in English common law from whence our legal traditions have their origins.

2.1 THE ORIGINS OF *STARE DECISIS*

The Plea Rolls represent the earliest records of English court proceedings. These documents were not public and only certain individuals had access to them (Lewis 1930a). It is unclear from the historical record when officials first began recording court proceedings in the Plea Rolls, although some remain today from as early as the twelfth century (Richardson 1922). The few remaining Plea Rolls, some records of litigation in monastic annals (Maitland 1907), and other miscellaneous sources of scattered records illustrate that attempts at preserving case law prior to the thirteenth century were haphazard at best. Therefore, while the historical evidence shows that some court records were clearly kept, the lack of a systematic method for doing so indicates that they were not used in the same way they are in the modern day.

Things began to change in the thirteenth century, first from the work of Henry de Bracton and later with the development of the first collections of case law in the Year Books. Yet, these first efforts at compiling records of court proceedings bore little resemblance to their modern-day counterparts. Change came slowly over the course of centuries as the Year Books gave way to the period of unofficial court reporters. From the sixteenth through the nineteenth centuries, case records in the English courts, as well as the American colonies (and later states), vary widely in quality, style, accuracy, and thoroughness. However, the best of these reporters laid the groundwork for modern case reporting and the evolution of *stare decisis*. Tracing this evolution is essential for understanding the role of precedent in the common law courts of today.

2.1.1 *The Earliest Systematic Court Records: Bracton and the Year Books*

Historians generally credit Bracton, a thirteenth-century jurist, as the first to compile large numbers of case records. He produced two works of note. The first, *Legibus et Consuetudinibus Angliae*, contains citations to around 500 cases and was the sole treatise to undertake an explanation of the whole of English law until Blackstone (Zane 1907). Second, his *Note Book* provided summaries of 2,000 cases from various English common law courts of his day (Lewis 1930a). Bracton's view of the authority of these decisions was not the same as today. His usage of past court decisions was in large part due to his personal belief that the judges of his day were inferior to those of the past and were perverting the law (Lewis 1930a; Plucknett 1929). Bracton thus saw his compilation of past cases as more of a teaching tool than as something to be cited in court (Lewis 1930a). Nor did he venerate precedents that he disliked, as he would frequently interject criticisms of the cases he compiled (for examples, see Lewis 1930a, 211).

Despite these qualifications, Bracton did lay the groundwork for the eventual development of precedent in its modern form in two ways. He was the first to actively cite past cases as evidence, albeit not as authority, for a particular legal rule or principle (Lewis 1930a). Second, and more indirectly, Bracton's writings had a significant influence on his contemporaries and likely influenced the development of the Year Books that would follow shortly after his time (Plucknett 1929).

Beginning in 1268, the first year of the reign of Edward I, a quasi-systemic collection of some English court decisions began in the form of the Year Books. These were a precursor to modern case reports, although they were quite different in form and style. Rather than simply reporting the decision of a court, the Year Books would contain aspects of the case that today would not be part of the record, including "the arguments of counsel, the remarks of the judges during argument, the skillful plea of the one lawyer, the adroit shift of the other" (Zane 1907, 650–651).[1] They also included commentary by the reporters that would criticize the quality of arguments, decisions, and even the habits of particular jurists, thus supporting the conclusion that despite some historical confusion, the reporters who compiled the Year Books did not do so in any official capacity (Holdsworth 1907; Lewis 1930a; Zane 1907).

While there are some examples of specific references to the importance of individual decisions in the Year Books (for examples see Holdsworth 1907, 111; Plucknett 1929, 345–346), there was no expectation that the cases reported in the Year Books would be treated as precedent in the modern sense, nor that citations to specific cases would be made. In fact, Lewis (1930a, 221–222; see also Holdsworth 1907, 111) highlights some examples in the Year Books of judges specifically stating that precedents were not to be considered authorities. Moreover, even when cases were cited, the form was very different than in the modern day. Rather than referencing cases by the parties or a formal citation, they

> usually took the form of an appeal to memory. Judges and counsel gave their recollections of what had happened in cases in which they themselves had taken part, or which they had heard, when such cases resembled the one before the Court, and it was presumed that all present would remember them. The personal element was predominant, as opposed to the reference by time and place. (Lewis 1930b, 341)

Thus, it is relatively clear that nothing approaching modern reliance on precedent existed in England by the end of the Year Book period in 1535. Yet to treat all the Year Books as identical would be a disservice. Clearly, there was evolution toward something more modern over the course of the nearly 300 years in which the Year Books were produced. Lewis (1931) notes several differences in the Year Books beginning during the reign of Henry VI in the fifteenth century. Specifically, he describes the Year Books during this time and afterward as providing more information about the arguments made and greater detail about the "points of law," explaining this as a result of the reporters "becoming masters of their art" (Lewis 1931, 357). However, in later years, the publication of the Year Books became more sporadic

---

[1] The remarks recorded can make one wonder if judges of that time shared the same directness as some of today's television judges. For example, Holdsworth (1907, 117) provides an account of a fourteenth-century judge telling a defendant to "go to the great devil."

(Holdsworth 1907), and eventually were stopped altogether in 1535 as part of Henry VIII's attacks on the common law system (Plucknett 1932).

2.1.2 *The Gradual Modernization of Case Reporting*

The same year that saw the last of the Year Books also saw the beginning of private, unofficial court reports as the primary mechanism for providing access to the records of court decisions. For nearly 250 years, these reports largely mirrored the Year Books in their more informal style as compared to the modern system. Lacking any official court reporter,[2] hundreds of different reporters, of various quality, published their notes during this period (Veeder 1907b). Despite these issues, this still shows an evolution toward a more modern idea of precedent, as the importance of maintaining records of cases was in large part responsible for the explosion in the number of individuals privately publishing court reports. It is worth briefly highlighting three key reasons why the historical record supports this claim.

First, the timing of these earliest reports is itself a clear indication of the importance of maintaining records by this point in legal history. As Lewis (1932, 230) observes, "[t]he fact that Plowden and Dyer took up the work of reporting when the last manuscript Year Book appeared in 1535, is a good illustration of the dependence of the law upon judicial decisions." The first reporters began their work in line with the old adage that necessity is the mother of invention. Despite their flaws, the Year Books had, by this point, become an indispensable resource to judges, attorneys, and law students. Thus, when their publication ceased, it became essential that something replaced them.

Second, we know that the reporters during this period included judges, clerks, and attorneys of various rank and quality. As such, the reports these individuals published were largely a collection of their private notes from cases they cited, were party to, or heard about from their professional colleagues (Veeder 1907b). In fact several reporters, including two of the most prominent of this period – Plowden and Coke – noted that they never originally intended for their notes to be published (Lewis 1932, 230). The fact that the individuals kept such extensive records for their own use shows the importance of having access to records of cases for those same groups that rely upon them today.

---

[2]   While there was no regular official court reporter in England prior to 1865, there were brief moments when reporters were officially appointed with a salary paid by the Crown. For example, in 1617 King James I appointed an official reporter for the court at Westminster at the insistence of Lord Bacon (Holdsworth 1907). However, this practice was sporadic at best and represents an exception rather than the general rule.

This serves to explain the somewhat scattershot nature of these early reports as there was not yet any systematic attempt to collect all court decisions in a single place. It also accounts for the dramatic variation in the quality of the different reports.

Third, we can see from these reports an increased use of citations to prior cases in court proceedings. As discussed above, references to prior cases were scarce in cases discussed in the Year Books, and on the rare occasion that such a reference did occur, it was generally a vague reference rather than a citation of a specific case as in modern fashion. However, by this period, citations to prior cases had grown in frequency. Between the time of Plowden and that of Coke the number of cases cited had increased by a factor of 16 (Lewis 1932, 236). Moreover, the form of those citations had evolved as well. At least by the time of Coke in the early seventeenth century, citations to specific cases had replaced references to general principles as the routine approach of counsel (Lewis 1932). To this end, Coke is credited as being among the first to rely on a substantial number of citations to past cases, including Year Book cases (Healy 2001). Even though precedent was not viewed as binding at this point, this was still a key step in the evolution of *stare decisis*. Direct citation of past cases provided strong evidence that the individual cases were viewed as important rather than simply examples of general principles.

The fact that many reporters of lesser quality and ability were publishing reports simultaneously should not detract from the fact that the best published during this period approximated something much closer to modern case reports than to the Year Books. In providing a summary description of the major reporters of this period, Lewis describes the work of Plowden, the first of these reporters, as reporting cases with "absolute clearness [on] the points at issue, the arguments of counsel, the judgments and the grounds therefor" (1932, 232). Similarly, Veeder describes Plowden's work as "accurate and complete" and "sparing in comment" (1907b, 130). Plowden also started the modern norm of providing a title for each case with the date, names of the parties, and other information (Veeder 1907b). Like Plowden, modern legal historians hold Coke in high esteem. However, Veeder (1907b, 130) notes that unlike Plowden, Coke often added his own commentary, including editing the opinion of the court in line with his personal views. Nonetheless, Coke was still respected such that no other reporters published competing reports during his time.

Moreover, the increased usage of citations to precedents – whether a product of improved case reporting or simply a coevolving trend facilitated by better reporting – led to the view of precedents as clearly authoritative by the early seventeenth century. Yet, precedents were still not considered binding, even in hierarchical fashion, at this point (Lewis 1932). Even Coke did not view precedents as binding (Wise 1974). Additionally, following Coke, the trend of multiple reporters of various quality and reliability publishing different, and sometimes conflicting,[3] reports resumed (Lewis 1932). Thus, while some of the improvement in the quality of reports was retained during this period, the continued variation in quality and dependability – combined with the continuing belief in natural law as the highest guiding principle – hampered the development of a strong view of binding precedent (Healy 2001, 67–69).

The establishment of the modern system of systematic reporting under the authority of the Incorporated Council of Law Reporting formed by the Bar to overcome the problems already discussed did not occur until 1865 (Veeder 1907b). Yet, the importance of precedent and the need for more modernized court reports continued to evolve throughout this period. Two final items from this time period are worth attention, the first being the publication of Blackstone's *Commentaries on the Laws of England* in the 1760s. Blackstone was among the first to take a strict view of the role of precedent, writing that it was "an established rule to abide by former precedents, where the same points come again in litigation," with the only exception being for those precedents that are "flatly absurd or unjust" (quoted in Lewis 1932, 246). Blackstone's strong view of the binding nature of precedent was not widely shared in his time (Lewis 1932). This is perhaps best illustrated by his contemporary, Lord Mansfield, who would frequently depart from existing precedents in line with his view that "precedent, though it be Evidence of law, is not Law itself, much less the whole of the Law" (quoted in Healy 2001, 72; see also Lewis 1932). Nonetheless, Blackstone's *Commentaries* would go on to have a strong influence on the future development of the common law in both England and the United States, with the former continuing to rely on his work even to the present day and the latter using it as the "repository of the common law" from which its own law had its genesis (Brunner 1907, 51).[4] Thus, while his strong view of precedent was a minority view in his own day, it would eventually play a substantial role in the evolution of *stare decisis*.

The second was the continued modernization of the style in which cases were reported. The fact that Coke's reports were looked to as the height of excellence during his time – despite haphazard organization and some inaccuracies (Veeder 1907b) – shows how far from the modern style reports

---

3 For an example, see Fix's (2016a, n.7) discussion of the differences in *Le Roy* v. *Sedley*, 1 Sid 168 (1663) and *Sir Charles Sydlyes's Case*, 1 Keble 620 (1663).

4 Even in the twenty-first century, the US Supreme Court still makes reference to Blackstone in its discussion of the history of various legal doctrines. See, e.g., *Obergefell* v. *Hodges*, 135 S.Ct. 2584, 2595 (2015); *McDonald* v. *City of Chicago*, 130 S.Ct. 3020, 3036–3037 (2010); *Gamble* v. *United States*, 139 S.Ct. 1960, 1969 (2019).

remained in the early seventeenth century. However, a major change in stylistic focus came only a few decades after Coke. Burrow, whose reports cover the period from 1757 to 1771, hearkened back to Plowden in terms of purpose by focusing on maintaining a high degree of accuracy.[5] Yet, perhaps more impactful was the modernization in style adopted by Burrow. Veeder concisely describes Burrows as: "the first reporter to appreciate the advantage of prefixing to the report of each case a statement of the facts and issues separate from the opinion of the court, and following in regular order with the arguments, the opinions of the judges, and the judgment of the court" (1907b, 144).

Thus, by the end of the eighteenth century, changes in attitudes towards precedent and the nature of case reports had paved the way for the development of modern notions of *stare decisis*. While not widely adopted at this point, one of the period's most prominent jurists was already promoting the idea of a strong view of binding precedent. Moreover, increased accuracy in reports and the modernization of style had made it easier for judges and attorneys to rely on precedents with reduced concern for errors in the reports.

2.1.3 *Precedent and Case Reporting in the American Colonies and the Early Post-independence Period*

The courts of the US colonies largely mirrored the English courts of the eighteenth century, with a weak reliance on precedent. Some historians go so far as to describe the view of seventeenth- and eighteenth-century colonial courts toward precedent as being even weaker than their English contemporaries (Healy 2001; Reinsch 1907). Clearly, the origins of American law lie in the common law of England, yet the law of the colonies was written and implemented in a way that was quite different than that from whence it derived. In the early colonial period, the legal needs of the colonies were much different than those of England. Small populations with few, if any, formally trained lawyers led to the de facto development of a "rude, popular, summary kind" of administration of justice (Reinsch 1907). In such an environment, precedent carried even less weight than in the English courts of the time. Rather than viewing themselves as bound by either the precedents of English courts, or even their own prior decisions, the courts of the pre-independence colonies "demonstrated a marked preference for adaptability over certainty, for latitude over restraint" (Healy 2001, 73).

---

[5] Veeder (1907b) does note that while Burrow is considered to have been highly accurate in his reporting, he only paraphrased the opinions of the judges rather than reporting them verbatim so there are potential errors in his reports.

Three factors largely drove this weak view of precedent in the early colonies. First, as noted above, the legal needs of the early colonies necessitated a more flexible approach to the law that was adaptable to the unique needs of the colonies. Second, during the colonial period, many of the judges lacked formal legal training and access to legal reference materials and other resources (Healy 2001). This created a scenario where many did not know that relevant precedents existed or, in some cases, even that precedent was a core component of the common law system. Finally, many of the colonies placed religious doctrine at the core of their system of laws. In Massachusetts, the elevation of God's law over the common law is exemplified in the *Body of Liberties*,[6] which proscribed that "[i]n all criminal offenses where the law hath prescribed no certain penalty, the judges have power to inflict penalties according to the rule of God's word" (quoted in Reinsch 1907, 374).

As the colonies grew, and the population with formal legal training expanded, the law grew more formal in its administration. Yet, even as this occurred, the degree to which the colonies faithfully incorporated the English common law or their own precedents varied greatly. Some colonies, such as the Carolinas, Maryland, and Virginia, formally adopted the English common law as governing in absence of legislation (Reinsch 1907). Conversely, others, like Massachusetts and Pennsylvania, continued to use religious scripture as the guiding principles for judges to follow (Reinsch 1907). Yet, even in those colonies that formally adopted English common law, the colonies often allowed themselves to diverge from it when it was antithetical to their own customs and established practices (Healy 2001).

After independence, all of the the original colonies formally adopted the common law (Healy 2001). Additionally, the US Supreme Court made it clear early on that the origin of American law was in the English common law. Yet, this was never seen as absolute. The dominant theory of the relationship between English common law and early (post-independence) US law is perhaps best summarized in the US Supreme Court's 1829 decision in *Van Ness* v. *Pacard*. Writing for a unanimous Court, Justice Story declared:

> The common law of England is not to be taken in all respects to be that of America. Our ancestors brought with them its general principles, and claimed it as their birthright; but they brought with them and adopted only that portion which was applicable to their situation.[7]

---

[6] The Massachusetts *Body of Liberties* was the first legal code to be established in any of the New England colonies. Written in 1642 it heavily reflected the values of the Puritans who founded the colony.

[7] 27 U.S. 137, 144 (1829).

Thus, the US Supreme Court saw English common law as the progenitor of American law, while recognizing that much as any organism changes over successive generations to fit its environment, so too does the law.[8] Likewise, in the courts of the states there was a recognition that while the law had its origins in the English common law, it was necessary to depart from those traditions when they would lead to outcomes that were "illogical, unreasonable, or inconsistent with public policy" or when they were decided by an English court *after* 1776 (Healy 2001, 79–80).

In practice, the use of English case law by post-independence state courts was varied. Despite the apparent clarity of standards like those discussed above, flexibility remained the de facto rule. Healy (2001, 78–81) provides numerous examples of instances where the courts of New York, Pennsylvania, Connecticut, and Virginia specifically decline to apply relevant English precedents due to their incompatibility. The most extreme example is Kentucky, where the state legislature prohibited the use of English law in the commonwealth by statute (Kempin 1959). Interestingly, the Supreme Court of Pennsylvania in the 1786 case of *Kerlin's Lessee* v. *Bull* cites English precedent to justify the right of a court to ignore what it considers an erroneously decided precedent. The Court here quotes directly, writing that "if a judge conceives that a judgment given by a former court is erroneous, he ought not in conscience to give the like judgment."[9] Yet, the same court felt perfectly justified a few years later in relying heavily on English precedent in upholding a conviction for the exhibition of an indecent picture, justifying the decision as part of the obligation of courts to protect public morals under the common law.[10]

With respect to their own precedents, the American courts of the early nineteenth century mirrored the English courts of that time in viewing them as strong authorities, but not as completely binding. In part this was a function of a lack of available information. Court reporting in the United States during this period was largely compiled by unofficial reporters who varied in quality,

---

[8] See Fix (2016a; 2018) for a thorough discussion of the parallels between the evolution of the law and the evolution of biological organisms.

[9] 1 Dall. 175, 178 (Pa. 1786) (quoting Vaugh. 383).

[10] The Supreme Court of Pennsylvania in *Commonwealth* v. *Sharpless*, 2 Serg. & Rawle 91 (1815) directly cited the decision of the Court of the King's Bench in *R.* v. *Curl*, 2 Str. 788 (1727). Additionally, as Fix (2016a) notes, the Massachusetts Supreme Judicial Court expressly relies on *Curl* in two cases dealing with the printing of obscene materials. These decisions are not outliers. In the area of obscenity law, U.S. state courts used English precedents in this area well into the twentieth century (for a thorough discussion, see Fix 2016a). This is especially interesting given that the decision of the Supreme Court of Pennsylvania in *Sharpless* came only five years after the Pennsylvania legislature adopted a statutory prohibition on the use of post-1776 English court decisions almost identical to the Kentucky law discussed above.

thoroughness, and speed of publication. Even the early US Supreme Court lacked an official reporter and the reporters from its earliest terms published incomplete records of the Court's decisions (Healy 2001; Joyce 1985). This was exacerbated by the fact that the Court itself did not issue written opinions in its early terms. The situation in the US states was even worse, with the absence of official reports continuing into the nineteenth century and most states not adopting official reporters until the 1840s and 1850s (Kempin 1959).

2.2 THE ADOPTION OF THE STRONG VIEW OF PRECEDENT IN ENGLISH AND AMERICAN LAW

It was not until well into the nineteenth century that a strong view of *stare decisis* took its place in the English and American legal systems.[11] In both the English and American systems, a strong view of vertical *stare decisis* took root by the mid-nineteenth century. Vertical *stare decisis* refers to the doctrine that lower courts were bound by relevant precedents of higher courts. However, the English and American courts took somewhat divergent evolutionary pathways with respect to their views on the binding nature of horizontal *stare decisis*, or the degree to which a court is bound by its own prior precedents. The English courts of the nineteenth century would adopt the view that horizontal precedent was equally as binding as vertical precedent. However, the American courts would only adopt the latter as absolutely binding. Even after backtracking from the view of absolutely binding horizontal precedent at the highest levels of the English court system, it would remain stronger there than in the United States.

2.2.1 *Toward an Absolute View of Precedent and Back Again: England in the Nineteenth and Twentieth Centuries*

In England, two major factors combined to bring about a significant evolution in the view of precedent. First, the *Judicature Act* of 1873 led to a massive reorganization of the court system in England. As part of this reorganization, several inefficiencies born of the historical development of the English courts were done away with, including the existence of several courts with overlapping jurisdiction and the separation of law and equity (Veeder 1907a;

---

[11] The use of the term *stare decisis* is almost exclusively American (Williams 1926). Nonetheless, we use that term when discussing the behavior of English courts when they conform to the principle, even if other terminology is used by the courts themselves and by English legal scholars and historians.

Wise 1974). The new Court of Appeals replaced the many overlapping appeals courts that had existed, allowing for more uniformity in the law (Plucknett 1929). This reorganization allowed for greater clarity in the judicial hierarchy and provided a necessary condition for the development of binding horizontal precedent.

Second, the House of Lords clarified its role as the highest court in the Empire and formally ruled that its precedents were binding on both lower courts and its own future decisions. Historically, the House of Lords had not clearly differentiated its legislative and judicial functions, but in the nineteenth century it made this distinction with the judicial function being set apart and handled solely by the Law Lords (Leach 1967; Plucknett 1929; Veeder 1907a). With this role more firmly established, the Judicial Committee of the House of Lords could cement its place at the pinnacle of the judicial system whose decisions were binding on all lower courts (Goodhart 1930; Leach 1967; Veeder 1907a). The decision in *Beamish v. Beamish* established this point. Here it was held that "The law laid down as your ratio decidendi, being clearly binding on all inferior tribunal."[12] However, the *Beamish* decision did not stop with solely holding that the decisions of the House of Lords were binding on all lower courts, but went on to declare that "if it were not considered as equally binding upon your Lordships, this House would be arrogating to itself the right of altering the law, and legislating by its own separate authority."[13] Thus, the *Beamish* case established that the strong view of *stare decisis* – or what scholars of British law refer to as the self-shackling rule (see, e.g., Leach 1967) – would go so far as to bind the Judicial Committee of the House of Lords to its own decisions.

While the language in the *Beamish* decision was clear and direct in establishing the principle of strong *stare decisis*, it did not immediately receive universal acceptance in all circumstances. Some believed that there were extraordinary or exceptional cases in which the House of Lords would be free to revisit its prior holdings (Leach 1967). As such, the absolute application of this view remained somewhat in flux for nearly forty more years until the question was finally settled in *London Tramways Company v. London County Council*.[14] Here, the Lord Chancellor stated, with the concurrence of the other Law Lords, that:

it is totally impossible ... to suppose that what some people call an "extraordinary case," an "unusual case," a case somewhat different from the common,

[12] 11 Eng. Rep. 735, 761 (1861).
[13] Id. at 761.
[14] [1898] AC 375.

in the opinion of each litigant in turn, is sufficient to justify the rehearing and rearguing before the final Court of Appeal of a question which has been already decided. Of course I do not deny that cases of individual hardship may arise, and there may be a current of opinion in the profession that such and such a judgment was erroneous; but what is that occasional interference with what is perhaps abstract justice as compared with the inconvenience – the disastrous inconvenience – of having each question subject to being reargued and the dealings of mankind rendered doubtful by reason of different decisions, so that in truth and in fact there would be no real final Court of Appeal?[15]

The *London Tramways* case thus firmly adopted a strong view of *stare decisis* in the English courts. While the was some criticism among the Law Lords and among legal academics over the rule (Leach 1967), it nonetheless appears to have been universally accepted in the courts. This remained the case until 1966, when the Lord Chancellor declared, on behalf of the Law Lords, in a formally issued Practice Statement:

> Their Lordships regard the use of precedent as an indispensable foundation upon which to decide what is the law and its application to individual cases … Their Lordships nevertheless recognize that too rigid adherence to precedent may lead to injustice in a particular case and also unduly restrict the proper development of the law. They propose, therefore, to modify their present practice and, while treating former decisions of this House as normally binding, to depart from a previous decision when it appears right to do so.[16]

While this is clearly a significant step back from the rule announced in *Beamish* and amplified in *London Tramways*, it was heavily conditioned. The Lord Chancellor's statement continued, noting that the Lords would "bear in mind the danger of disturbing retrospectively the basis on which contracts, settlements of property and fiscal arrangements have been entered into and also the especial need for certainty as to the criminal law."[17] Moreover, the statement concluded by noting that change was "not intended to affect the use of precedent elsewhere than in this House."[18] Thus, the strong view

---

[15] Id. at 380.

[16] Practice Statement (Judicial Precedent) [1966] 1 W.L.R. 1234.

[17] Id.

[18] Id. The Court of Appeals has since ruled, in *Young v. Bristol Aeroplane Co. Ltd.*, [1944] KB 718, that it also has some limited flexibility in departing from its own prior precedents, although it is still bound to the decisions of the House of Lords (and today the Supreme Court).

of precedent remains central to English law in terms of the application of hierarchical precedents and also with respect to departing from past precedents in only the most extraordinary of circumstances.[19]

2.2.2 *The View of Precedent in the US Courts*

As discussed above, the post-independence US Courts faced the same dilemma as their contemporary English counterparts with respect to precedent. As Lee cogently summarizes, the state of affairs was one in which:

> On one hand, the framing generation perceived the importance of stability and certainty in the law, and thus embraced a rule of following past decisions. On the other hand, a declaratory understanding of the common law gave rise to an exception permitting some form of reexamination of the merits of a prior decision. The unresolved tension involves the interplay between these two propositions. A strong rule threatens permanently to enshrine the errors of the past with no hope for internal correction, while a pure declaratory exception swallows the rule and its aim of stability. (1999, 667)

The US Supreme Court would eventually adopt a sort of middle ground between these two extremes. The Court viewed vertical *stare decisis* in absolute terms, while the binding nature of its own precedents was never seen as absolutely binding to the degree that was adopted in *London Tramways* (Gerhardt 2011; Goodhart 1930). While this view of precedent is weak compared to *London Tramways* standard, the historical evidence shows that by the mid-nineteenth century US courts had nonetheless begun to view *stare decisis* as a general rule to be followed except in rare circumstances (Gerhardt 2011; Goodhart 1930; Kempin 1959).

Beginning with the Marshall Court, the US Supreme Court simultaneously noted the importance of its own precedents while eschewing any absolute notions of *stare decisis*.[20] One of the earliest examples of this comes in *Cohens* v. *Virginia*,[21] where the Court holds dicta from *Marbury* v. *Madison*[22]

---

[19] See, for example, the decision of the Supreme Court of the United Kingdom in *Knauer* v. *Ministry of Justice*, [2016] UKSC 9 at [23], where the Court declares that it "should be very circumspect before accepting an invitation to invoke the 1966 *Practice Statement*" to overturn a decision of the House of Lords.

[20] During the Jay, Rutledge, and Ellsworth Courts, none of the Court's decisions discussed the role of precedent nor did any overturn existing precedent (Banks 1991; Gerhardt 2011; Lee 1999).

[21] 19 U.S. 264, 299 (1821).

[22] 5 U.S. 137 (1893).

to be inapplicable. In doing so, the Court presents a general rule that only the *ratio decidendi* from an opinion holds value as precedent. This rule continues through to the present day.[23] Specifically, the Court in *Cohens* held that:

> It is a maxim not to be disregarded, that general expressions, in every opinion, are to be taken in connection with the case in which those expressions are used. If they go beyond the case, they may be respected, but ought not to control the judgment in a subsequent suit when the very point is presented for decision.[24]

In addition to the notion that principles from precedents should only be held as authoritative for future cases in the same context in which they were applied in the precedent, the Court also limited the potential breadth of *stare decisis* in other ways. For example, in *Propeller Genesee Chief* v. *Fitzhugh*, the Court noted that if a precedent should "decide any question of property, or lay down any rule by which the right of property should be determined" then "stare decisis is the safe and established rule of judicial policy, and should always be adhered to."[25] By placing precedents dealing with issues of property rights into a special category, the Court implied that precedents in other areas must lack this protection, thereby freeing it to overturn a precedent dealing with admiralty jurisdiction.[26]

This is not to say that the US Supreme Court has no respect for its own precedents. Rather, the Court continually reaffirms the need to respect the norm of *stare decisis* to maintain consistency and uniformity in the law. This view of precedent is perhaps best summarized with an often quoted line by Justice Brandeis in dissent in *Burnet* v. *Coronado Oil & Gas Company*, where he declared that "*Stare decisis* is usually the wise policy, because in most matters it is more important that the applicable rule of law be settled than that it be settled right."[27] Thus, this form of *stare decisis* informally binds the Supreme

---

[23] See, e.g., *Arkansas Game & Fish Commission v. United States*, 568 U.S. 23 (2012); *Parents Involved in Community Schools v. Seattle School District No. 1*, 551 U.S. 701 (2007); *Central Virginia Community College v. Katz*, 546 U.S. 356 (2006); *Landgraf v. USI Film Products*, 511 U.S. 244 (1994).

[24] *Cohens*, *supra* note 21, at 299.

[25] 53 U.S. 443, 458 (1852).

[26] The Court still noted that precedents outside of the narrow domain of property rights were to be respected and only departed from when necessary. Specifically, the Court justified its departure from precedent by explaining that "We are sensible of the great weight to which it is entitled. But at the same time we are convinced that, if we follow it, we follow an erroneous decision into which the court fell, when the great importance of the question as it now presents itself could not be foreseen." Id. at 456.

[27] 285 U.S. 393, 406 (1932) (Brandeis, J., dissenting).

Court to its past decisions even when they disagree with those decisions, and even when a majority considers them to be in error.[28]

While this view of *stare decisis* as a strong norm constrains the justices, the fact that it exists as a norm rather than an absolute rule – as the House of Lords adopted in *London Tramways* – provides the justices with the flexibility to depart from precedents whenever "special circumstances" justify it (Healy 2001; Nelson 2001). Moreover, since the Court itself determines when these special circumstances are present, this means that the norm applies only when a majority of the Court wants it to apply, thus making *any* precedent a potential victim of special circumstances.[29] This notion that no precedent is truly sacred is abundantly clear from the refusal of Supreme Court nominees to state that even *Marbury v. Madison* could not be reconsidered if a future litigant were to bring that question before the Court.[30]

Keeping with its reasoning in *Propeller Genesee Chief*, the Court has continually reinforced that while departing from precedent always requires special justification, there is variability in the degree to which they find their precedents binding. The Court has held on numerous occasions that "the burden borne by the party advocating the abandonment of an established precedent is greater where the Court is asked to overrule a point of statutory construction,"[31] but weakest with regard to those precedents involving the interpretation of the Constitution as the "interpretation can be altered only by constitutional amendment or by overruling our prior decisions."[32] However, it is important to note that in practice, the Court rarely overturns its own precedents; thus the norm does appear to be one the Court goes to great lengths to follow in form, if not always in spirit (Gerhardt 2011).

---

[28] See, e.g., *Kimble v. Marvel Entertainment, LLC*, 135 S.Ct. 2401, 2409 (2015) ("Respecting *stare decisis* means sticking to some wrong decisions").

[29] While the US Supreme Court has never held that any of its precedents can ever achieve such a status as to make them nonrenewable, some judges and commentators have proposed that some precedents are essentially untouchable. See, e.g., *Richmond Medical Center v. Gilmore*, 219 F.3d 376 (4th Cir. 2000). See also Gerhardt (2005).

[30] See the comments by then Judge Scalia at his hearings before the Senate Judiciary Committee during an exchange with Senator Spector on page 83 of the official transcript available from www.loc.gov/law/find/nominations/scalia/hearing.pdf.

[31] *Patterson v. McLean Credit Union*, 491 U.S. 164, 172 (1989). See also *Hilton v. South Carolina Public Railways Commission*, 502 U.S. 197 (1991); *Square D Company v. Niagara Frontier Tariff Bureau*, 476 U.S. 409 (1986).

[32] *Agostini v. Felton*, 521 U.S. 203, 235 (1997). See also *Seminole Tribe of Florida v. Florida*, 517 U.S. 44 (1996); *Payne v. Tennessee*, 501 U.S. 808 (1991); *Garcia v. San Antonio Metropolitan Transit Authority*, 469 U.S. 528 (1985); *United States v. Scott*, 437 U.S. 82 (1978); *Smith v. Allwright*, 321 U.S. 649 (1944).

In contrast to horizontal *stare decisis*, vertical *stare decisis* has always been viewed as binding in the US federal system despite the fact that such a requirement is not formally stated in the Constitution.[33] Regardless of the source of this principle, lower federal court judges recognize the strict nature of vertical *stare decisis* even when it forces them to follow a precedent with which they disagree. Examples abound of US Courts of Appeal and even district court judges criticizing a Supreme Court precedent, while simultaneously noting that they are bound by it nonetheless.[34] We also see this in their extrajudicial writing. For example, Judge Posner of the Seventh Circuit described this as one of the "rules of the judicial game" (2008, 45).

Conversely, the US Supreme Court has held that while lower federal courts were bound by the Court's decisions, they were not bound by their own precedents in any absolute sense unless they so chose. This principle was clearly stated in *Hertz* v. *Woodman*, where the Court ruled that a circuit court was not bound by one of its own prior precedents, holding that "[t]he rule of stare decisis, though one tending to consistency and uniformity of decision, is not inflexible."[35] Moreover, the Court provided no formal rules whatsoever to limit the discretion of lower courts in this matter, stating in rather clear terms that "[w]hether [precedent] shall be followed or departed from is a question entirely within the discretion of the court."[36] However, most of the circuits have adopted rules that largely mirror the Supreme Court's own interpretation of horizontal *stare decisis* for their own precedents with the obvious addition of the ability to depart from circuit precedent that conflict with a subsequent Supreme Court precedent.[37]

While the US Supreme Court was relatively quick to adopt the principle of *stare decisis*, albeit a flexible version thereof, many state courts of last resort were more hesitant to accept their own precedents as binding. Even among the apparent earliest adopters, the language used often makes it difficult to tell

---

[33] The actual source of binding vertical *stare decisis* in the US federal courts remains a topic of some debate among legal scholars. While a full discussion of this is unnecessary for our purposes, interested readers can find a thorough overview of the debate in Caminker (1994).

[34] See, e.g., *United States* v. *Kennerley*, 209 F. 119 (S.D.N.Y. 1913) (Judge Learned Hand heavily criticizing the application of the *Hicklin* rule by US courts but declaring that he is bound to follow it); *Sojourner* v. *Roemer*, 772 F. Supp. 930 (E.D. La. 1991) (Judge Duplantier sympathetically quotes from Justice White's dissent in *Roe* v. *Wade*, but holds that the he is bound by the majority opinion).

[35] 218 U.S. 205, 212 (1910).

[36] Id.

[37] See, e.g., *Williams* v. *Ashland Engineering Company*, 45 F.3d 588 (1st Cir. 1995); *United States* v. *Ianniello*, 808 F.2d 184 (2nd Cir. 1986); *Owen* v. *Commissioner of Internal Revenue*, 652 F.2d 1271 (6th Cir. 1981); *Save Our Cumberland Mountains, Inc.* v. *Hodel*, 826 F.2d 43 (D.C. Cir. 1987) (Ginsburg, R., J., concurring).

whether the courts are simply viewing precedents as evidence of what the law is or actually viewing them as law itself (Kempin 1959). However, it would not necessarily be appropriate to assume this meant that early state courts felt that precedents had less intrinsic value than did their federal counterparts, or that they valued the importance of stability in the law any less. Rather, several key mechanisms worked to erect a barrier to the development of a strong version of *stare decisis* in state courts of last resort in the late eighteenth and early nineteenth centuries.

Perhaps chief among these reasons was the lack of accurate records. As discussed above, in many states, official reporters did not exist until the middle of the nineteenth century and the unofficial reporters present in most states were of varying quality and reliability. Additionally, many state courts lacked the resources to have a proper record of the relevant precedents, and it is likely that many members of the bar did as well. This left some state judges in the position of their English counterparts centuries earlier who had only their memory of prior cases to go by. This problem was especially pronounced in Georgia, where there was no state-level appellate court until 1845 (Almand 1943). For example, Kempin (1959, 41) highlights the 1808 case of *Grimball v. Ross* where the judge notes the lack of access to law books but refers to a group of precedents he remembers.[38]

Beyond these more practical issues, the nature of the US states has always been one of great variation. States have often served as laboratories of democracy, experimenting with new ideas in law and policy. Among the earliest states to adopt a more strict form of *stare decisis* was Kentucky, where in a pair of 1828 opinions the Kentucky Court of Appeals held that its precedents were binding even when wrong. First, in *South's Heirs* v. *Thomas' Heirs* the Court held that "whatever might be the opinion of the court, was the question new, this court can not depart from the former adjudications."[39] The basis for this strong adherence to precedent was rooted in the same argument that Justice Brandeis would make a hundred years later in *Burnet*, as the Court declared "it is not so important that the law should be rightly settled, as that it should remain stable after it is settled."[40] That same year, in *Trimble v. Taub*, this strong view of *stare decisis* was reaffirmed with even more direct language:

> If we were convinced that on this point the law was settled wrong originally, we should not feel ourselves at liberty to depart from it; aware, that it is of

[38] Charltons Reports (1805–1810), 175 (Liberty County Super. Ct. 1808).
[39] 23 Ky. 59, 62 (Ky. 1828).
[40] Id.

greater importance to society, that the rule should be uniform and stable, than that it should be the best possible rule that could be adopted.[41]

While several state high courts lagged behind Kentucky in accepting the binding nature of their own precedents, and a few even struggled with issues of lower court adherence to their precedents,[42] by the middle of the nineteenth century most had adopted the core principle of *stare decisis*. However, like the US Supreme Court, few were willing to view it in such absolute terms, and even the Kentucky Court of Appeals would eventually back off from the absolutist language in *South's Heirs* and *Trimble* as early as 1898.[43]

2.3 ARE STATE COURTS BOUND TO US SUPREME COURT DECISIONS?

In essence, we are left today in a situation where at all levels of the US federal and state judiciary there is a strong rule of vertical *stare decisis* combined with a respected, but flexible, horizontal *stare decisis*. However, issues related to federalism add additional complexity to the mix. Specifically, are state high courts bound by the decisions of the US Supreme Court? Further, if they are, then to what degree must the states adhere to US Supreme Court precedent?

While the Supreme Court established the doctrine that the Supremacy Clause of the US Constitution rendered invalid state laws that conflicted with federal treaties as early as 1796,[44] and that the Court had constitutional authority to review the decisions of state courts involving questions of federal law,[45] state responses to this doctrine were mixed. Some state high courts willingly accepted the supremacy of the federal constitution and treaties

---

[41] 23 Ky. 455, 456 (Ky. 1828).

[42] Even the vertical application of precedent was questioned at times in the early period of US law post-independence. For example, Kempin (1959, 48) provides an illustrative example of the Illinois Supreme Court in 1839 dealing with an attempt by a lower state court to de facto reverse one of its prior decisions.

[43] The Kentucky Court of Appeals s recognized the need to depart from precedent under very limited, special circumstances in *Montgomery County Fiscal Court v. Trimble*, 104 Ky. 629 (Ky. 1898). However, in *Hilen v. Hayes* the (since renamed) Supreme Court of Kentucky adopted a significantly more flexible approach, declaring that "stare decisis directs us to 'stand by' our previous decisions unless there are sound legal reasons to the contrary. Every case must be decided with a respect for precedent. But the doctrine of stare decisis does not commit us to the sanctification of ancient fallacy." 673 S.W.2d 713, 717 (Ky. 1984).

[44] *Ware v. Hylton*, 3 U.S. 199 (1796).

[45] While it would seem that *Ware v. Hylton* settled this question, it was not directly addressed in the opinions of any of the justices. However, the specific question was eventually raised and settled in the affirmative. See *Smith v. Maryland*, 10 U.S. 286 (1810); *Martin v. Hunter's Lessee*, 14 U.S. 304 (1816); *Cohens v. Virginia*, 19 U.S. 264 (1821).

over state laws. Perhaps the earliest example of this came in 1796, when the Supreme Court of North Carolina acknowledged that a federal treaty was not "to be restrained in its operation by any statute or any particular State, but that 'it ought to be interpreted in such manner as that it may have its effect, and not be found vain and illusive.'"[46] Moreover, several state courts of last resort showed a willingness to invalidate state laws or actions that were contrary to the federal constitution, including multiple instances where state courts invalidated state laws under various provisions of the Bill of Rights *prior* to the US Supreme Court's own adoption of the doctrine of selective incorporation.[47] Additionally, several state courts of last resort recognized the authority of the US Supreme Court to invalidate state laws early in the nineteenth century and, along with that, the corresponding obligation to recognize that "the judges of the respective States have no right to overrule or impugn such decision."[48] But it is worth noting that there was not universal acceptance of this principle at least as late as 1815.[49]

Yet missing from all of the above discussion is any indication in these early cases as to whether the decisions of the US Supreme Court are binding on state courts in future cases under the doctrine of *stare decisis*. The Supreme Court did not specifically address this question until the 1830s, when in *Green* v. *Lessee of Neal* the Court held that:

> On all questions arising under the constitution and laws of the union, this court may exercise a revising power; and its decisions are final and obligatory on all other judicial tribunals, state as well as federal. A state tribunal has a right to examine any such questions and to determine them, but its decision must conform to that of the supreme court, or the corrective power may be exercised.[50]

While clear, it is possible that the above-quoted language might only have served as dicta, as the principal focus in *Green* was on the opposite situation, whether the Supreme Court was bound by a state court of last resort's interpretation of state law. However, a similar holding was again reached about thirty years later in a similar context in *Provident Institute for*

---

46 *Hamilton* v. *Eaton*, 1 N.C. 641, 684 (N.C. 1796). See also *Jones* v. *Wheelis*, 4 La. Ann. 541 (La. 1849) (state court lacks authority to question a grant of land by the United States).

47 See, e.g., *State* v. *Moor*, 1 Miss. 134 (Miss. 1823) (applying the Double Jeopardy provision in the Fifth Amendment), *Nunn* v. *State*, 1 Ga. 243 (Ga. 1846) (invalidating a state law under the Right to Keep and Bear Arms in the Second Amendment).

48 *Linn* v. *State Bank of Illinois*, 2 Ill. 87, 89 (Ill. 1833). See also *Mather & Strong* v. *Bush*, 16 Johns. 233 (N.Y. 1819).

49 See *Hunter* v. *Martin*, 18 Va. 1 (Va. 1815), rev'd, *Martin* v. *Hunter's Lessee* 14 U.S. 304 (1816).

50 31 U.S. 291, 298 (1832).

Savings v. Massachusetts,[51] and finally in a case directly addressing the issue in *Chesapeake & Ohio Railroad Co. v. Martin* in 1931.[52] State high courts have largely accepted this general rule.[53] However, this logic does not apply to lower federal courts whose decisions are not binding on state high courts.[54]

Simultaneously, state courts have virtually unrestrained freedom when dealing with questions of purely state law. Not only will the US Supreme Court not override state courts' interpretation of their own laws and constitutions, but the Court has long recognized that it must give deference to the decisions of state courts with respect to questions arising under state statutes or state constitutions. In the early part of the nineteenth century, the Court frequently applied state court interpretations of their own statutes,[55] holding that "the construction given by the Courts of the several States to the legislative acts of those States, is received as true, unless they come in conflict with the constitution, laws, or treaties of the United States."[56] Nor did the Supreme Court limit itself to following state court interpretation of state law solely in matters of statutory interpretation. In *Jackson ex dem. St. John v. Chew*, the Court held that it would also follow the common law decisions of state courts in cases involving questions of property rights, reasoning that "[t]his Court adopts the State decisions, because they settle the law applicable to the case;

---

[51] 73 U.S. 611 (1868).

[52] 283 U.S. 209 (1931) ("The determination by this court of [a federal] question is binding upon the state courts and must be followed, any state law, decision, or rule to the contrary notwithstanding").

[53] See, e.g., *Mealey v. Martin*, 468 P.2d 965 (Alaska 1970); *Day v. Chicago & N. W. R. Co.*, 188 N.E. 540 (Ill. 1933); *Zahn's Executor v. State Tax Commission*, 47 S.W.2d 925 (Ky. 1932); *Morris v. Metriyakool*, 344 N.W.2d 736 (Mich. 1984); *Reichman-Crosby Co. v. Stone*, 37 So. 2d 22 (Miss. 1948); *Youngbluth v. Youngbluth*, 6 A. 3d 677 (Vt. 2010); *Schwartz v. Atlas Van Lines, Inc.*, 976 P.2d 145, 149 (Wash. 1999) (relying on a US Supreme Court precedent to apply the correct interpretation of a federal statute "although neither party cites any federal authority").

[54] Technically this remains an open question as the US Supreme Court has not directly addressed it, although it has stated in dicta that the decisions of the courts of appeal are not binding on state high courts. See *Johnson v. Williams*, 568 U.S. 289 (2013). However, several state courts have emphatically held that they were not bound to the decisions of the US Courts of Appeal even in cases dealing with a federal question. See, e.g., *Danner v. MBNA American Bank*, 255 S.W.3d 863 (Ark. 2007); *Carnival Corp. v. Carlisle*, 953 So. 2d 461 (Fla. 2007); *Abela v. General Motors Corp.*, 677 N.W.2d 325 (Mich. 2004); *Skelly Oil Co. v. Jackson*; 148 P.2d 182 (Okla. 1944); *Ratliff v. Norfolk Southern Railroad Co.*, 680 S.E.2d 28 (W. Va. 2009). For a thorough discussion of the case law in this area see Frost (2015).

[55] See, e.g., *Polk's Lessee v. Wendal*, 13 U.S. 87 (1815); *Shipp v. Miller's Heirs*, 15 U.S. 316 (1817); *Thatcher v. Powell*, 19 U.S. 119 (1821).

[56] *Elmendorf v. Taylor*, 23 U.S. 152, 160 (1825). See also *Shelby v. Guy*, 24 U.S. 361, 367 (1826) ("a fixed and received construction of their respective statute laws in their own Courts, makes, in fact, a part of the statute law of the country, however we may doubt the propriety of that construction").

and the reasons assigned for this course, apply as well to rules of construction growing out of the common law."[57]

To a degree, the deference of the US Supreme Court to state common law decisions ended with the Court's decision in *Swift v. Tyson*, where the Court held that the Rules of Decision Act applied only to the "positive statutes of the state, and the construction thereof adopted by the local tribunals, and to rights and titles to things having a permanent locality."[58] Yet, in the *Swift* decision limiting the Court's obligation to follow state common law decisions regarding commercial affairs, the Court still held that in these areas "the decisions of the local tribunals upon such subjects are entitled to, and will receive, the most deliberate attention and respect of this Court."[59] Thus, following *Swift* the Court would often take it upon itself to discover federal common law to guide its rulings,[60] while still holding itself bound to follow state high court interpretation of state statutes.[61] Nonetheless, even during this period, the Court sometimes continued to rely on state high court interpretations of common law within their state.[62]

While *Swift* and the federal common law it created did significantly alter the relationship between the U.S Supreme Court and state high courts for nearly a hundred years, once *Swift* was overruled by *Erie Railroad v. Tompkins*[63] there was essentially a return to the status quo ante at least with respect to substantive legal questions.[64] In the Court's opinion in *Erie*, Justice Brandeis wrote that:

> Except in matters governed by the Federal Constitution or by Acts of Congress, the law to be applied in any case is the law of the State. And whether the law of the State shall be declared by its Legislature in a statute

---

57 25 U.S. 153, 167 (1827). See also *Waring v. Jackson*, 26 U.S. 570 (1828); *Henderson v. Griffin*, 30 U.S. 151 (1831).

58 41 U.S. 1, 18 (1842).

59 Id. at 19.

60 See, e.g., *Railroad Co. v. Lockwood*, 84 U.S. 357 (1873); *Hough v. Railroad Co.*, 100 U.S. 213 (1880); *Burgess v. Seligman*, 107 U.S. 20 (1882); *Myrick v. Michigan Central Railroad Co.*, 107 U.S. 102 (1882); *Baltimore & Ohio Railroad Co. v. Baugh*, 149 U.S. 368 (1893); *Black & White Taxicab & Transfer Co. v. Brown & Yellow Taxicab & Transfer Co.*, 276 U.S. 518 (1928).

61 See, e.g. *Christy v. Pridgeon*, 71 U.S. 196 (1866); *Randall v. Brigham*, 74 U.S. 523 (1869); *Louisiana v. Pilsbury*, 105 U.S. 278 (1881); *Morley v. Lake Shore & Michigan Southern Railway Co.*, 146 U.S. 162 (1892).

62 See, e.g., *Beauregard v. New Orleans*, 59 U.S. 497 (1856); *Suydam v. Williamson*, 65 U.S. 427 (1861); *Detroit v. Osborne*, 135 U.S. 492 (1890).

63 304 U.S. 64 (1938).

64 The Court's decisions following *Erie* largely held that federal procedural rules applied even when federal courts had to enforce state substantive rights. See, e.g., *Guaranty Trust Co. v. York*, 326 U.S. 99 (1945). The determination of a proper rule for whether to apply federal versus state law after *Erie* is rather complex and well beyond the scope of this book. For a thorough discussion see Steinman (2008).

or by its highest court in a decision is not a matter of federal concern. *There is no federal general common law.*[65]

Despite the lack of citations to earlier cases, the language used here largely mirrors that of pre-*Swift* precedents. Moreover, recent decisions of the US Supreme Court have continued to reaffirm the rule that when "relevant state law is established by a decision of the State's highest court, that decision is binding on the federal courts."[66]

2.3.1 *When State and Federal Questions Are Mixed*

The decisions of the US Supreme Court make it clear that state high courts are bound to the Supreme Court's interpretation of federal law, but that the federal courts – including the Supreme Court – are bound by state high court interpretations of state law. However, even if we assume that things are as simple in practice as the above doctrine implies, it does not negate the fact that the majority of cases arising in state courts are not guided purely by state law or federal law alone. In such cases, the duty of state courts to follow the precedents set by the US Supreme Court is significantly less clear, although there are specific mechanisms that work to expand the freedom of state courts even in this situation.

Perhaps most significant in this respect is the adequate and independent state grounds doctrine. First adopted by the US Supreme Court in *Klinger* v. *Missouri*,[67] this doctrine states that "where the judgment of a state court rests upon two grounds, one of which is federal and the other non-federal in character, our jurisdiction fails if the non-federal ground is independent of the federal ground and adequate to support the judgment."[68] This doctrine provides state high courts with the freedom to avoid basing their decisions on federal grounds, even when such grounds are relevant to the decision,

---

[65] Id. at 78 (emphasis added).

[66] *Animal Science Products* v. *Hebei Welcome Pharmaceutical Co.*, 138 S.Ct. 1865, 1874 (2018) (internal quotations omitted). See also *Wainwright* v. *Goode*, 464 U.S. 78 (1983) (*per curiam*); *Mullaney* v. *Wilbur*, 421 U.S. 684 (1975).

[67] 80 U.S. 257 (1871). Many commentators credit *Murdock* v. *City of Memphis*, 87 U.S. 590 (1875), as the first application of the adequate and independent state grounds doctrine, but it was first applied three years earlier in *Klinger*. Moreover, the roots of the doctrine lie in cases – primarily involving contract law – dating back to at least the 1830s. See, e.g., *Crowell* v. *Randell*, 35 U.S. 368 (1836); *Gill* v. *Oliver's Executors*, 52 U.S. 529 (1850); *Railroad Co.* v. *Rock*, 71 U.S. 177 (1867); *Insurance Co.* v. *Treasurer*, 78 U.S. 204 (1871).

[68] *Fox Film Corp.* v. *Muller*, 296 U.S. 207, 210 (1935).

if they can base their decision instead on state grounds that meet the dual requirement of adequacy and independence. Thus, in practice, it offers a potential mechanism for state courts to avoiding applying Supreme Court decisions they find distasteful.

While the adequate and independent state grounds doctrine provides great flexibility to state high courts, it is not absolute and does have significant exceptions. First, the state grounds in which the decision was based must be adequate in the sense that it is "sufficient" or "broad enough" alone to justify the decision without the need to address the federal question, even if the federal question would compel a different outcome if it were addressed.[69] Additionally, adequacy requires that the state grounds must be real in the sense that they are more than a mere rationalization created to avoid addressing a federal question. As the US Supreme Court declared in *McCoy* v. *Shaw*, it will assert jurisdiction in cases where the state grounds were "essentially arbitrary or a mere device to prevent the review of a decision upon the federal question."[70]

Second, the state grounds must be independent from any federal ones in the sense that they provide an entirely separate basis for the decision. The independence would not be met, for example, in situations "where the non-federal ground is so interwoven with the [federal grounds] as not to be an independent matter."[71] The Court has also held that independence is lacking when a state court's application of state law is based on its interpretation of the requirements of the federal constitution.[72] Thus, independence requires that the state grounds be separate from any federal ones even when they involve the interpretation of statutory or constitutional provisions with similar, or even identical, language.

Third, there must be clarity in the source of law serving as a basis for the state court judgment. While the US Supreme Court has changed course throughout history with respect to what it should do when it is unclear from

---

[69] *Eustis* v. *Bolles*, 150 U.S. 361, 366 (1893)("the decision of the [non-federal] question is sufficient, notwithstanding the Federal question, to sustain the judgment"); *Giles* v. *Teasley*, 193 U.S. 146, 160 (1904) ("upon a ground broad enough to sustain it without deciding the Federal question raised"). For further elaboration see Fountaine (1998).

[70] 277 U.S. 302, 303 (1928).

[71] *Enterprise Irrigation District* v. *Farmers Mutual Canal Co.*, 243 U.S. 157, 164 (1917). See also *Abie State Bank* v. *Bryan*, 282 U.S. 765 (1931).

[72] *Zacchini* v. *Scripps-Howard Broadcasting Co.*, 433 U.S. 562, 568 (1977) ("felt compelled by what it understood to be federal constitutional considerations to construe and apply its own law in the manner it did"). See also *Delaware* v. *Prouse*, 440 U.S. 648 (1979); *Michigan* v. *Long*, 463 U.S. 1032 (1983).

a state court decision whether the basis for a decision is rooted in federal or state law, it has consistently held that it "cannot refuse jurisdiction because the state court *might* have based its decision ... upon an independent and adequate non-federal ground."[73] In *Michigan v. Long*, the Court took this requirement one step further and held that in cases where there is ambiguity or where federal and state law are interwoven, it "will accept as the most reasonable explanation that the state court decided the case the way it did because it believed that federal law required it to do so."[74] However, in such cases state courts can avoid this if they "make clear by a plain statement ... that the federal cases are being used only for the purpose of guidance, and do not themselves compel the result."[75] Since *Long*, state high courts have frequently included explicit "plain statements" in decisions where they assert an adequate and independent basis in state law for a decision that might not have been reached were the state court to decide the case solely on federal grounds under relevant US Supreme Court precedents.[76]

Today, we most often see state high courts use adequate and independent state grounds to avoid US Supreme Court precedent when using their state constitutions as a mechanism for expanding rights. While state courts have historically interpreted the guarantees embedded in their own constitutions as affording greater rights than the federal constitution,[77] the frequency

---

[73] *Indiana ex rel. Anderson v. Brand*, 303 U.S. 95, 98 (1938) (emphasis added). The Court has similarly held that this applies when there is "ambiguous or obscure adjudications by state courts" with respect to the basis for the decision, *Minnesota v. National Tea Co.*, 309 U.S. 551, 557 (1940).

[74] 463 U.S. 1032, 1041 (1983).

[75] Id.

[76] See, e.g., *State v. Rodrigues*, 286 P.3d 809, 811, n. 8 (Haw. 2012) ("The federal cases herein are used only to provide guidance as to the issues raised by Petitioner. Therefore, this case is not decided under the Fourth and Fourteenth Amendments of the United States Constitution. Article I, section 7 of the Hawai'i Constitution as opposed to federal law compels the result reached herein"); *Doe v. Department of Public Safety & Correctional Services*, 62 A.3d 123, 130, n.11 (Md. 2011) (after quoting the relevant language from *Long*, the Court then states: "Our judgment is based exclusively upon our interpretation of the protections afforded by Article 17 of Maryland's Declaration of Rights"); *Commonwealth v. Cass*, 709 A.2d 350, 358 (Pa. 1998) ("The decision of the United States Supreme Court in *Michigan v. Long* requires that we make a 'plain statement' of the adequate and independent state grounds upon which we rely, to avoid any doubt that we have rested our decision solidly upon Pennsylvania law. To that end we developed in *Commonwealth v. Edmunds*, a four pronged methodology that we will follow").

[77] See, e.g., *Cox v. GE Co.*, 85 S.E.2d 514, 519 (Ga. 1955) ("We are here, however, dealing with the statutes of this State and with the question of whether or not they violate the Constitution of the State of Georgia ... this is one of the few powers left to States to decide for themselves regardless of what the Supreme Court of the United States may or may not have decided.

of decisions of this nature have increased rapidly since Justice Brennan's well-cited article in the *Harvard Law Review* urging state court judges to remember that US Supreme Court decisions "are not, and should not be, dispositive of questions regarding rights guaranteed by counterpart provisions of state law" (1977, 502). When interpreting provisions in their state constitutions, state courts generally recognize a need to give careful consideration to US Supreme Court precedents interpreting corresponding provisions in the federal constitution, yet those courts also generally recognize that they are not bound by those precedents.[78]

Frequently referred to as new judicial federalism, this legal doctrine provides state high courts with a mechanism to circumvent the application of US Supreme Court precedents that they disagree with, provided that the state court's preferred legal doctrine expands individual rights as compared to the US Supreme Court's approach. Since the publication of Brennan's article, state high courts have repeatedly recognized the principle that "state courts are absolutely free to interpret state constitutional provisions to accord greater protection to individual rights than do similar provisions of the United States Constitution."[79] Myriad examples of this abound from a host of areas including same-sex marriage,[80] anti-sodomy laws,[81] the protection of obscene

We are also familiar with the modern trend to allow the government to encroach more and more upon the individual liberties and freedoms. So far as we are concerned, we will not strike down the Constitution of our State for this purpose").

[78] The discussion of the Supreme Court of New Jersey's decision in *State v. Hempele* in Chapter 1 provides a clear example of this. See also *State v. Glass*, 583 P.2d 872, 876 (Alaska 1978) ("In construing similar provisions of Alaska's Constitution, we, of course, give careful consideration to the holdings of the United States Supreme Court, although we are not bound by them"); *Horton v. Meskill*, 376 A.2d 359, 371 (Conn. 1977) ("the decisions of the United States Supreme Court defining federal constitutional rights are, at the least, persuasive authority, although we fully recognize the primary independent vitality of the provisions of our own constitution"); *CDA Dairy Queen, Inc. v. State Insurance Fund*, 299 P.3d 186, 190 (Idaho 2013) ("this Court will consider federal rules and methodology when interpreting parts of the Idaho Constitution that have an analogous federal provision. However, it is clear that the state constitution sometimes provides greater protection than the federal constitution. In those cases, this Court does not 'blindly apply United States Supreme Court interpretation and methodology' when interpreting the state constitution").

[79] *Arizona v. Evans*, 514 U.S. 1, 8 (1995). See also *PruneYard Shopping Center v. Robins*, 447 U.S. 74 (1980); *Oregon v. Hass*, 420 U.S. 714 (1975); *Vogel v. State*, 426 So. 2d 882 (Ala. 1982); *Bock v. Westminster Mall Co.*, 819 P.2d 55 (Colo. 1991); *State v. Schultz*, 850 P.2d 818 (Kan. 1993); *State v. Havlat*, 385 N.W.2d 436 (Neb. 1986).

[80] See, e.g., *Goodridge v. Department of Public Health*, 798 N.E.2d 941 (Mass. 2003); *Varnum v. Brien*, 763 N.W.2d 862 (Iowa 2009); *Kerrigan v. Commissioner of Public Health*, 957 A.2d 407 (Conn. 2008).

[81] See, e.g., *Commonwealth v. Wasson*, 842 S.W.2d 487 (Ky. 1992); *Gryczan v. State*, 942 P.2d 112 (Mont. 1997); *Powell v. State*, 510 S.E. 2d 18 (Ga. 1998).

materials,[82] probable cause requirements,[83] eminent domain,[84] and many other areas.

2.4 CONCLUSION

If judges on state high courts were mere automata, following principles of mechanical jurisprudence in their cases, then the application of US Supreme Court precedents would be clear. When the case dealt solely with federal questions, they should apply Supreme Court precedent. When the case dealt solely with state questions, they should apply only state precedents. When the case dealt with a mix of federal and state questions, they should apply Supreme Court precedent unless there were clear adequate and independent state grounds.

However, state high court judges are not automata, and the idea that judges apply mechanical jurisprudence is long dead. In practice, state courts will sometimes apply Supreme Court precedents in their decisions even when they are not bound to do so, while other times they will ignore – or even criticize – relevant precedents that they ought to be bound by. As such, a familiarity with legal doctrine is only the first step in our understanding of how, when, and why state court judges use US Supreme Court precedent.

In the next chapter, we present our theoretical explanation of US Supreme Court precedent usage by state high courts. Our theoretical framework recognizes that legal doctrine matters and sets out the parameters under which judicial decision-making should occur. Yet, it also recognizes that legal doctrine alone is insufficient to explain the decision by state high court judges in individual cases regarding whether and how to apply a relevant US Supreme Court precedent. Rather, this decision is a function of the legal and ideological preferences of the state court, the institutional design of the state judicial system, the political context of the state, and specific aspects of the individual case before the court.

---

[82] *State* v. *Henry*, 732 P.2d 9 (Or. 1987).

[83] See, e.g., *State* v. *Jackson*, 688 P.2d 136 (Wash. 1984); *State* v. *Jones*, 706 P.2d 317 (Alaska 1985); *People* v. *Johnson*, 488 N.E.2d 439 (N.Y. 1985); *State* v. *Cordova*, 784 P.2d 30 (N.M. 1989).

[84] See, e.g., *AFT Michigan* v. *State*, 866 N.W.2d 782 (Mich. 2015); *City of Norwood* v. *Horney*, 853 N.E.2d 1115 (Ohio 2006); *Board of County Commissioners of Muskogee County* v. *Lowery*, 136 P.3d 639 (Okla. 2006).

3

A Theory of State High Court Usage of US
Supreme Court Precedent

State high courts occupy a unique place in the American political system. Like state legislatures and governors, they hold a place of power and prestige within their state at the pinnacle of their branch of state government. Yet, unlike state legislatures and state governors, that are not bound in any way to implement the pronouncements of their federal counterparts,[1] state courts are technically bound by US Supreme Court decisions related to interpretation of federal law or the US Constitution.

In the last chapter, we discussed how this formal requirement becomes less clear in practice. Rarely do state high courts see cases where, there are solely federal questions. Rather, the majority of cases coming before state high courts involve issues of state law only (where US Supreme Court precedents have no more value than those of the courts of other states) or involve a mix of federal and state issues. In the latter scenario, state high courts can often rely on doctrines such as adequate and independent state grounds to ignore the federal law questions and focus solely on the state ones. Thus in many cases, state high courts are under no legal obligation to follow US Supreme Court precedent at all. What remains are those cases where only federal questions exist or where the federal and state questions are too intermingled to separate one from the other. We argue that state high courts possess a remarkable degree of flexibility with respect to their usage of US Supreme Court precedent even in these cases.

---

[1] While Congress and the president have various tools to encourage states to adopt certain policies, there are also clear constitutional limits on their ability to force state officials to take particular actions. These limits are crystallized in the form of the modern anti-commandeering doctrine crafted by the US Supreme Court in *New York v. United States*, 488 U.S. 1041 (1992) and *Printz v. United States*, 521 U.S. 898 (1997), which states that Congress cannot force state or local government officials to enforce federal law. See Adler (2001) for additional discussion of the anti-commandeering doctrine.

Our central argument is that while US Supreme Court precedent serves a vital role in shaping legal policy in the states, that role is dynamic and conditional on a host of state-level factors. Few scholars today would argue with the assumption that judges on state courts of last resort are motivated by a desire to formulate legal policy consistent with their personal values and beliefs. Yet, this does not make them mere politicians in robes. As we define the concept, legal policy is not purely outcome oriented, but focused on shaping the future application and evolution of doctrine in a given area of the law. In other words, the policy preferences of these judges matter, but so does the law. Additionally, we recognize that none of this occurs in isolation. As such, we borrow from neo-institutionalist theories applied to various aspects of law-making and judicial behavior (see, e.g., Brace and Hall 1995; 1997; Gillman and Clayton 1999; Hall and Brace 1992; Hoekstra 2005; Langer 2002). Simply put, we assert that a theoretical explanation of state high court usage (or nonusage) of US Supreme Court precedent must account for the myriad of factors that affect the decision-making of individual courts in individual cases. Specifically, we present a theory of state high court decisions regarding whether and how to use US Supreme Court precedent that defines this choice as a function of legal factors, the political context of the state, and audience considerations stemming from the institutional design of the state judicial system.

Prior to providing a full explanation of our new theoretical framework, we must first offer an overview of the existing literature on state high court decision-making generally and on prior empirical studies of state high court usage of US Supreme Court precedent. This chapter then turns to a discussion and justification for three core assumptions of our theory, and provides a detailed account of our theory of precedent usage by state high courts. The chapter concludes with a discussion of the observable implications of our theory and how that should impact the translation of federal precedent into state legal policy.

3.1 DECISION-MAKING ON STATE HIGH COURTS

Contemporary studies of state high courts focus primarily on a general research paradigm known as neo-institutionalism. This approach aims to combine many of the "best" features of traditional studies of formal institutional rules and political behavior. In a neo-institutionalist framework, researchers focus on how differences in institutional structures and rules impact individual behavior. Applied to state high courts, this often involves examining how differences in institutional structures or aspects of a court's political environment may affect the behavior of either individual state high court justices or (as in our case) decisions by a body of judges as a whole. The neo-institutionalist paradigm remains the predominant one with regard to contemporary studies of state high court behavior and understanding how differences in institutions may affect the behavior of courts that might previously been viewed as simply idiosyncratic. By doing so, it gives researchers and policy experts additional tools to understand the behavior of people within specific institutions, while accounting for the structure of those institutions.

The application of neo-institutionalism to state high courts began in the late 1980s with work by Hall (1987), which showed that institutional features and reelection concerns mediated ideological voting behavior. Building on this initial work, Hall and Brace found that differences in electoral structure, individual case-specific facts, ideological factors, and contextual features of the state's political environment combined to affect how state high courts would make decisions when it came to death penalty decisions (Brace and Hall 1995; 1997; Hall and Brace 1992; 1994; 1996), patterns of dissensus on state high courts (Brace and Hall 1990; 1993; Hall and Brace 1989), and the application of party capability theory to state high courts (Brace and Hall 2001). Recent work has expanded the focus of these neo-institutionalist studies in several ways. The largest changes include expanding the scope of analyses beyond death penalty decisions (Langer 2002), by examining different types of issues and postulating about how differences in issues would affect how state high court justices would vote.

One new direction for this line of research involves a greater focus on the role of elections (which the vast majority of state high court justices face in some way) and perceived electoral accountability on the behavior of state high court justices (Bonneau and Hall 2003; 2009; Caldarone, Canes-Wrone, and Clark 2009; Canes-Wrone, Clark, and Kelly 2014; Hall 2001); these works are part of a larger debate as to what types of elections elicit the most accountability from state high court justices (in particular, partisan versus nonpartisan elections).[2] Finally, other recent work examines how state high court justices craft opinions differently for different audiences depending on the circumstances (Romano and Curry 2019). Romano and Curry (2019) apply text analysis techniques to find systematic explanations for how state high courts alter the language in their opinions based upon variation in audience concerns. They also find evidence for strategic behavior (responding to their

---

[2] Of course, there is an implicit assumption that having a high degree of accountability is a good thing. This assumption is juxtaposed with that of Article III federal courts, of which any judge appointed under Article III of the Constitution is entitled to de facto life tenure.

colleagues and to external actors) broadly affecting the language used in state high court opinions.

3.2 STATE HIGH COURTS AND US SUPREME COURT PRECEDENT

Scholars of public law have been interested in state high court reactions to US Supreme Court precedents since at least the 1950s (Murphy 1959). Early studies on the topic came in a period of growing intrusion by the US Supreme Court into many aspects of the law that were previously left to the states, especially with respect to criminal procedure issues, and this was noted in many early studies as a motivation for the research. For example, both Murphy (1959) and Canon (1973) observe that there was a great deal of pushback from state high courts to this trend during the period, including a strong rebuke from the Conference of State Chief Justices in 1958 when it adopted, by a 36-8 vote, a resolution that criticized the Supreme Court for "an accelerating trend towards increasing power of the national government and correspondingly contracted power of the state governments" (quoted in Canon 1973, 109). Moreover, in reviewing the literature on the topic in 1978, Baum observes that most of the research in the area has focused on a few important Warren Court precedents that were particularly controversial.

Much of this early work was done through the lens of judicial impact studies. However, as Songer (1988) observes, studies falling under the umbrella of judicial impact took an array of approaches. Some of these early studies simply focused on the narrow question of whether lower courts implemented a Supreme Court decision reversing an earlier decision from that court (Beatty 1971; Wilkes Jr 1973). Other studies were more interested in the impact of precedent on the development of legal policy in the states (Canon 1973; Romans 1974). Finally, another large group of early studies on state high courts and US Supreme Court precedent focused on the more specific question of compliance, or whether the state court followed the standards set by the Supreme Court in its precedent (Canon and Kolson 1970; Manwaring 1968; Tarr 1977).

Moving forward, it was this last approach that appears to have made the greatest impact on future scholarship. Compliance studies recognized that while technically bound by US Supreme Court precedents involving interpretation of the US Constitution, state high courts have a variety of motivations and audiences that make their decision calculus more complex. Thus, later work on state high courts and US Supreme Court precedent was largely focused on isolating the determinants of compliance (Fix, Kingsland, and Montgomery 2017; Kassow, Songer, and Fix 2012). Combining studies with a specific focus on state high court compliance with those focused on compliance by lower courts generally, this collective literature has shown a wide array of factors which assert a systematic influence on compliance, including the age of the precedent, the vitality of the precedent, the type of question presented, ideological factors, case-specific factors, and an array of other factors related to the precedent (Black and Spriggs 2013; Fix, Kingsland, and Montgomery 2017; Hansford and Spriggs 2006; Hansford, Spriggs, and Stenger 2013; Hinkle 2015; Johnson 1979; Kassow, Songer, and Fix 2012; Masood and Lineberger in press; Pacelle Jr and Baum 1992; Songer and Sheehan 1990). Yet, this theoretical focus on compliance alone has limited our ability to fully understand the nature of the process. The decision of state high courts regarding how to use (or not use) a relevant US Supreme Court precedent is significantly more complex.

In contrast to this focus on compliance, two contemporary studies have taken a more nuanced approach to the question of state high court responses to US Supreme Court precedent. Both Hoekstra (2005) and Comparato and McClurg (2007) merge together aspects of the literature on neo-institutionalist models of state high court decision-making and the constraining effect of US Supreme Court precedent on lower courts to develop a more theoretically coherent explanation. Specifically, Hoekstra (2005) examines how US Supreme Court precedent, along with core variables from prior neo-institutionalist scholarship, impact state court decisions on the validity of wage and hour laws, while Comparato and McClurg (2007) look at the effect of shifts in US Supreme Court precedent on the ideological direction of state high court search and seizure rulings. Both of these studies break new theoretical ground in bridging the gap between the rich literature on state high court decision-making generally and studies of the impact of US Supreme Court precedent on state high court decision-making. However, the choice of outcome measure in these studies limits our ability to see whether a direct connection exists between the contextual, institutional, ideological, and legal factors in their models and how the state high court uses or elects not to use a given US Supreme Court precedent. Thus, the ability to learn about the connection between US Supreme Court precedent and state legal policy change from these studies is indirect.

In this chapter we will introduce a new theory that builds on the existing work on state court reactions to US Supreme Court precedent and state high court decision-making more broadly. Like Hoekstra (2005) and Comparato and McClurg (2007), we recognize the importance of borrowing from the neo-institutionalist paradigm in building a comprehensive explanation of the impact of US Supreme Court precedent on state high court decision-making. However, we depart from this work by recognizing the importance of focusing on the response of the state court to the precedent as the outcome of interest. While this approach has largely been used by studies focused on compliance in recent years (see, e.g., Fix, Kingsland, and Montgomery 2017; Kassow, Songer, and Fix 2012), it was also one of the earliest approaches for scholars concerned with how state high courts choose their responses to US Supreme Court precedent in order to affect the evolution of legal policy in their state (Canon 1973). Thus, our approach bridges the gap between studies that adopt neo-institutionalist explanations of why state high courts use precedent in a particular way and studies that focus on reactions to individual precedents in individual cases as pieces in the larger puzzle of how state high courts shape legal policy within their states. As we will discuss in greater depth later in this chapter, this shift in focus has important implications for both individual decisions and our understanding of how legal policy evolves over time.

3.3 CORE ASSUMPTIONS

Prior to presenting our theory of state high court usage of US Supreme Court precedent, it is first necessary to provide a brief discussion of the underlying assumptions central to our theory and a conceptual definition of what we mean by "legal policy." Our theory is predicated on three simple but fundamental assumptions. First, state high court judges care about creating legal policy that aligns with their own preferences and that lower court judges in their state will faithfully implement. Second, when considering whether and how to use a relevant US Supreme Court precedent, state high court judges recognize that this decision to use (or not use) a precedent can serve to facilitate or impede their ability to achieve their goal of crafting good legal policy. Finally, both of the other assumptions will be more pronounced when the legal policy area involved is a salient one.

Scholars have written much about courts as policy-making bodies, yet much of this literature is focused on the ability of courts to impact social policy (see, e.g., Dahl 1957; Feeley 1992; Horowitz 1977; McCann 1992; Rosenberg 1991). Social policy, as it is used in much of this literature, tends to focus on the types of policy change that have a broad, sweeping impact (e.g., public school desegregation). While it is important to understand the impact that courts have (or fail to have) on major social policy change, that question is beyond the scope of this book. Rather, our conceptual focus is on legal policy. Legal policy as a theoretical concept is narrower than social policy, but equally important. Specifically, when we refer to legal policy in this book, we mean *the authoritative pronouncement of the meaning of a particular statutory, constitutional, or common law provision or principle designed to guide the future application of that provision or principle by other legal actors.* This definition carries with it three key implications that make it ideally suited for our theoretical purposes.

First, this definition focuses on the procedural aspects of law, while retaining clear substantive implications. One major factor limiting the ability of courts to significantly alter social policy is their dependency on actors outside of the judicial branch to implement substantive policy (Canon and Johnson 1999; Hall, M. E. K. 2014; Rosenberg 1991). Conversely, courts exercise more direct control with respect to policy change focused on procedural aspects of the law. Procedural policy dictates only the rules or standards that must be followed, while leaving some freedom of action in the substantive policy space. Simultaneously, altering procedural policy still constrains the range of substantive choices available to other legal actors. Thus, it allows courts the ability to move substantive policy closer to their preferences in a way that gives them greater control over those actors who will implement the policy.

Second, it is consistent with how courts make policy. Unlike other policy-making actors, courts make decisions in the context of a specific case, with a limited choice set, and must provide a written justification for their decision. These characteristics do not simply serve as limits on what courts can do as policy-makers; rather, they shape the type of policy a court is likely to be most successful in making. Substantively, a court has great freedom in determining who wins and loses in a given case, but that outcome matters little to those without a direct connection to the parties. However, the written rationale for that decision often requires the court to apply some statutory, constitutional, or common law provision or principle and, in doing so, to define that provision or principle in a way that adds to the body of law in that area. Law is evolutionary in nature (Fix 2016a; 2018; Robinson 2013), and each time a statutory, constitutional, or common law provision or principle is interpreted, the law gradually changes. Our definition of legal policy recognizes these core characteristics of the judicial process and their role in shaping the type of policy a court is capable of producing.

Third, this definition is normatively consistent with the role of courts in a democracy. As Judge Frank noted long ago, we want to believe judges to be "oracles of an impersonal higher law, a body of law absolute and infallible" (Frank 1945, 12). In other words, we mythologize them as apart from the muck and mire of politics. Yet, Dahl's observation that "Americans are not quite willing to accept the fact that [the Supreme Court] *is* a political institution and not quite capable of denying it" (1957, 279) was no less true at that time than was Judge Frank's. Additionally, it is relatively clear that both remain true today.[3] While the goal of judges altering legal policy may often be to impact substantive policy, couching those changes in the language of law allows the public to continue to believe in the myth of judges as apolitical actors much like small children can convince themselves that Santa Claus just happens to look surprisingly similar to their fathers when they see him placing presents under the Christmas tree.

Given this conceptual definition of legal policy, we do not think our core assumptions should be particularly controversial. Our first assumption simply states that state high court judges care about legal policy that is both in line with their preferences and likely to be implemented by lower court judges. What this does *not* assume is in many ways equally important as what it does assume. Neither this assumption nor our definition of legal policy in any way diminishes the role that a desire for substantive social policy may play in decision-making on these courts. It would be quixotic to attack decades of research findings that support the notion that judges care about substantive social policy. However, it is possible to simultaneously recognize that this is true, while being cognizant that any ability a court has to shape social policy is indirect and largely a function of their ability to craft an opinion with a rationale that key audiences will accept (Baum 2009; Black et al. 2016; Romano and Curry 2019). Most importantly, their opinions must be convincing to the lower courts charged with applying them in later cases. In much the same way that animal species occasionally hit evolutionary dead-ends, so does the law, and judges know that those decisions best suited for their legal and political environments are the ones most likely to survive and thrive (Fix 2016a; 2018). Conversely, those that are poorly suited to their political and legal environments are likely to have little impact. Thus, while judges may have policy goals in mind when they are crafting opinions, the only tool they have to shape general policy changes is by shaping legal policy. When this occurs, a court (or set of judges) are able to shift the law gradually to allow for more desirable outcomes to occur over an extended period of time.

The second assumption is essentially a logical extension of the first. Just like state high courts need lower courts in their state to implement the rationale from their decisions in future cases to maximize the impact of those decisions, the US Supreme Court likewise depends on state high courts

---

3 Wading into the debate over the implications of this for the Court's legitimacy is beyond the scope of this book. For our purposes, it is sufficient to acknowledge that many in the mass public do view the Court as political. For a recent substantive study of this topic, see Gibson and Nelson (2017).

both to implement their decisions directly and to provide guidance to lower state courts regarding how those precedents apply. Moreover, we know that state high courts have a wide array of mechanisms to enhance their discretion with respect to the application of US Supreme Court precedents (see Chapter 2 for an in-depth discussion of these mechanisms). Taken together, these conclusions further imply that when faced with a relevant US Supreme Court precedent, state high courts will (1) have a great deal of discretion in how they use (or elect not to use) that precedent, (2) recognize that the choice they make regarding how to use (or not use) a given precedent will have a direct impact on the legal policy content of their decision (and potentially an indirect impact on the social policy implications thereof), and (3) understand that the implications of this choice will affect the perception of their own opinion by relevant audiences based on those audiences' own views of the precedent. Thus, the decision of how to use (or not use) a US Supreme Court precedent will both directly impact the legal policy content of the state court's opinion and also shape the perception of that opinion by the state's lower court judges who play a role in determining the extent of the opinion's impact on state law.

The final assumption is a recognition that all legal policy is not created equal. Judges, like other politicians and the general public, consider some issue areas to be more important than others (see, e.g., Collins and Cooper 2016; Epstein and Segal 2000; Fix 2014; Unah and Hancock 2006; Vining Jr and Wilhelm 2011). Given that judges face significant time and resource constraints, they cannot devote the same amount of time or allocate the same level of resources to every case, and those cases dealing with more salient issues are likely to receive a greater share of their time and resources than cases dealing with less salient issues. Moreover, this assumption magnifies the effects of the other two. First, it seems likely that judges will care more about ensuring legal policy in these areas aligns with their preferences and is likely to be faithfully implemented (Fix 2014). Second, judges are likely to give greater thought to how they deal with precedents in cases involving salient issues. In part this is due to the fact that their greater willingness to expend time and resources in these cases will give them a greater ability to sort through alternative precedents. However, it may also simply be easier to determine whether and how to engage with precedents in more salient areas. US Supreme Court precedents in salient legal policy areas are more likely to be already familiar to other judges, including those on state high courts. While this third assumption does not lead us to dismiss the applicability of our theory to how state high courts react to US Supreme Court precedent in cases dealing with nonsalient issue areas, we do expect it to have greater utility for our understanding of cases involving salient issues. Thus, this assumption helps to guide our case selection in Chapters 5, 6, and 7. Specifically, we select cases from highly salient areas of legal policy as those offer the most direct test of our theory.[4]

3.4 A THEORY OF PRECEDENT USAGE BY STATE HIGH COURTS

Recognizing the importance of state high court usage or nonusage of US Supreme Court precedent in shaping legal policy "on the ground" in each of the fifty states, we introduce a new theory to explain this decision process that better reflects the choice set state high courts select from when faced with a relevant precedent and the specific factors that influence their choice among these options. Our theoretical focus is on the decision of a given state high court in an individual case regarding a specific, relevant precedent. However, we do not view the importance of this decision in isolation. Rather, our theoretical approach mirrors older work in the sense that it is focused on how individual decisions about precedent usage are made based on their implications for the development of legal policy (see, e.g., Canon 1973; Romans 1974). This theoretical approach represents a departure from much of the recent research on state high court usage of US Supreme Court precedent in three key respects.

First, as discussed above, most existing work examining this question views it through the lens of compliance (Fix, Kingsland, and Montgomery 2017; Kassow, Songer, and Fix 2012). This conceptual focus on compliance implies the relationship between state high courts and the US Supreme Court is best understood through a principal-agent framework. Yet, this is an inaccurate reflection of the nature of the system of legal federalism in the United States. Legal doctrines and practical realities provide substantial freedom of action for state high courts to shape legal policy, including determining whether and how to use precedent. Our theoretical approach recognizes this and asserts that state high courts will use US Supreme Court precedents in ways that help them create their preferred legal policy, given the structural limits imposed by the legal system and their political environment.

Second, we recognize that the choice facing state high courts is not simply one of how to treat US Supreme Court precedents, but in many instances

---

[4] In the concluding chapter we discuss how a relaxation of this assumption impacts our theoretical expectations and provide some brief supporting evidence to show that our theory still applies to precedents in nonsalient policy areas. In fact, examining *Alden* v. *Maine*, 527 U.S. 706 (1999) descriptively in the concluding chapter, we find results generally in line with the other cases discussed in the book.

whether to engage with the precedent at all. Existing studies implicitly assume a two-step process whereby courts first decide whether they must engage with a precedent and then decide how to engage. This prior work enhanced our understanding of the process by examining factors that influence the likelihood a state court will attempt to actively distinguish or criticize a US Supreme Court precedent (Fix, Kingsland, and Montgomery 2017). However, we strongly question the implicit assumption that courts select among various treatment options for all precedents they must engage with. Rather, we argue that the decision not to engage with a precedent at all is itself a type of treatment. This approach recognizes that the most common way for state high courts to avoid US Supreme Court precedents they find distasteful is not to attack them, but to simply ignore them altogether. Given the prevalence with which state high courts opt to simply ignore a relevant precedent,[5] we argue that reality better fits with our conceptualization of this as a simultaneous process than it does a sequential process. Additionally, this implies that many existing empirical studies are potentially flawed due to a reliance on the wrong universe of cases, a point that is discussed at greater length in Chapter 4.

Finally, we depart from the assumption in most previous work that state high courts make a simple dichotomous decision to follow (or not follow) a precedent. As Hinkle (2015) does in her study of the US Courts of Appeal, we view the manner in which state high courts use precedent as nominal (i.e., in a way that cannot be ordered). While this measurement decision and its implication are discussed more thoroughly in Chapter 4, it is sufficient at this point to note that this approach contrasts with most of the existing work on precedent, which assumes that the way in which lower courts use US Supreme Court precedent can be ordered. While this may seem like a trivial distinction (between ordered and not), it has important implications when considered in combination with the prior point. Expanding our theoretical conceptualization of the choices judges face when deciding how to deal with a relevant precedent by including the option to ignore that precedent is more in line with reality. However, how would one rank order ignoring a precedent versus criticizing it? Which behavior is less compliant? In other words, even if one might argue that the choice among different treatments can be rank ordered, figuring out where on that scale ignoring fits is rather difficult and any choice will be somewhat arbitrary. This significantly affects how we shape our theoretical approach and the research designs we use in our empirical analyses in Chapters 5–7. By adding additional flexibility into our theory as to

---

5 For example, in Chapter 5 we show that state high courts ignore *Lemon v. Kurtzman*, 403 U.S. 602 (1971), nearly 50 percent of the time that it is relevant to the case they are deciding.

how state high courts (and actually all lower courts) use US Supreme Court precedent, we are better able to account for the real-world flexibility that state high courts have in choosing to ignore potentially relevant precedents.

Our theoretical approach is distinct from existing studies of this specific topic in many ways, yet our theory of precedent usage is influenced by work on state high court decision-making more generally. Specifically, we argue that state high court usage or nonusage of US Supreme Court precedents should be influenced by legal, contextual, and institutional factors akin to other aspects of state high court decision-making (Brace and Hall 1995; 1997; Comparato and McClurg 2007; Hall and Brace 1992; Hoekstra 2005; Langer 2002).

While state high courts clearly care about the potential policy impact of their decision in the traditional political or social policy sense, our theory assumes that their primary concern is with the legal policy content of their decisions. Recall that we define legal policy as the authoritative pronouncement of the meaning of a particular statutory, constitutional, or common law provision or principle designed to guide the future application of that provision or principle by other legal actors. As discussed in greater depth above, courts know that their ability to impact policy is contingent on their ability to craft opinions that convince key audiences. Crafting a convincing legal opinion requires taking legal factors seriously. As such, we give theoretical primacy to three key legal factors.

First, as a general rule, precedents tend to receive fewer citations as they age (Black and Spriggs 2013; Boyd and Spriggs 2009; Hansford, Spriggs, and Stenger 2013; Westerland et al. 2010). Yet, the effect of age is not universal for all precedents. In the context of the US Supreme Court, Hansford and Spriggs (2006) find that those precedents with a higher vitality (i.e., those that have received more positive treatment) tend to be treated positively over time compared to low-vitality precedents. Additionally, Masood, Kassow, and Songer (2017) show that vitality affects treatment of US Supreme Court precedents by the US Courts of Appeal. However, this effect appears to be somewhat dependent on the federal context, as Fix, Kingsland, and Montgomery (2017) show that a given state high court's use of a US Supreme Court precedent is heavily influenced by how *that* court has used the precedent in the past rather than how the US Supreme Court has used its own precedent.

When state courts adopt US Supreme Court precedents, they maintain the power to interpret those decisions as they incorporate them into state law (Canon and Johnson 1999; Fix, Kingsland, and Montgomery 2017). The translation of any idea into words is always imperfect at best, thus requiring the reader to interpret the text as they engage with it. This is true in the law as much as with news, popular fiction, or any other type of writing. Therefore, even when the US Supreme Court desires to set a clear precedent to guide lower courts, "any realistic view of the judicial process must make it clear that no authority can ever be binding in this sense" (Merryman 1953, 620). There are numerous reasons for this. Perhaps most obvious, is the fact that no two cases will ever be factually identical. This alone provides courts with sufficient room to distinguish the case before them from a relevant precedent based on factual differences between the two cases, thus allowing them the ability to avoid applying that precedent. Additionally, even when the state court feels bound to apply the US Supreme Court precedent, the impossibility of perfect linguistic precision ensures that the state court will have some flexibility in determining how the rule from the precedent is to be applied to the case at hand, allowing it to alter the precedent to better fit the legal and political climate of their state. For this reason alone, it is recognized that the meaning of precedents is not only ambiguous to some degree, but also that they are not static. This continual interpretation that comes with repeated application of a precedent will alter its meaning over time (Black and Spriggs 2013; Fix 2016a; 2018; Hansford and Spriggs 2006; Landes and Posner 1976; Merryman 1953). Moreover, once a state high court decision integrates a US Supreme Court precedent into state law, the state court can then ignore the original US Supreme Court precedent in future cases, choosing instead to rely solely on its own precedent where the altered version of the US Supreme Court's standard was first adopted (Fix, Kingsland, and Montgomery 2017).

Second, the application of precedent often turns on the specific facts of the case and how closely those mirror the facts of the precedent. Whether and how a state high court uses a US Supreme Court precedent in the same general area of the law is likely to be influenced by the level of factual similarity between the case at hand and the precedent. To illustrate, imagine that a hypothetical state high court had two different free speech cases involving students in public high schools on their docket in the same term. In the first, a school suspended a student for wearing a shirt that criticized US military action in the Middle East. In the second, a student received a suspension for holding up a sign at a football game promoting the legalization of marijuana. In the court's opinion for the first case, it is more likely that they will cite *Tinker* v. *Des Moines Independent Community School District*,[6] a case dealing with symbolic political speech by students, than *Morse* v. *Frederick*,[7] a case dealing with a student expressing a pro-drug message at an event outside of school hours. However, in the second

---

[6] 393 U.S. 503 (1969).
[7] 551 U.S. 393 (2007).

case, the opposite is likely true as the facts in *Morse* are more akin to that case than to *Tinker*.

Third, the nature of individual precedents also leads to variation in their application. Scholars have found that whether a Supreme Court decision sets a hard rule versus a flexible standard impacts compliance with the decision (Bueno de Mesquita and Stephenson 2002; Jacobi and Tiller 2007). Precedents that create a hard rule provide little flexibility by setting a line that must be followed. For example, the Court crafted hard rules in some of its early 2000s death penalty cases. In *Roper* v. *Simmons*,[8] the Court set an absolute prohibition on the execution of individuals under the age of eighteen. Similarly, in *Kennedy* v. *Louisiana*,[9] the Court prohibited the use of the death penalty for the crime of raping a child. In both instances, a sharp cutpoint was established that provided lower courts with guidance as to what was and was not acceptable under the Eighth Amendment. When a US Supreme Court precedent contains a clear rule, such as in *Roper* or *Kennedy*, it will be harder for lower courts – including state high courts dealing with a federal question – to avoid following the precedent. Avoiding a precedent with a rule will likely require the court to actively find a way to distinguish the precedent on the facts or find an alternative way to justify a failure to apply it.

Conversely, standards provide greater freedom in terms of their interpretation and application of precedent. Standards often consist of vague guidelines or tests that allow lower courts a great deal of flexibility in determining whether and how to apply them. An example of a standard is the three-part test for determining whether material is obscene – and thus lacking First Amendment protection – from *Miller* v. *California*.[10] Some have argued that the standard from *Miller* is so vague that it is impossible to have consistency and uniformity in its application (Fix 2016b; Scott, Eitle, and Skovron 1990). Thus, compared to rules, it is likely that lower courts will feel less constrained in having to justify a departure from a precedent that adopts a vague standard. Alternatively, it is possible that in some cases the ambiguous nature of a standard could increase adherence to a precedent, as it enables a court to reach a wide range of results while claiming faithful adherence to the precedent (Fix, Kingsland, and Montgomery 2017).

Moving beyond legal factors, our theory also incorporates contextual factors related to a state's political environment and institutional features of the

---

[8]　543 U.S. 551 (2005).
[9]　554 U.S. 407 (2008).
[10]　413 U.S. 12 (1973).

state judiciary as part of a multifaceted explanation of state high court use of precedent. Courts are a part of the political and legal environments they inhabit and must be cognizant of both the environment in which they render their decisions and the potential impact of their decisions on that environment. Judges, even at the federal level, generally come from the states in which they serve. While we may like to mythologize them as high priests of the law, their views are often shaped in part by cultural values shared with their community (Hamilton 1973; Peltason 1971; Schmidhauser 1961). This is likely to be even more true of state high court judges. As such, our theory incorporates the notion that the overall political climate of a state should exert an independent influence on the way its state high court judges decide to use (or not use) US Supreme Court precedents in politically charged areas of the law (Romans 1974). For example, a state high court judge in a relatively conservative state is likely to share many of the values of the mass public of that state. When faced with a case dealing with abortion, that judge – mirroring the views of the overall state population – may try to avoid reliance on a relatively liberal precedent such as *Roe v. Wade*,[11] even though it is potentially relevant to the case at hand.

Additionally, institutional variation in the states is likely to influence state high court usage of US Supreme Court precedents. Unlike their counterparts on the federal bench, most state high court judges serve limited terms. As such, these judges should be concerned with how key audiences view their decisions. Specifically, in states that use popular elections to retain judges, they may be concerned with the policy views of the mass public, whereas in states where retention decisions are made by elite actors, judges may more concerned with the views of those actors. While most research on the impact of retention methods on state high court decision-making has focused on case outcomes (see, e.g., Brace and Hall 1995; 1997; Hall and Brace 1992; Langer 2002) or broader institutional concerns (see, e.g., Bonneau and Cann 2015; Goelzhauser 2016; Tarr 2012), there is evidence that it also affects the content of opinions (Romano and Curry 2019).

It seems logical that audience considerations that are at least partially driven by the need for retention may also affect how state high courts use US Supreme Court precedent. For some state high court justices facing reelection or reappointment pressures, ignoring – or even vehemently criticizing – a US Supreme Court precedent antithetical to the preferences of their state may come with benefits for the likelihood of their retention that outweighs any possible cost suffered if the US Supreme Court rebukes them. While atypical,

[11] 410 U.S. 113 (1973).

two relatively extreme examples help illustrate this behavior. First, in *Salt Lake City* v. *Piepenburg*[12] the Utah Supreme Court issued an extremely harsh criticism of the US Supreme Court's *Miller* v. *California* precedent, describing the standard adopted therein as "an argument [that] ought only to be advanced by depraved, mentally deficient, mind-warped queers." The Utah Court went on to add that state court judges who followed the decision "should be removed either by impeachment or by the vote of the decent people of their constituency." This language goes well beyond what was necessary to immunize legal policy in Utah from the effects of *Miller*. However, this highly charged language would show members of their attentive audiences that the Court's values mirrored those of the average Utah resident.

Perhaps even more direct than the Utah example above is one from Alabama. While not in the context of an opinion, this example further illustrates the principle of how institutional factors may lead state high court judges to criticize US Supreme Court precedents as a signal to their retention constituency. After the Alabama Supreme Court issued a decision that followed the clear rule against the application of the death penalty to minors established in the US Supreme Court's decision in *Roper* v. *Simmons*, Alabama Supreme Court Justice Tom Parker – who recused himself from the case for having worked on it as assistant attorney general – wrote an scathing op-ed in the *Birmingham News* criticizing both the US Supreme Court and his brethren on the Alabama Supreme Court. Of *Roper* itself, Justice Parker wrote that the "liberal activists on the US Supreme Court" were "forc[ing] foreign legal fads on America" (Parker 2006). He then went on to criticize the Alabama Supreme Court, which "gave in to this unconstitutional activism without a word of protest," arguing that it should have unabashedly ignored the precedent since "[t]he proper response to such blatant judicial tyranny would have been for the Alabama Supreme Court to decline to follow *Roper* ... defend[ing] both the U.S. Constitution and Alabama law (thereby upholding their judicial oaths of office)" (Parker 2006).

In short, our theory of state high court use of precedent posits that the decision calculus of state high courts is a function of an array of factors acting in complex and interdependent ways. Specifically, we argue that state courts of last resort seek to use US Supreme Court precedents in such a way as to set legal policy in their state as close as possible to their preferences. Yet, these courts must also consider core legal factors, the political context of the state, and the institutional design of the state judicial system. Additionally, our theory accounts for the unique cross-pressures placed on state high courts by

---

[12]   571 P.2d 1299, 1300 (Utah 1977).

the federalist nature of our legal system. Unlike state legislatures or governors that operate largely independent of their federal counterparts, state courts are bound to follow the US Supreme Court's decisions with respect to federal law. Yet, federalism also provides state high courts with a great deal of flexibility in whether or how they apply US Supreme Court precedents through formal legal doctrines such as adequate and independent state grounds and informally through the US Supreme Court's limited ability to engage in formal oversight of how its decisions are implemented.

3.5 FROM FEDERAL PRECEDENT TO STATE POLICY

In this chapter, we introduce a new theoretical perspective for understanding how state high court use US Supreme Court precedents. Under our theoretical framework, it is helpful to think of state courts of last resort serving as a filter between the US Supreme Court and the lower appellate and trial courts in their states. Intuitively, we can think of US Supreme Court policy as freshly ground coffee. It contains the potential to have a significant impact, but needs additional steps to unlock that potential. State high courts are the baristas who brew and serve the coffee, determining how strong to make it, whether to sweeten it, and whether it needs other additives. Just as these choices dramatically alter how a cup of coffee will taste, the parallel decisions made by a state high court in interpreting and applying US Supreme Court precedents play a major role in determining how that precedent will be used by the lower courts in that state.

We recognize that baristas are not interested in getting the most out the coffee just to make the coffee look good, but rather to ensure that their customers view the product they produce as the best. The baristas want their customers to tell their friends that they make the best latte in town, so they will also get their coffee from that particular cafe. Similarly, the goal of state high courts is not simply to implement US Supreme Court precedents in a manner that maximizes the Supreme Court's policy goals. Instead, their focus is on how to use those precedents to shape legal policy in their state in line with their own goals. In doing so, they have a great deal of freedom. Doctrines such as adequate and independent grounds give state high courts legal cover for avoiding faithful implementation of precedents they find distasteful. Yet, an array of legal, contextual, and institutional factors combine to limit the freedom of action available to state high courts. While they may have a high degree of legal independence from the US Supreme Court, they also do not operate in isolation from the broader legal and political environments of their state and the broader United States.

In the next chapter, we will discuss some of the measurement issues associated with testing observable implications of our theory of precedent usage by state high courts. Due to the theoretical departures from existing studies of this topic, we must make several important departures in terms of our approach to case selection (both the US Supreme Court precedents we select for our applications and how we define the universe of relevant state high court cases where that precedent was cited or *could have been cited*), measurement of our key variables of interest, and the modeling techniques used. Thus, Chapter 4 consists of a discussion of the prior approaches used to study this topic, why these approaches are inappropriate to test our theory, our alternative approach, and why our approach is ideally suited to our theory.

Chapters 5–7 will then test our theory of precedent usage by state high courts with three different applications. Chapter 5 will examine state high court responses to *Atkins* v. *Virginia* in line with the approach detailed in Chapter 4. Chapter 6 will mirror Chapter 5 and offer an examination of state high court responses to *Lemon* v. *Kurtzman*. Finally, Chapter 7 will look at state high court responses to *District of Columbia* v. *Heller* and *McDonald* v. *City of Chicago* using a case study approach that allows for a more in-depth examination than the statistical analyses in Chapters 5 and 6.

4

Conceptualizing and Measuring How State High Courts Use US Supreme Court Opinions

A substantial amount of literature exists that examines how lower courts in the United States discuss and address US Supreme Court precedents over time. As we discussed in the preceding chapters, the primary focus of our book is to examine and test when, why, and how state high courts use US Supreme Court precedent. And, to the degree that they do not mechanistically follow US Supreme Court precedent, why do they not do so? In particular, one of our main foci in this book is examining the full range of options that state high courts have to use US Supreme Court precedent.

In this book, we put forth a new theory to explain whether and how state high courts use relevant US Supreme Court precedent. In Chapter 3, we laid out our theory and argument why this approach is necessary for a complete understanding of state high court policy-making. However, our new theoretical approach requires that we revisit the concepts and measures used in the existing literature. The goal of this chapter is twofold. First, we outline the existing literature with regard to existing measurements from studies that examine how courts (especially state high courts) use US Supreme Court precedent. Examining the strengths and deficiencies of these existing measures, we continue with a discussion of our reasoning as to why a new measurement approach for examining how lower courts use precedents is necessary. We conclude this chapter by introducing our new measure and discussing what this new measure allows us to do that earlier measurements of precedent treatment cannot.

4.1 BRIEF HISTORY OF COMPLIANCE STUDIES IN TERMS OF MEASUREMENT THEORY

Early works in the literature, which attempted to examine how state high courts used US Supreme Court precedent over time, focused on precedent usage as a way to understand whether lower courts comply with US Supreme Court rulings or whether lower courts were disobeying requirements put in place by the US Supreme Court. Compliance was examined in one of several methods in this research. Some scholars used a legal perspective to simply note whether lower courts were using US Supreme Court opinions and discussing them in their own opinions (what would be viewed as legal-based compliance). Others used a policy-based measure of compliance by noting whether lower courts decided similar cases in the same ideological direction in the US Supreme Court. The classic example given for policy-based compliance is from *Brown v. Board of Education*,[1] where lower court opinions would be examined to see whether they ruled that segregation in a particular state was unconstitutional based on the Equal Protection Clause of the Fourteenth Amendment (if not, a lower court would be ruled as noncompliant with precedent). Given that much of this literature reached the conclusion that state high courts generally comply with US Supreme Court decisions from a policy-making perspective, this second approach of analyzing policy-based compliance is largely no longer commonplace in the literature. Additionally, for our purposes, we are more interested in how state high courts use specific precedents in their opinions for determining compliance. A policy-based measure of compliance or precedent usage is conceptually problematic for this approach.

Other research focused on examining single precedents with the goal of determining whether state high courts shifted their policies to be in line with what the US Supreme Court had required, to minimally comply with the precedent (follow it in a minimal way), or to attack the precedent. For example, Canon (1973) finds that state high courts varied dramatically in how they responded to *Mapp* v. *Ohio*,[2] with some states applying it broadly, others applying it minimally, and with a few (about 20 percent) refusing to apply the *Mapp* test at all. While the work by Canon (1973) is important, it focuses on compliance using a policy construct and policy-related definitions rather than a legal treatment-based definition, such as we use. Johnson (1979), using a legal-compliance measure from *Shepards' Citations*, finds essentially no effect for US Supreme Court variables in explaining how lower courts respond to US Supreme Court precedent. But in this work, Johnson ultimately speculates that explaining lower court reactions to Supreme Court decisions may be based solely on lower-court variables.

---

[1] 347 U.S. 483 (1954).
[2] 367 U.S. 643 (1961).

Finally, Romans (1974) examined *Escobedo* v. *Illinois*[3] and *Miranda* v. *Arizona*,[4] finding that state high courts generally did not strongly comply with the Supreme Court's decisions until they received a clear command from the US Supreme Court. When the Supreme Court issued a vague standard in *Escobedo*, policy compliance by state high courts was quite weak. Interestingly, Romans finds that upon receipt of a clear command by the Court in *Miranda*, it is primarily those courts that would have been opposed to the policy that comply most strongly (conservative courts in his case). In contrast, he finds that liberal courts were relatively unenthusiastic users of *Miranda*, essentially ignoring the decision at times. Romans chalks up this change to institutional loyalty: state high courts that had *already* developed standards similar – but not identical – to *Miranda* may have felt a certain degree of loyalty due to being involved in their states' processes for making their own policy, separate from what the US Supreme Court demanded. The measurement used for this study is a policy-based one, that primarily examines how broadly state high courts were using *Escobedo* and *Miranda* and assessing to what degree state high courts would rely on these two opinions in cases with somewhat different fact patterns.

The most recent study that uses this policy compliance frame, with a policy-based dependent variable, is Comparato and McClurg's (2007) study. They examine state high court responses to a series of search and seizure cases, using a liberal or conservative decision outcome. This study has a variety of interesting findings, including describing the fact that state high courts can cite a liberal (or conservative) precedent, and then make a decision ideologically opposite to that of the Supreme Court precedent. What this effectively means, according to the authors, is that US Supreme Court precedents are flexible, which raises the potential concern that state high courts are simply using US Supreme Court precedents as a way to rationalize their desired outcomes. However, Comparato and McClurg's (2007) study is ultimately interested in policy compliance rather than legal treatments of precedent, making the scope of the article inherently differently from what our book aims to do.

Much of the early literature focuses on the fact that state high court decisions generally comply with US Supreme Court decisions (Canon 1973; Canon and Johnson 1999; Johnson 1979; 1987, but see Comparato and McClurg 2007). Yet, this approach ultimately fails to provide a full picture of how state high courts use US Supreme Court precedents in terms of

---

[3] 378 U.S. 478 (1964).
[4] 384 U.S. 436 (1966).

policy-making goals, as well as what compliance looks like from a measurement perspective.[5] Rather, many of these early studies define compliance too narrowly from a legal perspective (by assuming that compliance only occurs if a liberal Supreme Court decision elicits a liberal lower court decision). This creates a theoretical confusion as to what compliance actually means. This confusion occurs because it is rather uncommon for lower courts to get factual patterns that are identical to US Supreme Court decisions later on, meaning that lower court judges must use their discretion when determining how closely a fact pattern fits a US Supreme Court precedent.

However, these early studies still provide valuable insights into how to set up an appropriate research design for precedent compliance and usage, compared with newer studies that eliminate useful attributes and theoretical richness from these earlier studies. One especially useful feature of these early compliance studies for our purposes is that they define a set of relevant cases in a relatively broad sense. Returning to the *Brown* v. *Board of Education* example, if one were constructing a compliance study examining whether lower courts abided by *Brown* v. *Board*, one might conduct a search examining all cases dealing with segregation based on race or ethnicity in the United States in a given time period, as opposed to simply looking at those cases that may have treated *Brown*. By using this broader choice set of cases, one casts a relatively wide net to examine how lower courts ruled in cases that were at least moderately similar to *Brown*. Compared with later studies – which primarily examine how lower courts would discuss *Brown* among those cases where it was mentioned in the opinion – this early approach of gathering data (at least in theory) would allow for a set of cases that better reflects the actual universe of cases.

4.2 NEWER RESEARCH CONTRIBUTIONS: THE GIFT OF *SHEPARD'S CITATIONS*

More recently, mostly due to efforts by Hansford and Spriggs (2006; Spriggs and Hansford 2000), many scholars have shifted approach from a traditional model of policy-based compliance to one that examines how lower courts treat and use precedent more broadly with more of a legal-based focus. The central premise behind the use of examining lower court treatments in this way is the ability to examine the degree to which lower courts are faithful to US Supreme

---

[5] The one major exception to this is Johnson (1979), which defines compliance as being equivalent to positive treatments and thus is able to use a more generalizable method of determining compliance compared with most other early works.

Court precedent. These recent works provide an interesting mix of findings that are highly important for understanding how courts deal with precedent. First, this literature finds that the way the US Supreme Court treats its own precedents impacts how the Court discusses those precedents in the future. It also finds evidence that suggests that US Supreme Court treatment of its own precedents may affect how lower courts use the same precedent.[6] Finally, this literature creates a new measure, called precedent vitality, which measures the strength of a precedent.[7]

In *The Politics of Precedent*, Hansford and Spriggs (2006) argue that understanding how the US Supreme Court discusses and treats its own precedents over an extended period of time is essential for understanding a variety of factors that relate to judicial politics. These include examining how often lower federal courts use Supreme Court precedents, how the US Supreme Court treats its own precedents into the future, and whether the manner in which a precedent is treated by the US Supreme Court impacts its probability of being overruled in the future. In their book, they create a novel measure that is based on data from a tool that provides information to attorneys and judges about the strength of precedent, known as *Shepards' Citations*. Their purpose was to measure the "strength" of precedent, or what they call precedent vitality. This measure captures the sum of the number of positive treatments of precedent subtracted by the number of negative treatments of precedent to create a score comprised of integers ranging from negative infinity to positive infinity, at least in theory.

For both positive and negative treatments of precedents, they obtain this information from *Shepards' Citations*. For the number of positive treatments, they simply count the number of "Followed" treatments in *Shepards' Citations* for a given period of time. For negative treatments, they count the number of "Distinguished," "Criticized," "Limited," and "Overruled" treatments of precedent for a given period of time. Then they subtract the latter from the former to create a precedent vitality score. Editorial staff at Thompson-Reuters code individual treatments based on established criteria. Many applications rigorously tested this coding, providing strong evidence as to its facial and construct validity (Spriggs and Hansford 2000). This score has several advantages

---

6 Recent work by Fix, Kingsland, and Montgomery (2017) (for state high courts) and Masood, Kassow, and Songer (2017) (for federal appeals courts) raise strong question as to this latter finding, as both articles find that the way that the US Supreme Court treats its own precedents over time does not impact lower court treatment of Supreme Court precedents.

7 Fix, Kingsland, and Montgomery (2017) create a similar measure for state high courts, which is referred to as "state-specific precedent vitality," and Masood, Kassow, and Songer (2017) create a similar measure for Court of Appeals circuits, which is referred to as simply "circuit vitality."

over using the earlier measures of state high court treatment and discussion of US Supreme Court precedent by providing substantially more nuance to the precedent usage literature.

Importantly, this approach gives researchers a more nuanced measure that allows for courts to reach different conclusions as to the merits of a case, while still being considered in legal compliance. Specifically, if a decision follows the rationale of a case, but reaches an ideologically divergent result from the original precedent, it would still be in compliance. This increased nuance provides researchers with a broader definition of precedent treatment and provides for multiple ways for courts to respond to and use Supreme Court precedents. It also shifts the focus of precedent usage by lower courts away from a policy-based model to one that more effectively accounts for factors involved in legal reasoning (Braman 2009; 2012), and more closely resembles the process that judges use when examining potential precedents to discuss in their opinions. So from a construct validity and facial validity standpoint, this measure seems to be more useful for a variety of studies than earlier measures of precedent treatment.[8]

The use of precedent vitality is rather common in the contemporary judicial politics literature, including by the authors of this book in previous works (Fix, Kingsland, and Montgomery 2017; Kassow, Songer, and Fix 2012; Masood, Kassow, and Songer 2017). However, we believe that there are several concerns with the measurement, in its purest form, for this particular project. The most critical concern is a well-established one in the literature, which is how to address a *lack* of citation by a lower court, and what a lack of citation means both theoretically and empirically. This concern has been a long-standing one in the literature, with Klein (2002) finding that US Court of Appeals judges almost never fail to cite a relevant precedent, as long as they are aware of it. Similarly, in a contemporary article, Benesh and Reddick (2002) use this argument to assert that US Court of Appeals' panels should not fail to cite relevant precedents, but will cite and discuss a precedent in all cases where it is relevant for the Court of Appeals to do so. However, beyond Klein's book, no research has explicitly tested this assumption. So one of the preliminary questions we address here is whether this assumption is tenable when examining how state high courts respond to US Supreme Court

---

[8] One of the tricky aspects of discussing this topic is that prior to Hansford and Spriggs' (2006) book, most of the literature simply used a compliance frame to examine how lower courts used Supreme Court precedent (two exceptions to this include Johnson 1979; 1987). We generally use the word "treatment" to describe these earlier studies, except for those using a political definition of compliance (i.e., whether a liberal Supreme Court decision was followed by a liberal lower court decision on a similar topic).

precedent. As evidence in Chapters 5–7 show, the answer is definitely "no." Based on the theory that we propose in Chapter 3 and our examination of state high court-US Supreme Court interactions in Chapter 2, this is hardly surprising.

As we note in Chapters 2 and 3, state high courts are in an especially unusual position by virtue of their partial insulation from the US Supreme Court, as well as frequently not being insulated from stakeholders in the state where they are a high court justice. This ultimately places state high court justices in a position where they may be relatively willing to flout Supreme Court precedent, at least if they believe they are able to get away with doing so. While state high court justices are certainly socialized in the "language of law" – including the idea that following precedent is important – these justices may feel pressure or may outright disagree with a decision that the Court made at some point in the past. Even more so, as we noted in the last chapter, state high courts have an easy tool in their toolkit if they do not believe that a US Supreme Court opinion applies in a specific case (or if they believe it should be narrowly tailored).

This creates the need for the usage of another relatively new measure for our theory: namely, what we call state-specific vitality. This measure originates from Fix, Kingsland, and Montgomery (2017), who created a precedent vitality measure that is based on the idea that states themselves can interpret US Supreme Court precedent over time in a similar manner to the US Supreme Court. While this concept is relatively new in the context of state high courts, several studies have similar findings as applied to the federal courts of appeal (Masood, Kassow, and Songer 2017; Westerland et al. 2010). In both of these articles, directly comparing the substantive effect of Supreme Court precedent vitality with that of lower court vitality, the lower court vitality patterns of treatment over time mattered significantly more. Given this burgeoning evidence that state and lower federal courts have the ability to largely interpret precedents in a way that they desire, we believe it is important to rely on state-specific vitality for our theory.

In the remainder of this chapter, we create a measure that accounts for a lack of citation (as well as citation in different forms). We define the measure and explain how it is operationalized. We then continue with a brief descriptive exploration of the measure, as it is defined and examined in three empirical applications of our theory. We then conclude the chapter with a brief discussion of the empirical chapters that make up the remainder of the manuscript. The first two empirical chapters consist of two quantitative analyses, with the third empirical chapter consisting of a qualitative case-study-based approach.

4.3 OUR MEASURE OF STATE HIGH COURT RESPONSES
TO US SUPREME COURT PRECEDENTS

As we noted previously in this chapter, most works examining how state high courts apply US Supreme Court precedent treat the choice of using a particular precedent in a dichotomous manner: choosing to follow (or cite) a precedent or not to do so. We believe this choice of dichotomizing all possible outcomes that a state high court may select from regarding a US Supreme Court precedent is acceptable *if* the variation lost in dichotomizing such a variable is not theoretically meaningful. Because most scholars typically focus theoretically on the simple act of policy compliance (i.e., whether a state high court complies with a US Supreme Court precedent), assuming state high court treatments of precedent in terms of a dichotomous choice set is probably acceptable. Yet, for the larger question in this book of examining how state high courts apply US Supreme Court precedent, there are several theoretical reasons to believe that dichotomizing how state high courts examine precedent is not ideal. We provide an example below showing why we argue this distinction is important.

Suppose that a hypothetical state high court A exists, and that this hypothetical court generally decides social issues in a very conservative manner. These conservative patterns of decisions make sense given that State A is rather conservative. Imagine that, in contrast, state high court B exists, which tends to decide important social issues in a very liberal manner. Again, in this example, that fact is rational and makes sense, given that both the justices in State B and the populace in State B are relatively liberal. Assume that both states have an abortion case on their docket that challenges the states' new abortion laws under both the federal and state constitutions of each state. Even more importantly for our example, let us assume that the US Supreme Court recently handed down a new abortion precedent at the end of the previous term that was quite moderate in an ideological sense and that used a very "middle-of-the-road" approach to determining whether an individual's rights were violated by state laws restricting abortion access and availability. As a result, both conservatives and liberals were frustrated by this decision and expressed their irritation.

Given this scenario (which we believe is not far-fetched), it seems reasonable to believe that the supreme courts in State A and State B would be rather unenthusiastic about such a US Supreme Court precedent and would have ideological reasons for not wanting to use this new precedent. State high court A, for example, might distinguish their case from the new Supreme Court precedent based on differing facts in an attempt to minimize the applicability of the new US Supreme Court precedent. On the other hand, state high court B might attempt to use adequate and independent state grounds and rule that State B's constitution protects abortion rights more than the federal constitution does under the US Supreme Court's new precedent. They could then distinguish their case from the Supreme Court case or perhaps ignore the Supreme Court's precedent altogether. In a traditional legal-based compliance study, we believe the two state high court decisions would be coded as observationally equivalent, although the outcomes of these two state high courts' decisions might be quite different from one another.[9]

We believe that a new approach for examining state high court reactions to US Supreme Court precedents is useful. Our approach is one that is consistent with traditional research studies about compliance and state high court examinations of precedent, yet allows for an examination of theoretically important variation unexplored to this point. Specifically, we argue that in studies examining treatments of US Supreme Court precedent, the potential choice set should consist of the following four categories: positive treatments, neutral treatments (including citation), ignoring a precedent altogether, and negative treatments of precedent.

The general approach we use follows many other studies of precedent compliance and treatments of precedent by lower courts (Corley 2009; Fix, Kingsland, and Montgomery 2017; Hansford and Spriggs 2006; Kassow, Songer, and Fix 2012), and their analyses of treatments using *Shepards' Citations*. First, as LexisNexis states, a decision follows a precedent if it "relies on the case … as controlling or persuasive authority" (quoted in Dear and Jessen 2007, 690). Second, for citations and neutral treatments, we include all precedents that get cited and/or neutrally treated (such as "Explained" or "Harmonized") if they include no additional positive or negative treatments. Third, we consider a precedent ignored if it is relevant, but rather than treating a precedent or even citing it, a state high court decision simply excludes any mention of the precedent altogether. In doing so, the court hopes that a certiorari petition is not filed and/or that the US Supreme Court denies certiorari to such a petition. Finally, the fourth possibility we include is to negatively treat a precedent. As Hansford and Spriggs (2006) note, this choice is rather straightforward to address. Simply put, we code as a negative treatment any case where a precedent is "Criticized," "Distinguished," "Limited," or "Questioned" according to *Shepards' Citations*.

---

9   A second more worrying possibility is that the case from State B would not be in the dataset if the US Supreme Court's precedent based on the federal constitution was simply ignored.

To accomplish our goal of expanding the theoretical choice set for our empirical analyses, we must alter the way in which we select the state high court cases for our analysis. We use several techniques to establish the universe of cases for our purposes. The method of case selection varies somewhat in each of the three empirical chapters, but we follow the same general strategy in all three. We believe that the method we use to derive our set of cases is highly consistent with early works on lower court compliance with US Supreme Court precedents (e.g., Canon 1973; Romans 1974). For each US Supreme Court precedent we examine, we first create a large set of cases through LexisNexis searches for areas that are strongly related to that precedent. This large set of cases is then culled by hand to remove all cases that are not actually in the same issue area as the instant case. For example, if the phrase "intellectually disabled" is mentioned in an opinion and is found through a LexisNexis search, but is not used in a death penalty decision, we remove that case from the dataset in Chapter 4 (our chapter on *Atkins* v. *Virginia*).[10] To ensure that we have the true universe of state high court cases where a given US Supreme Court precedent was relevant, we also *Shepardize* the precedent via the *Shepards'* Report feature in LexisNexis. *Shepards'* Reports provide coding of each treatment for a case that is substantively related to the original case. After these two steps, we end up with a dataset that contains all cases heard by state high courts since the creation of a Supreme Court precedent dealing with the specific issue and observations of all treatments of a specific precedent according to *Shepards' Citations*.[11] By creating this type of dataset, we are able to accomplish our key goal from the research design and analysis standpoint, which is to ensure that a systematic method exists for determining the universe of state high court cases in which a given US Supreme Court precedent was relevant. This case selection method allows for us to examine not only treatments of those precedents, but also when a state high court would ignore a US Supreme Court precedent.[12]

---

[10] As we note in Chapter 5, the LexisNexis searches that we use are actually broader than solely the word "intellectual disability."

[11] An important caveat applies to Chapter 6. Due to *Shepards' Citations* being vastly underinclusive of state high court treatments of US Supreme Court precedents prior to 1993 (see Kassow, Songer, and Fix 2012), we code all state high court treatment types by hand for observations prior to 1992 when examining state high court responses to *Lemon* v. *Kurtzman*.

[12] Recall that if earlier works – which assume that lower courts never (or almost never) ignore US Supreme Court precedent – are correct, we should have almost no observations where a state high court ignored US Supreme Court precedent. However, that is not what we find. While this conflicts with some more recent research, this finding is broadly consistent with earlier works, which explicitly allow for this possibility (Canon 1974; Johnson 1979).

We believe that expanding the theoretical choice set that we use in this book has several benefits. The largest benefit is developing an empirical model that better aligns with the real choices that state high court justices have when addressing US Supreme Court precedent. Additionally, this approach redefines the appropriate universe of cases that should be examined in studies of US Supreme Court precedent usage. Rather than looking solely at cases that treat precedents (Kassow, Songer, and Fix 2012), all cases that cite a precedent (Fix, Kingsland, and Montgomery 2017), or all cases that reference a precedent in a litigant's briefs (Hansford and Spriggs 2006), we are able to account for the universe of cases where a precedent should be cited regardless of whether a precedent was actually cited. We do this by focusing on all state high court decisions in an issue area that was the same as a given US Supreme Court precedent. We believe that a failure to account for these additional cases where state high courts ignore Supreme Court precedents overlooks important, and significant, variation by neglecting to account for a key legal mechanism (or choice) that state high court justices have in their opinions. This choice is not simply random in our view, but rather is a theoretically viable choice for a state high court that does not like a US Supreme Court precedent, yet wants to avoid getting the attention of the Court in later decisions on review.

Empirically, we use what we describe as a "full choice set" for the dependent variable in our analyses. By full choice set, we mean that our measure of state high court response to a US Supreme Court precedent includes all categories found in a typical lower court precedent treatment study, but which also includes the additional category of "ignored." However, in order to obtain a useful comparison of cases that allows for the ignored category to have any utility, we have to use a larger set of cases compared with typical precedent treatment studies. In particular, for each issue area that we focus on in terms of precedent, we have to include all cases within that issue area to see whether a state high court ignored a relevant precedent or mentioned it in some way. Again, if it is mentioned, we code it as either positively treated, neutrally treated/cited, or negatively treated. A careful selection of issue areas is key for our understanding of the ignored category, and we choose the following issue areas: executions of those who are intellectually disabled (*Atkins* v. *Virginia*), Establishment Clause cases (*Lemon* v. *Kurtzman*), and Second Amendment cases (*District of Columbia* v. *Heller* and *McDonald* v. *City of Chicago*). Beyond the general discussion in this section, we save the rest of the specific instructions as to how we selected the universe of cases for each of the specific empirical chapters (Chapters 5–7).

4.4 DESCRIPTIVE FINDINGS FROM THREE
EMPIRICAL APPLICATIONS

At this point, we conclude the chapter with a brief discussion of how state high courts treated the four precedents that we feature in this book. Again, these include citations and treatments for *Atkins* v. *Virginia*, *Lemon* v. *Kurtzman*, *District of Columbia* v. *Heller*, and *McDonald* v. *City of Chicago*. As we discuss in more detail later in the book, all four cases featured vary from each other in a variety of ways, but all four tend to be on the trickier side for lower courts to implement. In the case of *Atkins*, while the rule given by the Court was fairly clear on the surface, it still required some other body (whether it be a state legislature or a state high court) to implement appropriate standards. As we note in Chapter 5, this led to a large degree of ambiguity, in particular as relates to discussion of how to figure out an appropriate test to be used to determine whether an individual who was given the death penalty was intellectually disabled. However, most of the states ended up relying on tests that were at least somewhat similar to one another.[13]

We focus on *Lemon* v. *Kurtzman* as our second key case in Chapter 6 because it is an example of a precedent that provides maximum discretion to lower courts. We argue this to be the case for two reasons. First, *Lemon* provides an archetype for what we call zombie precedents. By this, we mean that it has had its validity eroded over time as multiple justices on the US Supreme Court have proposed alternative legal tests for dealing with Establishment Clause cases. This has led some of the justices to go as far as declaring *Lemon* dead on multiple occasions. Yet, like a zombie from *Night of the Living Dead*, it returns from the grave each time it is killed. However, this uncertainty regarding whether it remains good law makes it one potential case where a large proportion of state high court treatments may either ignore or attack it. In addition, even if one follows the basic rules from *Lemon* in a broad variety of cases, portions of the *Lemon* test are well known for being difficult to interpret. Both of these reasons (the legal-doctrine-based one and the political one) make it especially likely for state high courts to be reluctant across the board to rely too heavily on *Lemon* for strong precedential value. We believe that given both of these reasons (the vagueness of the test and the profusion of alternative Establishment Clause tests), state high courts would have an especially high interest in ignoring *Lemon* or at least attempting to limit the use of *Lemon* when dealing with Establishment Clause cases. State high courts, in our view,

---

[13] Having said that, in Chapter 5 we note some of the important differences among states' policies aimed at determining who is intellectually disabled.

have the greatest freedom to act as they like in this case of the three analyses included in our book.

Finally, in the case of Second Amendment issues, we take a more qualitative approach to analyzing how state high courts reacted to the precedent, given the relatively small number of cases that treat either *Heller* or *McDonald*. As we note in Chapter 7 of the book – which focuses on state high court responses to these recent Second Amendment cases – the precedent laid out in *Heller* is too narrow and subjective to apply outside of a very specific context (keeping a handgun in one's house, for the purpose of self-defense). Prior to *McDonald*, which formally incorporated the right to bear arms to the states, several states were unwilling to apply *Heller*, given that it was not incorporated. On the other hand, at least one state (Washington) applied it preemptively shortly after the *Heller* decision. After incorporation of the right to bear arms occurred in *McDonald*, some ambiguity (about whether *Heller* applied) was removed, yet more ambiguity in terms of how to apply it still remained. We ultimately argue that *Heller* and *McDonald* cumulatively give state high courts a moderate level of flexibility to interpret the precedents as they please. This moderate degree of flexibility is there in our view because the rule from *Heller* is somewhat complex to apply to real-world situations that differ from the facts in the instant case, but unlike in the case of *Lemon*, the US Supreme Court has supported *Heller* and *McDonald* since they were first issued by the Court.

In terms of descriptive statistics as to *how* state high courts treated each of the precedents, we find consistent evidence in the next three chapters that suggests state high courts quite frequently ignore US Supreme Court precedents in ways that are largely consistent with our overall theory. In all three sets of cases analyzed, we find that state high courts ignore US Supreme Court precedent in 10–50 percent of all potential opportunities they had to interpret one of these precedents. The frequency of available opportunities states had to interpret specific precedents given their dockets explains some of these differences.[14] Yet we believe that dockets alone are not sufficient to explain differences among the states in terms of how they interpret US Supreme Court precedent.

---

[14] Perhaps the most emblematic example from the next three chapters relates to Second Amendment cases. While the Massachusetts Supreme Judicial Court and Illinois Supreme Court had a relatively large number of cases dealing with the Second Amendment, many conservative states had few (or none), although the Louisiana Supreme Court had five Second Amendment cases between the years 2012 and 2015, largely due to other statewide changes that had occurred shortly post-*McDonald*, creating a potential new area of jurisprudence that the Louisiana Supreme Court felt obliged to address on several occasions in our data.

We also find initial evidence from the next three chapters suggesting that differences of flexibility in how state high courts can deal with US Supreme Court opinions influence how those precedents get treated over an extended period of time. Specifically, we find that *Lemon* was the precedent ignored most frequently in our analyses, with state high courts ignoring it 50 percent of the time it was relevant. Conversely, we find *Atkins* was the precedent ignored the least frequently among those we examine, although *Atkins* was still ignored in about 11 percent of all the opportunities state high courts had to treat it. Finally, *Heller* and *McDonald* had an intermediate degree of instances where state high courts ignored the precedent: with 34 percent of all state high court potential treatments of *Heller* being instances where the court ignored the precedent, and a slightly higher 40 percent of all state high court potential treatments of *McDonald* being instances where the court ignored the precedent.

This initial evidence is extremely important regarding the claim we make that having knowledge of when state high courts ignore Supreme Court precedent is crucial for a comprehensive understanding of how state high courts respond to US Supreme Court precedents. In fact, given that anywhere from roughly 10 to 50 percent of all observations for each of the precedents we examine were instances where a relevant precedent was ignored, studies that neglect to account for instances where a state high court ignored precedent are inherently incomplete. This particular issue of systematically missing ignored cases in earlier studies is a significant limit on the ability of that research to account for all possible treatments. Finally, by using a nominal measurement of precedent treatment type, we are able to show that the determinants of why state high courts use different treatment types may differ in terms of what variables matter for each individual treatment type, rather than assuming a linear or ordinal effect. In short, after using our new measurement and theoretical construct, we find strong evidence for the idea that existing studies of lower court responses to US Supreme Court precedent are incomplete, in terms of the theories used for their study, as well as the universe of cases being used to examine many common research questions.

5

State High Court Responses to *Atkins* v. *Virginia*

Characterized by Flexibility

Even though state high courts seldom criticize US Supreme Court precedents directly, they are also not simply mechanical jurists who faithfully apply any precedent handed down by the Court any time one is relevant. Empowered to implement and interpret the policy content of US Supreme Court opinions (Canon and Johnson 1999), state high courts have significant discretion in whether and how they apply the Court's precedents. This chapter continues as the first empirical application of our theory articulated in Chapter 3. Thus, we are testing both our general theory outlined in Chapter 3, and our new measure detailed in Chapter 4.

For this chapter, we examine how state high courts use US Supreme Court precedent in decisions that relate to the execution of those that are intellectually disabled. Specifically, we analyze the population of death-penalty cases post-*Atkins* where issues relating to intellectual disability/mental retardation was mentioned in the opinion. We find strong support for the idea that state high court decisions periodically do ignore relevant US Supreme Court precedents. We also find that specific fact patterns that relate to *Atkins* and its potential application strongly influence the likelihood of the presence, and type, of treatment. We also show that how state high courts have used *Atkins* in the past affects the degree to which *Atkins* gets used by the same state high court in the future. This suggests that a certain level of path dependence is endemic in the process of using *Atkins*, meaning that how a state high court discusses a specific Supreme Court precedent at a given time will have substantial effects on how the same state high court discusses that precedent in the future. Based on these results, we believe it is safe to say that the ignoring of relevant Supreme Court precedents by state high courts is both systematic and relatively common.

5.1 A BRIEF HISTORY OF DEATH PENALTY LITIGATION: POST-GREGG V. GEORGIA

As is well known by legal scholars and those interested in questions that relate to the substantive use of the death penalty, *Gregg* v. *Georgia*[1] allowed for the reinstatement of the death penalty by state governments after a short moratorium following *Furman* v. *Georgia*.[2] In *Gregg*, the state of Georgia had rewritten their death penalty statute to have a bifurcated trial, with the first stage finding for the guilt of the defendant, and the second stage determining whether the death penalty should be applied. In order to apply the death penalty, the jury was required to unanimously prove, beyond a reasonable doubt, one of ten aggravating conditions. They additionally could, but were not required to, consider mitigating conditions against the death penalty, in what would be considered a *non-weighting* application of the death penalty. Other types of death penalty statutes, which were also held to be constitutional, used a *weighting* application of the death penalty, which required jurors to weigh the number of aggravating factors and mitigating factors against one another. With the per se question of the constitutionality of the death penalty largely settled, the US Supreme Court found itself dealing with a variety of questions regarding the appropriateness of the death penalty for specific situations post-*Gregg*.

Many of the Supreme Court cases post-*Gregg* focused on what types of crimes could constitutionally be eligible for the death penalty. These include cases such as *Coker* v. *Georgia*[3] (which banned the use of the death penalty for rape of an adult), *Enmund* v. *Florida*[4] (which banned the use of the death penalty for second-degree murder), and *Godfrey* v. *Georgia*[5] (which declared an aggravating factor of being "outrageously or wantonly vile" unconstitutional as an arbitrary and completely subjective standard).

In *Coker*, Ehrlich Coker was a hardened criminal who had escaped from a prison in Georgia. After escaping, he raped Elnita Carver, and stole her family's car. Georgia state law at the time allowed for the death penalty to be used for rape cases, if there were aggravating circumstances that were proven beyond a reasonable doubt. At trial, the state proved two aggravating circumstances: having a previous conviction of a death-penalty eligible crime and having committed rape in the process of committing another similarly eligible crime

[1] 428 U.S. 153 (1976).
[2] 408 U.S. 238 (1972).
[3] 433 U.S. 584 (1977).
[4] 458 U.S. 782 (1982).
[5] 446 U.S. 420 (1980).

(armed robbery). Justice White authored the majority opinion in this case. Ultimately, the majority ruled in a 6–3 opinion that a national consensus had grown against allowing the death penalty for rape, as Georgia was the only state that allowed the it for the rape of an adult at that time. The Court concluded that use of the death penalty for rape was grossly disproportionate and excessive to the crime committed.

In the case of *Enmund* v. *Florida*, Earl Enmund was an accomplice to two individuals who intended to commit armed robbery. After one of the victims shot one of the armed robbers, the other armed robber (Sampson Armstrong) shot both victims. Mr. Edmund drove both of the individuals to and from the crime scene. All three individuals were indicted, and found guilty of first degree murder and sentenced to death by the trial court judge. On appeal, Mr. Enmund successfully argued before the Supreme Court that his punishment of the death penalty was unconstitutional given that he was neither directly involved in murder nor in the armed robbery, but was merely an accessory to the crime. Thus, he argued that the Eighth Amendment did not allow the death penalty to be applied in his specific case given that he was not a direct perpetrator with involvement in the murder. All three of the previously mentioned cases differ somewhat on the specific details involved in their cases. Yet, the common thread among all of these cases is that the death penalty itself was not challenged in terms of its constitutionality, nor were individuals of particular classes (in a legal sense) prohibited from receiving the death penalty (such as juveniles or those who are intellectually disabled). Rather, the questions the Supreme Court faced regarding the death penalty related to what types of crimes it could constitutionally be applied to.

5.2 INTELLECTUAL DISABILITY AND THE EIGHTH AMENDMENT: CONTROVERSY AND RESOLUTION

As the previous section notes, the US Supreme Court has not directly addressed the question of whether the death penalty is per se unconstitutional under the Eighth Amendment since *Gregg*.[6] Rather, the Court's more recent

---

[6] However, Justices Brennan and Marshall dissented on all cases where an application of the death penalty was ruled as constitutional post-*Gregg*. Both of these justices asserted a view that the death penalty was unconstitutional under all circumstances. Marshall would generally dissent, simply noting this and referencing his concurring opinion in *Furman*. See *Furman, supra* note 2, at 314 (Marshall, J., concurring). Similarly, Brennan would generally make a similar note with a reference to his *Gregg* dissent. See *Gregg, supra* note 1, at 227 (Brennan, J., dissenting). Additionally, in recent years, Justice Breyer has expressed an interest in revisiting death penalty jurisprudence by the US Supreme Court. See, e.g., *Glossip* v. *Gross*, 135 S.Ct. 2726, 2776–2777 (2015) (Breyer, J., dissenting) ("I believe it highly likely that

landmark death penalty cases address the constitutional validity of the death penalty in particular contexts.[7] The issue of the execution of those who are intellectually disabled is one of these specific applications of the death penalty. Questions as to the actual degree of culpability of those with intellectual disabilities have long been a part of discourse and policy related to the death penalty. Rigorous debate over this issue started in the late 1980s with the American Bar Association (ABA) calling for an end to the execution of those who were intellectually disabled. The ABA based its position on testimony from mental health experts who asserted that the intellectually disabled are especially prone to confessions (sometimes falsely) in an attempt to please individuals. As a result, they possess a diminished ability to stand up to even mild coercion. Additionally, intellectually disabled individuals often lack a full understanding of the magnitude and heinousness of any crime they may have committed.

The first US Supreme Court case dealing with the execution of those who are intellectually disabled came during this period in *Penry* v. *Lynaugh*.[8] In a 5–4 decision, the Court held that executing individuals deemed "mentally retarded" did not violate the Cruel and Unusual Punishment Clause of the Eighth Amendment of the US Constitution. The majority ruled that there was insufficient evidence of a "national consensus" that executing intellectually challenged individuals violated "evolving standards of decency."[9] At that time, only two states with the death penalty (Georgia and Maryland) banned the execution of those who were intellectually disabled. However, between 1989 and 2002, sixteen additional states and the federal government banned the execution of those who were intellectually disabled.[10] While this was not an overwhelming sense of consensus, it did represent just over half of all states that had the death penalty.

In 2001, the Court agreed to revisit the question of the constitutionality of this practice in *Atkins* v. *Virginia*. A Virginia trial court sentenced Atkins to death following his conviction for armed robbery and murder despite having

---

the death penalty violates the Eighth Amendment. At the very least, the Court should call for full briefing on the basic question").

[7] See, e.g., *Roper* v. *Simmons*, 543 U.S. 551 (2005) (death penalty unconstitutional for those under the age of eighteen); *Kennedy* v. *Louisiana*, 554 U.S. 407 (2008) (death penalty unconstitutional as punishment for rape of a minor).

[8] 492 U.S. 302 (1989).

[9] Id. at 340.

[10] The sixteen states were Arizona, Arkansas, Colorado, Connecticut, Florida, Indiana, Kansas, Kentucky, Missouri, Nebraska, New Mexico, New York, North Carolina, South Dakota, Tennessee, and Washington.

his IQ officially tested at 59.[11] After the Virginia Supreme Court, relying on *Penry* v. *Lynaugh*, held that his low IQ was not a barrier to the imposition of the death penalty, the US Supreme Court granted certiorari to revisit the constitutional question. In reversing the Virginia Supreme Court, the US Supreme Court relied heavily on the fact that significantly more states had banned the practice by 2002, making the case that there was sufficient evidence of a growing national consensus that this practice violates evolving standards of decency.

While the *Atkins* decision provided a clear rule in the form of an absolute prohibition on the execution of the intellectually disabled, it only *suggested* a potential three-prong test for determining whether an individual was to be considered "mentally retarded."[12] The first prong of the suggested test said that individuals claiming an *Atkins* exemption from the death penalty due to intellectual disability must have substantially subaverage intellect. While this prong was not defined in absolute terms in the opinion, it suggested that an IQ equal to or below 70 constitutes evidence of being of substantially subaverage intellect (which is two standard deviations below the average IQ score in the United States). The second prong states that individuals would need to show a significant lack of adaptive functioning; this determination would be made by experts in the field. Finally, the third prong of the suggested legal test in *Atkins* is evidence that the intellectual disability started prior to the age of eighteen. Therefore, if an individual satisfied the first two elements of *Atkins* but failed the third prong (e.g., due to having a severe brain injury in a car accident), that individual would not be considered intellectually disabled according to the test that was espoused in *Atkins*. Even more importantly, *Atkins* itself did not give highly specific directions to states as to how to determine who was intellectually disabled. Rather, Justice Stevens' majority opinion implied that such determinations should be made by state legislatures, or by state high courts in the absence of state legislative action.

As noted above, while *Atkins* provides a somewhat vague standard as to what constitutes intellectual disability, many of the laws passed by state legislatures mirrored the model provided in dicta from the *Atkins* opinion. Typically, this means using a standard of intellectual disability based on the Diagnostic and Statistical Manual of Mental Disorders, 4th Edition (DSM-IV).

---

[11] An IQ of 70 is approximately two standard deviations below the mean. Thus, an IQ of 59 would represent significant intellectual disability, with an IQ of 60 being roughly three standard deviations below the mean IQ score in the United States.

[12] We use this slightly unusual phrasing because the Court's opinion ultimately said that the states needed to determine who was intellectually disabled.

The DSM-IV standard has three parts, which are mirrored in *Atkins*: these include having substantial limitations in intellectual functioning, substantial limitations in adaptive behavior, and evidence of the condition prior to the age of eighteen. As we discuss later, while most state statutes and state high court decisions adhere closely to professional definitions from the DSM-IV for evidence of these three conditions, a few states (in particular, Florida, Georgia, and Texas) have placed substantially higher barriers for proving at least one of the three elements compared with *Atkins*. For example, the Texas Court of Criminal Appeals found the "substantial limitations in adaptive behavior" requirement exceedingly subjective and effectively replaced it with seven additional factors based on whether the outside community considered an individual to be intellectually disabled, rather than on psychiatric criteria.[13]

Interestingly, many state statutes written prior to *Atkins* closely followed the standard in *Atkins* itself. First, most state statutes banning the execution of intellectually disabled individuals define an IQ that is considered to be indicative of significant subaverage levels of intelligence. Most states define this as two standard deviations below the mean, which is approximately 70. Secondly, an individual generally must show an inability to be able to function effectively on their own in terms of things such as personal hygiene or the ability to hold a job. The third element requires that an individual be diagnosed as intellectually disabled prior to reaching the age of eighteen.[14] Additionally, in Georgia's case, the Georgia Supreme Court, while having a statute to rely on that is substantively quite similar to that in *Atkins*, decided that the standard of proof for an *Atkins* claim is "beyond a reasonable doubt." This standard is the highest standard of proof used by courts in the United States. While the US Supreme Court has not made a legal ruling on Georgia's *Atkins* test specifically, at least one other state high court has claimed that Georgia's "beyond a reasonable doubt" standard of proof is likely unconstitutional when constructing their own legal test to comply with the *Atkins* decision.[15]

5.3 HOW STATES HAVE DEALT WITH *ATKINS*

At this point, we believe it is useful to first examine in greater depth how states have dealt with *Atkins* and intellectual disability with regard to the

[13] *Ex parte Briseno*, 135 S.W.3d 1, 5 (Tex. Crim. App. 2004).
[14] Several states have increased the age to twenty-two.
[15] See *Bowling v. Commonwealth*, 163 S.W. 3d 361, 382 (Ky. 2005).

death penalty. Within a few years of the *Atkins* decision, a majority of state legislatures had either amended their death penalty statutes formally to be in compliance with *Atkins* or had already banned the execution of those who are intellectually disabled prior to *Atkins*. In fact, the only six states that had not done so within two years of the decision were Alabama, Mississippi, New Jersey, Oklahoma, Pennsylvania, and Texas.[16] The other eighteen states with the death penalty had already banned the execution of intellectually disabled individuals prior to the Supreme Court's opinion in *Atkins*.[17] However, these statutes, as well as policies that courts have created to comply with *Atkins*, vary in some substantively important ways.

Comparing two states with a relatively high number of death penalty cases illustrates how great these differences can be. In Pennsylvania, the Supreme Court of Pennsylvania adopted a relatively liberal policy, requiring merely a "subaverage intellectual capacity," which they define as an IQ score less than 65–75.[18] Additionally, Pennsylvania required a relatively low standard of proof, using a preponderance of the evidence standard to determine intellectual disability.[19] Conversely, Texas developed a strict test for determining whether an individual is intellectually disabled, requiring that fact-finders consider whether people in the community believed an individual was "mentally retarded" for that individual to be eligible for an *Atkins* claim consideration.[20] One of the strictest interpretations of *Atkins*, this highlights the extraordinary degree of flexibility that states felt empowered with through the vagueness of *Atkins*.[21]

In the case of Pennsylvania, as we noted above, to satisfy the first prong of *Atkins*, a defendant must show that they would have an IQ of 65–75 or below, along with significant adaptive functioning issues, to trigger *Atkins* protections in the state. This range of numbers recognizes the possibility of error in the IQ test itself, with a potential bias of up to five points in either direction (predicting IQ as higher or lower than its actual value), meaning that

---

[16] California, Delaware, Idaho, Illinois, Louisiana, Nevada, Utah, and Virginia all passed state statutes prohibiting the execution of the intellectually disabled within two years of *Atkins*.

[17] The first state to explicitly ban the execution of the intellectually disabled while still having the death penalty was New Mexico, which passed a state legislative ban against executing intellectually disabled individuals in 1978.

[18] *Commonwealth v. Miller*, 888 A.2d 624, 630 (Pa. 2005).

[19] *Commonwealth v. Sanchez*, 36 A.3d 24, 62 (Pa. 2011).

[20] *Briseno, supra* note 13.

[21] However, this was considered a step too far as the US Supreme Court declared Texas's standard from *Briseno* to be unconstitutional in *Moore v. Texas*, 137 S.Ct. 1039 (2017).

an individual with an IQ of 75 could potentially be considered as intellectually disabled. Additionally, the Pennsylvania Supreme Court noted that a proper test of intellectual disability primarily relies on an interaction between the first two prongs (IQ scores and adaptive functioning issues), rather than relying on either one of the two prongs in isolation for borderline cases. In particular, *Miller* states that an individual who is considered "mentally retarded" with an IQ of below 70 is automatically ineligible to receive the death penalty without regard for the second prong. However, in cases where individuals are considered "borderline mentally retarded" with an IQ between 70 and 75, it is the second prong that becomes critical for determining whether an individual is exempt from the death penalty (the court used the DSM-IV standard verbatim for the second prong). Finally, the Pennsylvania Supreme Court ruled in *Miller* that *Atkins* does apply retroactively to all individuals currently on death row. Thus, we consider this to be a relatively liberal interpretation of *Atkins* by a state high court, as it does not require the consideration of the second prong if someone has an IQ at or below 70, but allows for use of the second prong in borderline cases (where an individual *may be*, but is not necessarily, intellectually disabled).

In the case of Texas, the Texas Court of Criminal Appeals, in *Ex parte Briseno*, came to a dramatically different interpretation of how to best comply with *Atkins*, specifically in regard to evidence requirements for the second prong (substantial issues with adaptive functioning).[22] While the Texas Court of Criminal Appeals complied with the first and third prong of *Atkins*, it substantially modified the second prong, making it dependent on seven specific factors. These factors include whether family, friends, teachers, or employers believe the individual was intellectually disabled; if the individual is impulsive; if the individual shows leadership; if the individual responds to stimuli rationally; if the individual responds rationally to questions; whether the individual is capable of lying; and whether commission of a murder required complex thought and extended planning.[23] Unlike the Pennsylvania Supreme Court, which automatically considered an IQ of 70 or below as prima facie evidence in favor of intellectual disability, in Texas one had to prove both that a defendant had a significantly subaverage IQ score and evidence that the defendant had failed several of the *Briseno* factors. While the first and third prongs in *Ex parte Briseno* followed conventional norms post-*Atkins*, Texas's

---

[22] *Briseno, supra* note 13.
[23] Id. at 8–9.

interpretation of the second prong was extremely strict and made it difficult to classify individuals as intellectually disabled.

On several occasions in Texas, this led to highly unusual justifications for the use of the death penalty at both the appellate and trial court levels. For example, in *Ex parte Taylor*[24] the Texas Court of Criminal Appeals applied the death penalty to Mr. Taylor on the basis that he was able to drive a manual gear tractor while evading police, despite having an IQ that was estimated to be between 63 and 69. Additionally, the Court said that he passed one of the *Briseno* factors, specifically the leadership one, because he had boasted to several people about killing the victim. The Court gave no explanation as to how this behavior indicated leadership ability, and he was executed in 2008. On another occasion, an individual who was diagnosed as mildly intellectually disabled was sentenced to death by a jury on the basis of being able to fry chicken successfully when working at a Kentucky Fried Chicken restaurant despite overwhelming evidence that he had significant issues with adaptive functioning in society, such as failing first grade, being able to read at a fourth-grade level, being homeless for much of his adult life, and frequent firings from jobs throughout much of his adult life.[25] Thus, the implementation of *Atkins* by the Texas Court of Criminal Appeals has rarely allowed for an individual to be found intellectually disabled, due to the extremely strict requirement to find someone intellectually disabled based on the second prong of *Atkins*.

The specific test adopted by state legislatures and state high courts is an important choice, as descriptive evidence suggests that the specific test used has significant implications on the success rate of individuals with an *Atkins*-based Eighth Amendment claim. Blume et al. (2014) note that from the years 2002 to 2013, relatively few inmates brought up claims of intellectual disabilities, and the success of those claims varied dramatically depending on the state. While some states had relatively high success rates, such as North Carolina (82 percent) and Mississippi (57 percent), others were much worse, with Texas having an 18 percent success rate, Georgia having an 11 percent success rate, and Florida having a 0 percent success rate for individuals making *Atkins* claims in their state high courts (Blume et al. 2014). Specifically in the case of Georgia, a successful *Atkins* claim must survive a beyond a reasonable

---

[24] 2015 WL 5076811 (Tex. Crim. App. 2006) (unpublished opinion).
[25] *State v. Williams*, No. 114-1505-06 (114th Dist. Ct. Tex. 2006).

doubt standard of proof, which is the highest possible legal standard, so it is not surprising that their *Atkins* claim success rate was quite low.

As noted in the above paragraphs, in most states state legislatures have led the way towards determining how *Atkins* would be implemented. Yet, in six states it has been left exclusively to state high courts to determine and mold how *Atkins* should be integrated into state law. In some instances, state courts have felt obligated to set a standard in the absence of action by the state legislature despite repeated calls for legislative action.[26] Additionally, as Kastellec (2018) found, state high courts also have the power to modify existing state law and mold other state laws into a judicial policy in the absence of state legislation. Perhaps the best example of this is from the state of Mississippi, where the Mississippi Supreme Court reinterpreted an existing statute that related to civil commitments, and applied a test based on that statute to adjudicate *Atkins* claims given the lack of a standard provided by the state legislature. The Mississippi Supreme Court had asked for a "clear and convincing evidence" standard of proof for civil commitments in its prior interpretation of the legislation in question.[27] However, when the Mississippi Supreme Court molded that statute for use in complying with *Atkins*, it declared this standard of proof as violating the Eighth Amendment when applied to *Atkins* claims, and modified the test to require the defendant to merely prove a "preponderance of evidence" that they were intellectually disabled.[28]

Table 5.1 shows how states have dealt with *Atkins* over time in a more systematic fashion. We find evidence of substantial degrees of heterogeneity depending on the specific state, although many states have been willing to positively treat *Atkins* on numerous occasions.[29] States that tend not to have death penalty cases would obviously have fewer (if any) opportunities to treat *Atkins* in a case that is truly closely tied into what *Atkins* does, which is as we would expect. Thus, the regional clustering of *Atkins* treatments overall is somewhat expected.

---

[26] E.g., *State ex rel. Bourque* v. *Cain*, 876 So. 2d 744 (La. 2004). In this particular instance, the Louisiana state legislature created a standard shortly after the release of this opinion.

[27] See, e.g., *Chill* v. *Mississippi Hospital Reimbursement Committee*, 429 So.2d 574 (Miss. 1983).

[28] *Russell* v. *State*, 849 So. 2d 95 (Miss. 2003).

[29] The Mississippi Supreme Court, Texas Court of Criminal Appeals, Florida Supreme Court, and Louisiana Supreme Court have the most positive treatments of *Atkins* of the states, which is not surprising given that they have among the most death penalty decisions.

TABLE 5.1. *Treatment patterns by state high court of* Atkins

State	Positive treatment	Negative treatment	Cited	Ignored
Alabama	3	0	1	0
Arizona	4	0	4	0
Arkansas	0	0	7	4
California	3	3	3	5
Colorado	1	0	0	0
Connecticut	0	0	1	0
Delaware	0	0	0	0
Florida	8	7	37	21
Georgia	2	2	3	6
Idaho	1	1	2	0
Illinois	1	1	0	0
Indiana	5	1	6	2
Kansas	1	0	1	0
Kentucky	4	1	6	0
Louisiana	7	2	13	0
Maryland	0	0	0	0
Mississippi	20	3	15	0
Missouri	4	2	6	1
Montana	0	0	0	0
Nebraska	1	0	1	0
Nevada	0	0	2	0
New Hampshire	0	0	0	0
New Jersey	0	0	0	2
New Mexico	0	0	0	0
North Carolina	0	0	3	0
Ohio	5	2	9	0
Oklahoma CCA	4	1	13	3
Oregon	1	0	0	0
Pennsylvania	6	2	19	0
South Carolina	0	0	3	0
South Dakota	0	0	0	0
Tennessee	4	1	4	1
Texas CCA	11	2	79	1
Utah	1	0	0	0
Virginia	1	0	8	0
Washington	0	0	1	0
Wyoming	0	0	0	0

There is no entry for states that had no death penalty for the entire time frame of our study (Alaska, Hawaii, Iowa, Maine, Massachusetts, Michigan, Minnesota, New York, North Dakota, Rhode Island, Vermont, West Virginia, and Wisconsin). Additionally, the Oklahoma Supreme Court and the Texas Supreme Court are excluded as they do not hear death penalty cases.

5.4 SUPREME COURT POST-*ATKINS*

As we mention in the preceding paragraphs, the US Supreme Court decided two cases related to the methodology used by state high courts and state legislatures to determine which individuals are intellectually disabled: *Hall* v. *Florida*[30] and *Moore* v. *Texas*.[31] We provide a brief background of both cases at this point. In the case of *Hall*, Freddie Lee Hall sexually assaulted and murdered a seven-months pregnant woman by the name of Karol Hurst in 1978. After the *Atkins* decision, Hall asked to have his death sentence vacated due to intellectual disability. While Hall had previously scored 60 on an IQ test, he was unable to conclusively prove that he had an IQ of 70 or below at the time of his postconviction hearing. While Hall had also asked to show additional evidence of adaptive deficits as *Atkins* mandates, the Florida Supreme Court ruled that he could not do so. Hall further argued that the Supreme Court did not mandate a specific IQ range in *Atkins* that would constitute evidence for intellectual disability.

In the 5–4 majority opinion, authored by Justice Kennedy, the Court found that only nine states had a strict IQ cutoff of 70 or below. The opinion also stated that no state high court had interpreted a death penalty statute authored by a state legislature in a similar way to the Florida Supreme Court. Additionally, the majority opinion stated that the Florida Supreme Court's interpretation of its state statute was deficient because it failed to account for the standard error inherent in an IQ test (which suggests IQ is a range rather than a single number) and that it did not allow for additional evidence of intellectual disability to be considered, even though other types of evidence could give substantial weight in favor of (or opposed to) a factual finding of intellectual disability.

In *Moore* v. *Texas*, the Court addressed a similar issue to *Hall*. Again, this decision related to how states define individuals as being intellectually disabled, and therefore ineligible for the death penalty. In this case, Bobby Moore and two other men shot a store clerk at a supermarket in Houston in 1980. While he was sentenced to death in 1980, his case was later remanded on appeal due to a successful ineffective counsel claim. On his retrial in 2001, he was resentenced to death, but claimed that he was ineligible to be executed due to intellectual disability. While a Texas habeas court proceeding ruled in his favor, the Texas Court of Criminal Appeals reversed the habeas court on appeal based on an earlier Texas Court of Criminal Appeals precedent,

---

[30] 134 S.Ct. 1986 (2014).
[31] *Supra* note 21.

Ex parte Briseno. As discussed above, *Briseno* had seven questions that were designed to assess intellectual disability based on the impression of individuals who knew the suspect. The questions related to stereotypical behavior based on popular culture depictions of of intellectual disability, such as detailed in John Steinbeck's novel *Of Mice and Men*.[32] For instance, Texas stated that being able to play pool in a bar for money was evidence that Mr. Moore was not intellectually disabled. He had additionally scored an average IQ of 70.66 over six IQ tests (later rescaled to 74), which resulted in a potential IQ range of 69 to 79, post-rescaling. Similar to the earlier Florida case, the Texas Court of Criminal Appeals ruled that he was not intellectually disabled given that the point estimate for his IQ was greater than 70.

5.5 APPLICATION OF OUR THEORY TO *ATKINS*

The application of our general theory (from Chapter 3) to the issue of executions of intellectually disabled individuals is rather straightforward. As we note in Chapter 3, *Atkins* consists of the combination of a clear rule in a general sense (a categorical prohibition on the execution of the intellectually disabled) with a vague standard that has been somewhat complicated in its application. Evidence for this point can be seen by the fact that the US Supreme Court has invalidated two states' schemes regarding how to determine when an individual is intellectually disabled: Florida (2014) and Texas (2017). As a potentially useful tool, having a vague standard may actually make it easier for state high courts to comply with a precedent, as it gives state high court judges flexibility on how to use a precedent (Fix, Kingsland, and Montgomery 2017). Conversely, confusion about a precedent could simply lead to it being ignored, attacked, or stretched beyond reason as in the case of Florida and Texas.

Existing evidence suggests that states that have dealt with a precedent positively in the past are more likely to do so again in the future (Fix, Kingsland, and Montgomery 2017). Because we believe that state high court judges have substantial freedom to interpret precedents largely in the way that they desire without fear of interference by the US Supreme Court (Kassow, Songer, and Fix 2012), what a state high court has done in the past should have an especially large effect on how it treats *Atkins* in the future. Moreover, as state high courts continually interpret (and reinterpret) cases, the meaning of a precedent within the context of a state may change over time (Black and Spriggs 2013; Hansford and Spriggs 2006; Landes and Posner 1976; Merryman 1953). As an

---

[32] In fact, the Court ruled unanimously that the *Ex parte Briseno* test was unconstitutional, and the dissent was not based on this portion of the case.

additional corollary, we believe that if a state high court has shown a propensity to follow *Atkins* when it has had prior opportunities to do so, it will be less likely to ignore *Atkins* when there is a present opportunity for it to discuss the case. From this, we expect:

H_1:   If a state high court treated *Atkins* positively in the past, then it is more likely to treat *Atkins* positively and less likely to ignore *Atkins*.

Prior research shows that case-specific factors significantly influence state high court decision-making, especially in death penalty cases (Brace and Hall 1995; 1997). In the context of *Atkins*, we expect two case-specific factors to have a systematic impact on whether and how state high courts use the precedent. The first relates to whether a state high court opinion shows that an individual has an IQ lower than 70, as the first part of the standard from *Atkins* uses an IQ of "approximately 70" to determine intellectual disability. Thus, when a defendant's IQ is above 70 it is potentially easier for judges to argue that *Atkins* does not apply and that there is no need to follow it.[33] When a defendant's IQ is at or below 70, according to all statutes and legal tests adopted to deal with determinations of intellectual disability, one part of the *Atkins* test is satisfied. Thus, in this situation, state high courts have a situation that is at least fairly analogous to *Atkins*, suggesting that the conclusion reached in *Atkins* is now possible given the tight fit with the first part of the *Atkins* test. Thus, our second hypothesis:

H_2:   If a defendant's IQ is less than 70, the probability of a state high court ignoring *Atkins* will decrease and the probability of a state high court treating *Atkins* positively will increase.

The second case-specific factor relates to whether a claim of mental illness was made by the defendant. The issue of whether an individual having severe mental illness serves as a barrier to execution has been a controversial topic since *Atkins*. According to an article in an ABA newsletter, many of the attributes highlighted in *Atkins* to justify why the execution of the intellectually disabled was cruel and unusual punishment also apply to those with severe mental illness (Mangels 2017). Moreover, several unsuccessful recent attempts have been made to pass such restrictions through state legislatures.[34]

---

33 In particular, this was the case in Florida, where the statute for determining intellectual disability disallowed anyone being considered intellectually disabled if they had an IQ of 70 or higher. Thus, we would expect in Florida this relationship to be particularly strong, at least until this statute was overturned by the US Supreme Court in *Hall* v. *Florida, supra* note 30.

34 These include Indiana and Kentucky in 2009; North Carolina in 2011; and Indiana, Ohio, South Dakota, Tennessee, Texas, and Virginia in 2016–2017. As of 2018, only one state with

However, while this remains an evolving issue in death penalty states, during the time of our analyses neither the US Supreme Court nor any state high court had yet considered severe mental illness to be equivalent to being intellectually disabled.[35] Thus, if a defendant claims severe mental illness as being a valid reason for not being executed under *Atkins*, this creates an easy opportunity for state high court justices to distinguish an instant case from *Atkins*, or even to ignore *Atkins* entirely. Our third hypothesis reflects this:

H_3: If a case discusses mental illness as a separate issue from intellectual disability, the probability of a state high court distinguishing *Atkins* will increase and the probability of a state high court ignoring *Atkins* will also increase.

Additionally, we believe that the political environment that a state high court sits in may cause state high court opinions to use *Atkins* in particular ways. Specifically, we argue that in a state high court environment that is relatively conservative, state high court justices are especially likely to have reasons to attack *Atkins* or to ignore it based on political reasons. In particular, evidence suggests that state high court justices (and courts themselves) are somewhat constrained in their ability to act on their own ideological impulses. This leads to our fourth hypothesis:

H_4: State high courts in states that are relatively conservative will be especially likely to ignore *Atkins*, compared with state high courts in liberal states.

Finally, our general theory argues that institutional factors will influence state court decisions on whether and how to use US Supreme Court precedents. Specifically, in the context of death penalty cases, prior work has shown that individual state high court judges in areas of the country where elections may pose a real threat are more likely to vote to uphold death penalty sentences (Brace and Hall 1997). It seems logical to expect that these judges would also be more hostile to US Supreme Court precedents limiting the death penalty.

---

the death penalty had banned the execution of individuals with severe mental illness (Connecticut). However, Connecticut passed a non-retroactive ban of the death penalty in its entirety 2012.

[35] Two caveats are important to note here. First, some cases involve both claims of intellectual disability and severe mental illness where it is possible that a court will grant an *Atkins* claim irrespective of whether mental illness alone is grounds for such a claim. See, e.g., *Goodin v. State*, 102 So. 3d 1002 (Miss. 2012). Second, there is an important difference between "severe mental illness" and other types of neurological and/or brain disorders, as the latter can lead to intellectual disability of the sort recognized under the strictest applications of *Atkins*.

This observation is reinforced by the anecdote of Justice Parker of the Alabama Supreme Court – a state with partisan judicial elections – writing a hostile editorial in the state's largest newspaper to make a public attack against a US Supreme Court death penalty decision and his own court for following it (Parker 2006). This leads to our final hypothesis:

H_5: If a state uses partisan or nonpartisan elections to retain their high court judges then the likelihood that court will ignore or distinguish *Adkins* is higher than in states that use elite appointment or merit selection.

5.6 DATA AND METHODS

The data used for this project come from an original dataset containing the universe of state high court death penalty cases dealing with claims related to intellectual disability from 2003 (the year after *Atkins* was decided) through 2016. The data consist of information about each state high court case, how *Atkins* was treated (if it was), and state-level factors. To locate the universe of death penalty cases dealing with claims related to intellectual disability, we conducted a LexisNexis search for the following Boolean search term to ensure that we were able to examine the relevant population of cases where a state court could have been expected to cite *Atkins*: "death penalty" AND ("mentally retarded" OR "intellectually disabled" OR "mentally handicapped").[36] The resulting dataset contains all cases that cite *Atkins* and those where *Atkins* was relevant but the state court chose to ignore it. This yields a total of 421 cases with 46 (10.9 percent) representing cases where *Atkins* was not cited but could have been. These are cases that would have been excluded under case selection techniques generally used in research in this area.

Our dependent variable measures how a state high court used *Atkins*. We treat this as a four-category nominal variable as there is no clear ordering among the alternatives. We code our dependent variable "4" if *Atkins* is followed or treated positively, "3" for citation with no (or neutral) treatment, "2" if *Atkins* is ignored, and "1" if it is treated negatively. Our coding follows *Shepards' Citations* coding rules for treatments where followed means that the court explicitly relied on *Atkins* as the basis for its decision and a negative treatment requires that the court explicitly distinguish the case from *Atkins* due to factual differences or criticize *Atkins*. In our data, 98 cases are positive

---

[36] While the term "intellectually disabled" is the most appropriate term today according to medical professionals, judges have frequently used the other two terms that we searched for rather than using the phrase "intellectually disabled."

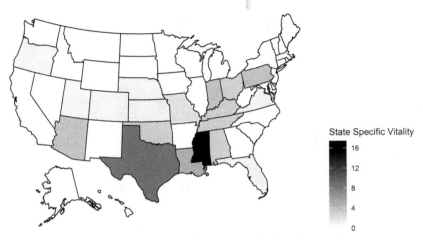

FIGURE 5.1. Variation in state-specific vitality for *Atkins* (2017)

treatments (23.3 percent), 246 just cite *Atkins* (58.4 percent), 46 ignore *Atkins* (10.9 percent), and 31 treat it negatively (7.4 percent).[37]

Our first independent variable measures prior treatment of *Atkins* in the state. This is related to the concept of precedent vitality developed by Hansford and Spriggs (2006) which focuses on how the US Supreme Court treats its own precedent over time. However, for our purposes, we believe that how a given state high court has treated a US Supreme Court precedent over time is more important than how the Supreme Court has treated its own precedent. Fix, Kingsland, and Montgomery (2017) created a measure of state-specific precedent vitality that mirrors the Hansford and Spriggs (2006) measure but in a way that is consistent with our theoretical needs. Our measure of *State-Specific Vitality* is the annual difference between the total number of prior positive treatments of *Atkins* and the total number of prior negative treatments in that state. This variable has a theoretical range from negative infinity to infinity, but in our data ranges from −2 (Georgia 2010–2011) to 17 (Mississippi 2015). Figure 5.1 shows how state-specific vitality varies among the states in our analysis of state high court treatments of *Atkins* in 2017. Figure 5.2 also shows how treatment types of *Atkins* have changed over time, as well as the frequency of overall treatments.

Our next two variables measure the key case facts in Hypotheses 2 and 3. The first, *IQ Below 70*, is coded "1" if the opinion specifically states that the

37 Of course, many of the states that have no positive treatments of *Atkins* are those that do not have the death penalty. This result is as one would expect – states that do not have the death penalty would not have any observations in our *Atkins* responses dataset.

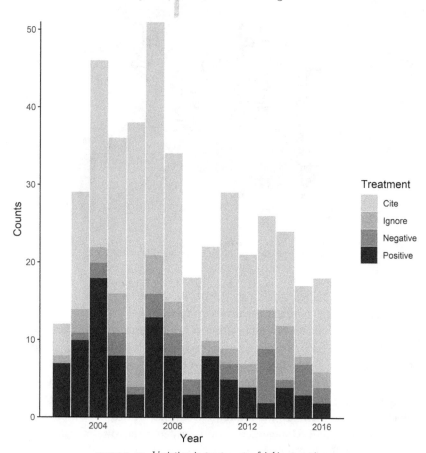

FIGURE 5.2. Variation in treatments of *Atkins* over time

individual's IQ is lower than 70. If the opinion states that the individual's IQ is 70 or higher, or if the opinion does not state the IQ score, then this variable is coded as a "0." The second, *Mental Illness Claim,* is coded "1" if the defendant makes an argument that their severe mental illness makes them ineligible for the death penalty. If no such claim is made, we code this variable "0."

For state ideology, we use the Berry et al. (1998; 2010) state ideology scores (updated through 2016 for our analysis). Specifically, we use the mass electorate ideology scores for states that retain judges via popular elections and elite ideology scores for states that use elite-based retention methods for state high court justices.[38]

[38] We do not include a state high court ideology variable in our analysis due to temporal limits with all currently existing state high court ideology measures (the most recent state high

Another important state-level factor relates to how judges are retained. For this, we include two dummy variables: one that denotes all states that use *partisan elections*, and a second that denotes states that use *nonpartisan elections*.[39]

Finally, we include a series of important control variables in our model specifications. First, we include an indicator of whether there is a *state statute* that bans the execution of the intellectually disabled. Data for this variable is derived from information obtained on **deathpenaltyinfo.org** (independently verified by searching information on statutes cited by the website). The reason for including this variable is that if a state legislature created a law or statutory scheme to ban the execution of those who are intellectually disabled, state high court justices would now have the option (and perhaps even obligation) to cite a specific state statute as legal grounds for a decision they make giving them additional flexibility with respect to *Atkins*. We code this variable "1" if a state has a relevant statute in a given year, and "0" otherwise. Next, we include the *Age of Atkins* (natural log) to account for potential decay in the rate of citations (Hansford, Spriggs, and Stenger 2013). We also include an additive index of *Aggravating Factors* including concurrent convictions of rape/sexual assault, robbery, kidnapping, different categories of victims (whether the victim is a law enforcement officer, a female, a senior citizen, or a child), and whether the defendant was found guilty of murdering multiple individuals (Brace and Hall 1995; 1997). Last, we include a dummy variable for all cases after 2014 when the US Supreme Court issued a follow-up precedent to *Atkins*, *Hall v. Florida*.

Our primary analysis uses a multinomial logit estimator.[40] While multinomial logit models potentially suffer from violations of the independence

court ideology score is measured from 2011). Due to the need to drop several years from our analysis, the loss of data would be unacceptably large. This is especially problematic as the US Supreme Court partially modified *Atkins* in 2014 (we even include a variable for this in our analysis). In total, roughly 30 percent of all state high court treatments would be eliminated by including this variable in the analysis. Other measures of state high court ideology, such as Brace, Hall, and Langer's (2000), have even greater temporal limitations.

39 We use this specific operationalization for two reasons. First, there is a theoretical debate in the literature as to how similar retention elections are to other types of elections. Second, there are very few observations in our data from states with gubernatorial or legislative reappointment.

40 In Chapter 3 we discussed how our theory requires a departure from prior theoretical accounts of this process as being sequential (courts first decide whether they have to engage with a precedent, then decide how to engage with it). Our choice of a multinomial logit is predicated on our assumption that this is a simultaneous process, where the choice to ignore a precedent is made at the same time as the choice of other treatment options. To test our assumption, we estimated a selection model. In this selection model, we used an indicator of where the precedent was ignored or not in the first stage (selection) equation. The second stage equation then estimated the type of treatment (positive, neutral, negative) among the set of cases that were not ignored. In this alternative model, we found no statistically

of irrelevant alternatives (IIA) assumption, the literature does not dictate a standard way of dealing with this issue. Some scholars ignore the IIA assumption, while others use a multinomial probit model which is less sensitive to violations of the IIA assumption but is prone to instability in coefficient and standard error estimates. This instability sometimes results in an artificial appearance of a lack of robustness in the results, due to the fragility of the model (Alvarez and Nagler 1998; Dow and Endersby 2004; Kropko 2007). The evidence is mixed as to whether multinomial logit models perform better than multinomial probit models even with severe violations of the IIA assumption, or whether multinomial probit models derive more accurate coefficient and standard error estimates than multinomial logit models.[41]

5.7 RESULTS AND DISCUSSION

Table 5.2 shows the results from a multinomial logit model comparing the three substantive categories (Ignored, Negatively Treated, and Positively Treated) with the modal baseline category of Cited. The reason for using the baseline category of being cited is twofold. First, precedents that are just cited or receive a neutral treatment are the most common in our data. Second, we believe theoretically comparing substantive outcomes is best conceptualized in comparison with neutral treatments (and mere citations), given that it is likely the default status given to the use of precedents by state high courts.

We begin with the examination of ignoring precedent presented in the first column of Table 5.2. Our results comparing ignored cases with cited ones show that three variables of interest matter with regard to the probability of ignoring *Atkins*. In particular, we find that as state-specific vitality increases, the probability of ignoring the precedent decreases, which gives support for Hypothesis 1. We also find that in states with partisan elections, the probability of ignoring *Atkins* is relatively small, consistent with Hypothesis 5. Finally, we find that the more aggravating factors present in a case, the less likely state courts are to ignore the precedent.

Looking at the baseline results putting all variables at their mean (continuous) or modal (categorical) values, we find that the probability of a given

---

significant selection effects, thus strongly indicating support for our assumption regarding the simultaneous nature of treatment choice.

[41] To test the robustness of our models, we additionally estimated a multinomial probit model. The results are substantively similar to the multinomial logit model presented in the next section.

TABLE 5.2. *Determinants of treatment types for* Atkins

Variable	Ignored	Negative	Positive
State Court Vitality	−0.161*	0.140*	−0.042
	(0.075)	(0.062)	(0.050)
IQ below 70	0.126	−1.063	0.643*
	(0.523)	(1.168)	(0.315)
Mental Illness Claim	−0.328	2.142*	−0.218
	(0.453)	(0.494)	(0.378)
Citizen Ideology	0.033	0.031	−0.009
	(0.024)	(0.031)	(0.015)
Partisan Elections	−3.792*	0.565	−0.478
	(1.218)	(0.731)	(0.386)
Nonpartisan Elections	−0.087	0.190	0.550
	(0.431)	(0.690)	(0.330)
State Statute	0.218	1.260	−0.090
	(0.669)	(0.727)	(0.400)
Age of *Atkins*	0.120	0.016	−0.068
	(0.065)	(0.075)	(0.046)
Aggravating Factor Scale	−0.587*	−0.261	0.008
	(0.150)	(0.157)	(0.084)
Post-*Hall* (2014)	−1.112	0.525	0.212
	(0.964)	(0.765)	(0.633)
Constant	−1.887	−5.252*	−0.048
	(1.221)	(1.931)	(0.711)
Observations		421	
X^2		119.23*	

Estimates are from a multinomial logit model comparing each outcome to a baseline of just cited or neutral treatment. Robust standard errors are in parentheses.
*$p < 0.05$.

treatment is as follows: 0.151 for ignoring *Atkins*, 0.011 for negatively treating the precedent, 0.605 for citing *Atkins*, and 0.233 for positively treating *Atkins*. The main result that predicts the incidence of ignoring an *Atkins* claim relates to state-specific precedent vitality. In fact, the substantive effect of state-specific precedent vitality on the probability of ignoring a case is profound. Specifically, we find that for state high courts with a state-specific precedent vitality of −2, the probability of ignoring *Atkins* is a sizable 0.262. For cases where *Atkins* has a vitality of 0, the probability of ignoring *Atkins* decreases to 0.207, and for a vitality score of +2, the probability of ignoring *Atkins* decreases to 0.163.

Turning to the other variables that reach statistical significance in this model, partisan elections have a substantively large negative effect on the probability of ignoring *Atkins* (0.151 for states with merit retention or elite retention methods, versus 0.004 for states with partisan elections). Additionally, the presence or absence of aggravating factors exerts a large substantive effect on the likelihood of ignoring *Atkins*. When no aggravating factors are present, state high courts have a 0.407 probability of ignoring the precedent. However, that drops to 0.020 when all six aggravating factors we measured are present.

The second column in Table 5.2 compares the category of negative treatments of precedent. Here we find support for the idea of mental illness claims increasing the probability of a negative treatment. Surprisingly, we find no support for any other hypothesis. The only other variable in the model to reach statistical significance is precedent vitality. Counter to our expectations, a defendant having an IQ of less than 70 appears to exert no significant effect. Results examining the substantive impact of a defendant claiming severe mental illness on the probability of a negative treatment are rather sizable. Specifically, we find that in cases where a defendant claims severe mental illness, the probability of a negative treatment of *Atkins* increases from approximately 0.011 to 0.093.

The final column in Table 5.2 compares the category of positive treatments of *Atkins* to the baseline category of being cited. Perhaps most surprising is the lack of results for state-specific vitality contrary to Hypothesis 1. The one variable that reaches statistical significance in this model is having a judge rule that an individual may have an IQ below 70, which automatically triggers the first prong of *Atkins*. We find that in cases where a judge (or court) has not ruled that a defendant has an IQ of less than 70, the probability of a positive treatment, *ceteris paribus*, is approximately 0.233, compared with a probability of 0.361 of a positive treatment where a defendant has officially been declared as having an IQ of less than 70.

Figure 5.3 graphically depicts the predicted probability a court will use each of the possible treatment outcomes based on whether there was a claim of severe mental illness, with all other variables held constant at their means (continuous variables) or medians (categorical variables). The figure shows that when an opinion cites severe mental illness as a reason given by a party for invoking *Atkins*, the court is significantly more likely to treat *Atkins* negatively than if such a claim is not made. Given that severe mental illness is not considered the same as being intellectually disabled, we expect (and find) evidence that suggests the likelihood of a negative treatment by *Atkins* will increase. These findings comport with expectations and fit within the general framework of our theory.

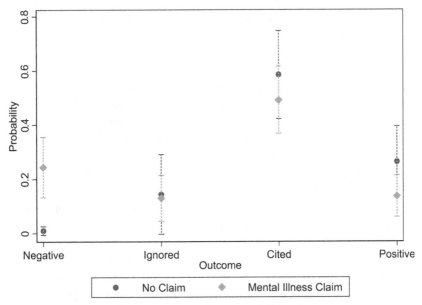

FIGURE 5.3. Effects of severe mental illness claim
Dots represent predicted probabilities for each possible outcome holding all other variables
at their mean (median for categorical variables). Errors bars are 95 percent confidence
intervals.

5.8 CONCLUDING THOUGHTS

In this chapter, we presented the first analysis testing our theory of state high
court responses to US Supreme Court precedents. According to our theoretical
account of state high court responses to Supreme Court precedents, we
assert that state high courts have one of four possibilities as to how they can
potentially respond to a relevant US Supreme Court precedent. They can
follow the precedent, mention it in a neutral light, attack (or distinguish) it,
or they can simply ignore it. We find evidence that the possibility of state high
courts choosing not to discuss a Supreme Court precedent is something that
is not just a potential possibility, but is something that occurs with significant
frequency even in an area where the US Supreme Court has set a clear rule.

In this chapter, we contended that the case of *Atkins* v. *Virginia* and
the policy area of the application of the death penalty to those who are
intellectually disabled, is useful for understanding the interplay between case
facts, state political environment, and the state legal environment. We believe
this to be the case because of the type of legal standard that the case uses.
Specifically, *Atkins* has *both* a clear rule that states those who are intellectually

disabled cannot be executed *and* gives substantial discretion to both state legislators and state high courts in terms of creating a statute or legal standard that satisfies *Atkins*. At the same time, the *Atkins* standard allows for states to mold legislation and precedents in such a way that fits their own needs and political interests. Effectively, this provides an encouragement for state high courts to interpret *Atkins* positively given that it allows for some flexibility in determining how it is best to apply the case.[42] Ultimately, we believe that examining legal policy in the area of the death penalty provides an excellent example of understanding how state high courts have the ability to make policy and how their decisions regarding the use of precedent play a key role.

When examining our empirical results, we find that case facts matter substantially for how state high courts treat *Atkins* over time. We find strong support for both of the factual elements which we hypothesize in this chapter: (1) claims of severe mental illness by defendant, and (2) a defendant having a verified IQ of 70 or less. In the case of severe mental illness claims, we find strong substantive support for the idea that when severe mental illness is discussed in the absence of a true intellectual disability claim, the probability of a state high court distinguishing such a case increases significantly compared to when this factual element is not mentioned in a state high court opinion. On the other hand, in the case of a defendant having a verified IQ less than or equal to 70, we find that the likelihood of a positive treatment of *Atkins* increases.

Somewhat surprisingly, we find less support for our political environment hypotheses, which suggests that the political environment does not seem to affect the types of treatments that state high courts give to *Atkins* in cases that relate to intellectual disability and the death penalty. However, the legal environment of a state high court does seem to affect treatment. In particular, lower levels of state-specific high court vitality have an effect on the probability of a state high court ignoring *Atkins*. As the state-specific high court vitality decreases over time, the probability of the same state high court ignoring *Atkins* increases substantially. This finding indicates that there is a large degree of path dependence in how state high courts use precedents, such as *Atkins*. Even more interestingly, the state political environment does not seem to either discourage or encourage the ignoring of *Atkins*. This may be the case, however, because of the flexibility that is innate within *Atkins*.

---

[42] On the other hand, with the two later decisions that reinforce *Atkins* and prevent states from acting with as much flexibility, this may have changed a bit post-*Hall*, despite our statistical evidence suggesting the contrary.

In the next chapter of the book, we are able to compare the results with *Atkins* to those of *Lemon* v. *Kurtzman*, a case where state high court discretion should be at its highest levels. *Lemon* combines a vague standard with a lack of clarity about whether it applies *at all*, due to subsequent US Supreme Court criticism of the precedent. In many ways, *Lemon* was an attempt by the Supreme Court "to find a grand unified theory of the Establishment Clause."[43] However, subsequent decisions of the Court not only question that broad purpose, but whether *Lemon* retains any value as precedent at all. These questions make *Lemon* an ideal case. In contrast to *Atkins*, where it was, at a minimum, clear that the precedent applied in a given area, state courts facing Establishment Clause cases lacked clarity on either the standard or whether it remains good law.

---

[43] *American Legion v. American Humanist Association*, 139 S.Ct. 2067, 2087 (2019).

6

State High Court Usage of *Lemon* v. *Kurtzman*
Examining a Case of Maximum Discretion

In the last chapter, we examined state high court responses to the Supreme Court's *Atkins* v. *Virginia* precedent. *Atkins* represented a case where the Court created a clear rule (no execution of the intellectually disabled) but a vague standard for determining when that rule applied to individual criminal defendants. In this chapter, we examine a Supreme Court precedent that is vastly different from *Atkins* in several key ways. Unlike *Atkins*, the Court in *Lemon* v. *Kurtzman* made no attempt to set a clear rule; rather it represents an attempt to craft a flexible, universal standard for cases arising under the Establishment Clause.

In addition to the rule versus standard distinction, *Atkins* and *Lemon* differ in another important way. While *Atkins* has been subsequently supported by the Supreme Court itself, *Lemon* is a different story.[1] As Justice Alito recently noted, any expectation that *Lemon* "would provide a framework for all future Establishment Clause decisions ... has not been met."[2] In fact, only two years after the decision, the Court held that the three prongs of the *Lemon* test "are no more than helpful signposts,"[3] and dissatisfaction with *Lemon* has only grown since. It has been subject to harsh scholarly criticism (See, e.g., Kurland 1979; McConnell 1992; 1997; Paulsen 1986; 1992) and direct attacks by several Supreme Court justices.[4] Criticism of *Lemon* is so extreme that it has

---

[1] The Supreme Court has never criticized or distinguished *Atkins* in any of its subsequent cases, but has done so to *Lemon* on seven occasions.

[2] *American Legion* v. *American Humanist Association*, 139 S.Ct. 2067, 2080 (2019) (while the majority opinion was authored by Alito, J., the part of Alito's opinion this quote comes from was joined only by three other justices).

[3] *Hunt* v. *McNair*, 413 U.S. 734, 741 (1973).

[4] Examples of this abound. See, e.g. *Wallace* v. *Jaffree*, 472 U.S. 38, 112 (1985) (Rehnquist, J., dissenting) ("If a constitutional theory has no basis in the history of the amendment it seeks to interpret, is difficult to apply and yields unprincipled results, I see little use in it"); *Board of*

essentially become a zombie precedent: one that has been effectively killed by subsequent Supreme Court decisions without being formally overruled, thus retaining the ability to be resurrected at any time.[5]

These features combine to make *Lemon* an archetype of precedent where state high courts ought to have maximum flexibility in determining whether and how to use it in cases where it is potentially relevant. While this uncertainty might lead one to expect that state high courts would simply abandon the use of *Lemon* altogether, this is not the case. State courts still routinely follow *Lemon* in their Establishment Clause cases, despite having ample freedom to avoid doing so. Additionally, while zombie precedents like *Lemon* are rare, they are often in areas of law that are politically important and contentious. Thus, understanding how state courts deal with *Lemon* is important not simply because it offers an extreme case for our theoretical examination, but also for its insight into understanding how state high courts deal with zombie precedents more generally.[6]

Education of Kiryas Joel Village School District v. *Grumet*, 512 U.S. 687, 720 (1994) (O'Connor, J., concurring in part) ("courts tend to continually try to patch up the broad test, making it more and more amorphous and distorted. This, I am afraid, has happened with *Lemon*"); *Roemer* v. *Board of Public Works of Maryland*, 426 U.S. 736, 768 (1976) (White, J., concurring in judgment) ("The threefold test of *Lemon I* imposes unnecessary, and … superfluous tests for establishing when the State's involvement with religion passes the peril point for First Amendment purposes"). *Edwards* v. *Aguillard*, 482 U.S. 578, 639 (1987) (Scalia, J., dissenting) ("Given the many hazards involved in assessing the subjective intent of governmental decisionmakers, the first prong of *Lemon* is defensible, I think, only if the text of the Establishment Clause demands it. That is surely not the case"); *County of Allegheny v. ACLU*, 492 U.S. 573, 655 (1989) (Kennedy, J., concurring in part and dissenting in part) ("I am content for present purposes to remain within the *Lemon* framework, but do not wish to be seen as advocating, let alone adopting, that test as our primary guide in this difficult area").

5   While we believe we are the first to use the term "zombie precedent," the concept is drawn from language used in a handful of Supreme Court opinions. See, e.g., *Hein* v. *Freedom from Religion Foundation, Inc.*, 551 U.S. 587, 636 (2007) (Scalia, J. concurring in judgment) ("honoring *stare decisis* requires more than beating *Flast* [v. *Cohen*, 392 U.S. 83 (1968)] to a pulp and then sending it out to the lower courts weakened, denigrated, more incomprehensible than ever, and yet somehow technically alive"); *Kisor* v. *Wilkie*, 139 S.Ct. 2400, 2445 (2019) (slip op., at 2) (Gorsuch, J., concurring in judgment) ("the doctrine [from *Auer* v. *Robbins*, 519 U.S. 452 (1997)] emerges maimed and enfeebled – in truth, zombified").

6   One important example of this is the Aguilar-Spinelli test abandoned by the US Supreme Court in *Illinois* v. *Gates*, 462 U.S. 213 (1983). Despite the Supreme Court's adoption of a new standard for probable cause, many state courts continued to use Aguilar-Spinelli, holding that their state constitutions required a higher standard than the US Constitution post-*Gates* under the doctrine of adequate and independent state grounds. See, e.g., *State* v. *Jackson*, 688 P. 2d 136 (Wash. 1984); *State* v. *Jones*, 706 P.2d 317 (Alaska 1985); *State* v. *Kimbro*, 496 A.2d 498 (Conn. 1985); *Commonwealth* v. *Upton*, 476 N.E. 2d 548 (Mass. 1985); *People* v. *Johnson*, 488 N.E.2d 439 (N.Y. 1985); *State* v. *Cordova*, 784 P.2d 30 (N.M. 1989); *State* v. *Jacumin*, 778

In this chapter, we apply our theoretical model to an original dataset of all state high court decisions from 1972 to 2016 in which *Lemon* was a relevant precedent, whether it was cited in the opinion or not. Our results show support for our broad theoretical claim that state high court decisions on whether and how to use a relevant US Supreme Court precedent is complex and the available choice set is not an ordered range of options, but one where specific factors drive the choice between options in different ways.

6.1 A BRIEF HISTORY OF ESTABLISHMENT CLAUSE JURISPRUDENCE

Like many of the guarantees in the Bill of Rights, the Establishment Clause of the US Constitution contains textual ambiguity, a lack of clarity as to the history and intent, and little early precedent to serve as a guide to its meaning. Legal scholars have written extensively on the intellectual history underlying the religion clauses in the First Amendment, the debates surrounding their drafting and ratification, and the writings of those most influential in shaping these guarantees (Feldman 2002; Kurland 1985; Levy 2017). Yet little clarity or consensus emerges from the studies to point to a single, historically grounded meaning for the phrase "establishment of religion." The search for the meaning of the Establishment Clause is made all the more difficult by the fact that the Supreme Court only decided a single case on the topic prior to 1947.[7]

While the Supreme Court had little to say about the Establishment Clause directly in its first 150 years of existence, one important early Free Exercise case played a significant role in shaping the modern debates over its meaning. In *Reynolds* v. *United States*,[8] the Court relied heavily on the writings of Jefferson and Madison and essentially wrote them into the First Amendment (Drakeman 2004). In the *Reynolds* opinion, the Court quoted the "wall of separation between church and state" – language from Jefferson's *Letter to the Danbury Baptist Association* – adding the commentary that "[c]oming as this does from an acknowledged leader of the advocates of the measure, it may

---

S.W.2d 430 (Tenn. 1989). Thus, despite being "killed" by the US Supreme Court, Aguilar-Spinelli has lived a long and full life as a zombie roaming the constitutional law of several states.

[7] That case, *Bradfield* v. *Roberts*, 175 U.S. 291 (1899), did not attempt to define the scope of the Establishment Clause. Rather, the Court relied on the fact that a hospital, while staffed by a church organization, was created via an act of Congress and thus not religious in nature.

[8] 98 U.S. 145 (1879).

be accepted almost as an authoritative declaration of the scope and effect of the amendment."[9]

Beginning in the late 1940s, the US Supreme Court made its first significant attempts to interpret the meaning of the Establishment Clause. In *Everson v. Board of Education*,[10] the Court first directly addressed the meaning of the Establishment Clause. Relying heavily on references to the writings of Madison and Jefferson along with Chief Justice Waite's historical interpretation of the two religion clauses in *Reynolds*, the Court concluded that "The First Amendment has erected a wall between church and state. That wall must be kept high and impregnable. We could not approve the slightest breach."[11] Despite adopting this strong view of the Establishment Clause as a prohibition against essentially any government support of religion, the Court simultaneously upheld a New Jersey law allowing local governments to reimburse parents for expenses incurred in transporting their children to school regardless of whether the children attended a public or church school.

The confusion fostered by this seeming disconnect was magnified when the following term the Court held that a "release time" program allowing public school children to spend part of their school day attending religion classes taught by outside instructors in their normal classrooms did violate the Establishment Clause.[12] Scholars at the time were highly critical of potential confusion sown by these decisions (Corwin 1949). Additional cases over the next few years continued this pattern of allowing some types of indirect aid to religion, while holding others in violation of the Establishment Clause. Four years after *McCollum*, the Court allowed a released time program where students were allowed to leave their public schools for a set period of time each day to receive religious education. In upholding this law, the Court emphasized that this case, unlike *McCollum*, did not involve the use of public institutions or facilities for religious instruction. The Court held this finding to be consistent with a strict separation of church and state.

Moreover, lacking from these cases was any sort of overarching standard that could be applied to a wide range of factual scenarios. These early cases established that a line clearly existed between acceptable government activity and activity that crossed over the line in violation of the Establishment Clause. These early school cases made it reasonably clear that the question would revolve around how direct the aid to religion was or where the activity

9 Id. at 164.
10 330 U.S. 1 (1947).
11 Id. at 18.
12 *McCollum v. Board of Education*, 333 U.S. 203 (1948).

occurred. Such a fact-intensive approach continued to be used into the 1960s and in the Court's decision in *Engel* v. *Vitale*,[13] which held that school lead prayer violated the Establishment Clause. However, this approach gave little guidance on where to draw that line in cases involving factual scenarios distinct from those the Court had directly addressed. This led to a bit of an ad hoc approach in Establishment Clause cases. In large part, this problem was due to the lack of a clear standard in any of these cases to provide guidance to other courts trying to ascertain the precise location of the line between aid to religion and actions or policy that might indirectly aid religion without damaging the wall of separation between church and state.

The beginnings of a meaningful standard came in *Abington Township* v. *Schempp*, where the Court held that "to withstand the strictures of the Establishment Clause there must be a secular legislative purpose and a primary effect that neither advances nor inhibits religion."[14] A few years later, the Court clarified the second part of the test from *Abington Township* in *Board of Education* v. *Allen*.[15] In *Allen*, the Court states that the effect prong of the test requires examining whether the "necessary effects of the statute ... [are] contrary to its stated purpose."[16] Then, in *Walz* v. *Tax Commission*, the Court added an additional requirement, recognizing that "[d]etermining that the legislative purpose ... is not aimed at establishing, sponsoring, or supporting religion does not end the inquiry," but that a statute must also not create an "excessive government entanglement with religion."[17]

6.2 *LEMON V. KURTZMAN*: A (FAILED) ATTEMPT AT A UNIVERSAL STANDARD

In *Lemon* v. *Kurtzman*,[18] the Court crafted a single standard from the pieces in *Abington Township* and *Walz*. In doing so, they created what is commonly referred to as the *Lemon* test:

> First, the statute must have a secular legislative purpose; second, its principal or primary effect must be one that neither advances nor inhibits religion; finally, the statute must not foster an excessive government entanglement with religion.[19]

---

[13] 370 U.S. 421 (1962).
[14] 374 U.S. 203, 222 (1963).
[15] 392 U.S. 236 (1968).
[16] Id. at 243.
[17] 397 U.S. 664, 674 (1970).
[18] 403 U.S. 602 (1971).
[19] Id. at 612–613 (internal citations and quotation marks omitted).

Seemingly simple on its surface, the *Lemon* test has proven difficult to apply in practice owing to the inherent ambiguity in all three prongs, but especially with respect to the entanglement prong. This inherent ambiguity in the standard itself is magnified by the US Supreme Court's post-*Lemon* Establishment Clause jurisprudence where the Court vacillated between applying and ignoring *Lemon*. In the decades following the *Lemon* decision, the Court would sometimes apply the test and other times ignore it in favor of some alternative standard. Dissatisfaction with the *Lemon* test on the Court itself is perhaps best exemplified by the fact that as many as ten alternative tests have been proposed by the justices for determining whether an Establishment Clause violation has occurred (Gey 2006).[20] Of these, three potential replacements to the *Lemon* test have received support from multiple sitting justices at various points since the 1980s: Justice O'Connor's Endorsement Test,[21] Justice Kennedy's Coercion Test,[22] and the Neutrality approach adopted by the Court majority in a handful of school funding cases.[23]

The Endorsement Test is perhaps best understood as a combination of purpose and effect prongs of *Lemon* presented in a cohesive and refocused way (Gey 2006). Most clearly defined by Justice O'Connor in her concurrence in *Lynch* v. *Donnelly*, this approach holds that the Establishment Clause is violated when the government "endorses" religion in a way that is relevant "to a person's standing in the political community" since "Endorsement sends a message to nonadherents that they are outsiders, not full members of the political community, and an accompanying message to adherents that they are insiders, favored members of the political community."[24] This approach garnered the support of a majority of the justices in *County of Allegheny* v. *ACLU*, with the majority opinion directly quoting relevant language from Justice O'Connor's concurrence in *Lynch*.[25] After *County of Allegheny*, some

[20] While Gey (2006) lists ten different "standards," some of these represent multiple variants on a single standard (e.g., broad coercion versus narrow coercion) and others are not really standards at all (e.g., the argument that the Establishment Clause should not be incorporated and should apply only to the states made by Justice Thomas in *Elk Grove Unified School District* v. *Newdow*, 536 U.S. 639 (2002)).

[21] The majority opinion in *County of Allegheny* v. *ACLU*, *supra* note 4, largely adopted this approach. See also Justice O'Connor's concurring opinions in *Lynch* v *Donnelly*, 465 U.S. 668 (1984) (O'Connor, J., concurring) and *Wallace* v. *Jaffree*, *supra* note 4 (O'Connor, J., concurring).

[22] The majority opinion in *Lee* v. *Weisman*, 505 U.S. 577 (1992) largely adopted the coercion approach. See also Justice Kennedy's concurring opinion in *County of Allegheny*.

[23] See *Mitchell* v. *Helms*, 530 U.S. 793 (2000) and *Zelman* v. *Simmons-Harris*, 536 U.S. 639 (2002).

[24] *Supra* note 21, at 687–688 (O'Connor, J., concurring).

[25] *Supra* note 4, at 590–597.

scholars declared the *Lemon* test dead and replaced with this approach (Choper 2002; Lewis and Vild 1989). However, such predictions turned out to be premature as it never gained the consistent support necessary to supplant *Lemon*.

Like the Endorsement Test, the Coercion Test saw its star rise to garner a support of the majority of the justices and for some scholars to prematurely declare its ascendancy as the replacement for *Lemon* (Pongrace 1993).[26] In *Lee* v. *Weisman*, the Court adopted the coercion approach in holding a prayer at a public high school graduation in violation of the Establishment Clause. The *Lee* Court defined the requirements of the Establishment Clause using the following language: "at a minimum, the Constitution guarantees that government may not coerce anyone to support or participate in religion or its exercise, or otherwise act in a way which establishes a [state] religion or religious faith, or tends to do so."[27] A few years later, the Court again used the coercion approach in another case dealing with prayer at a public school function.[28]

Finally, the Neutrality approach has gained support in recent years, but primarily in the narrow context of state funding for religious schools. Here the Court has focused on the nature of the aid as a benefit to students rather than religious institutions directly and that such programs allow "individuals to exercise genuine choice among options public and private, secular and religious."[29] This differs significantly from the endorsement or coercion approaches as it does not depend on either the purpose of the government action or its indirect effects. By far the most permissive of the three, some have criticized the Neutrality standard as "a scheme that amounts to little more than a framework of plausible deniability to cloak the constitutionally dubious consequences of certain government funding programs" (Gey 2006, 748). Yet it remains one of the few clear alternatives to *Lemon* to gain the support of a majority of justices.

The existence of multiple competing standards in the Court's Establishment Clause jurisprudence combined with the outright hostility of some

---

[26] Here we focus only on what is sometimes referred to as "broad coercion." Some scholars have differentiated this approach from what is termed "narrow coercion." We focus on the former here as it has achieved the support of a majority of the Court in two cases, while the latter has not. For a full discussion of the differences between the two approaches see Gey (2006, 740–746).

[27] *Supra* note 22, at 587.

[28] *Santa Fe Independent School District* v. *Doe*, 530 U.S. 290 (2000) (striking down a prayer at a high school football game).

[29] *Zelman, supra* note 23, at 662.

justices towards *Lemon* meant that relatively long spans of time would pass in which the Court would decide several Establishment Clause cases with no reliance on *Lemon*, leading some of its more virulent opponents to declare its death. For example, through the late 1980s and early 1990s, the Court decided six Establishment Clause cases with only one relying upon *Lemon* (McConnell 1997). As discussed earlier in this chapter, this makes *Lemon* a clear example of what we term a zombie precedent. Frequently abandoned in favor of the other tests discussed above, *Lemon* seemed to return each time it appeared to be gone forever from the Supreme Court's Establishment Clause jurisprudence. Justice Scalia summarized this idea well in a special concurrence in *Lamb's Chapel* v. *Center Moriches Union Free School District* – the one case referenced by McConnell (1997) as applying *Lemon* in the late 1980s and early 1990s – when he wrote that "[l]ike some ghoul in a late-night horror movie that repeatedly sits up in its grave and shuffles abroad, after being repeatedly killed and buried, *Lemon* stalks our Establishment Clause jurisprudence."[30]

Not only has the Supreme Court failed to provide further clarity in the years following Justice Scalia's colorful analogy, it has managed to muddy the waters even more. This is exemplified by a pair of decisions issued on the same day (June 27, 2005), dealing with the same religious symbol (the Ten Commandments), and the same legal question (whether the posting on government property violated the Establishment Clause). In *Van Orden* v. *Perry*, the Court ignored the larger questions regarding *Lemon's* value as a precedent, holding that "[w]hatever the fate of the *Lemon* test in the larger scheme of Establishment Clause jurisprudence, we think it not useful for dealing with the sort of passive monument that Texas has erected."[31] However, in *McCreary County* v. *ACLU*, the Court not only relied upon *Lemon*, but explicitly rejected a call by the petitioners to abandon the *Lemon* test.[32] Nor does it appear that clarity will come anytime soon. In its most recent Establishment Clause case, the Court again failed to apply *Lemon*, but seemed at a loss for a replacement standard.[33] Moreover, Justices Breyer and Kagan appeared to have given up *Lemon's* dream of a universal standard altogether, with Breyer noting in his concurring opinion (joined by Kagan) that "there is no single formula for resolving Establishment Clause challenges."[34]

---

[30] 508 U.S. 384, 398 (1993) (Scalia, J., concurring in judgment).
[31] 545 U.S. 677, 686 (2005).
[32] 545 U.S. 844, 861–863 (2005).
[33] *American Legion, supra* note 2.
[34] Id., slip op. at 39 (2019) (Breyer, J., concurring).

6.3 HOW STATES HAVE DEALT WITH *LEMON*

Before turning to a statistical analysis of our full dataset, it is useful to examine in depth how state high courts have used (or not used) *Lemon* in a few key ways. This approach allows us to see trends that are difficult (if not impossible) to capture via statistical tools. One observation that is revealed from an in-depth reading of the cases is that state high courts are well aware of the dissatisfaction with the *Lemon* test by a faction of the US Supreme Court and the broader legal community. Interestingly, this does not appear to have had a systematic influence on how *Lemon* is used by these courts. As Figure 6.1 shows, the rate at which state high courts ignore *Lemon* appears to fluctuate over time, both in terms of raw numbers and in proportion to other types of treatments.[35] Moreover, the rate of positive treatments tends to ebb and flow over time as well. Were the criticisms of *Lemon* having the effect one might intuitively expect, we would likely see the rate of cases ignoring *Lemon* monotonically increasing over time and the rate of positive treatments monotonically decreasing over time rather than what we observe in Figure 6.1.

Additionally, while several of the justices of the Supreme Court have frequently criticized *Lemon*, it is interesting to note the rarity of negative treatments in Figure 6.1. Across all state high courts, there is never more than one negative treatment in a single year, and these incidences of negative treatments are spread out evenly over the life span of *Lemon*. This is in part explained by the relative rarity of negative treatments of US Supreme Court precedents by state high courts in general.[36] In this specific application, this is further explained by the extremely high frequency with which *Lemon* is ignored. This suggests that state high courts that do not like *Lemon* may simply choose to ignore it altogether rather than taking the time to distinguish or criticize it.

While some state courts use the recognition of the US Supreme Court's own ambivalence toward *Lemon* as a justification to avoid applying *Lemon*, others make note of it while continuing to apply the *Lemon* test. The Utah Supreme Court's decision in *Society of Separationists* v. *Whitehead* exemplifies the former.[37] Here the Utah Supreme Court rejects a call by one of the parties to apply the *Lemon* test to their interpretation of Article I, Section 4 of the

---

[35] Perhaps one reason why the negative treatment rate for *Lemon* is so low relates to the fact that it is relatively easy to ignore if a state high court wants to do so.

[36] In each of our applications, we find negative treatments to be the least common outcome. This is supported by other studies of state court reactions to US Supreme Court precedent as well (see, e.g., Fix, Kingsland, and Montgomery 2017).

[37] 870 P.2d 916, n.36 (Utah 1993).

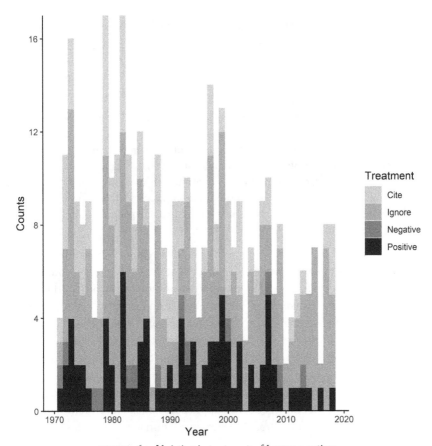

FIGURE 6.1. Variation in treatments of *Lemon* over time

Utah Constitution.[38] In doing so, they observe that the US Supreme Court "appears to apply [*Lemon*] rather opportunistically" and that when it "wants to reach a result that might not flow from a *Lemon* analysis, it seems quite willing

[38] It is worth noting that Utah is the only state where the constitution explicitly references a separation of church and state in the constitutional text (Wallace 2001). The full text of Utah Constitution Article I, Section 4 reads:

> The rights of conscience shall never be infringed. The State shall make no law respecting an establishment of religion or prohibiting the free exercise thereof; no religious test shall be required as a qualification for any office of public trust or for any vote at any election; nor shall any person be incompetent as a witness or juror on account of religious belief or the absence thereof. There shall be no union of Church and State, nor shall any church dominate the State or interfere with its functions. No public money or property shall be appropriated for or applied to any religious worship, exercise or instruction, or for the support of any ecclesiastical establishment.

to ignore *Lemon*."39 The Utah Court simultaneously rejects a call by the other party to emulate the interpretation of similar state constitutional provision by other state high courts. Instead, they elect to chart their own path, justifying this decision in the language of adequate and independent state grounds and the unique language and history of Article I, Section 4 of their constitution:

> The federal rulings set the floor for federal constitutional protections which we must respect in interpreting the scope of our own constitution's provisions. But the federal courts have an entirely different task before them than do we. They have only a cryptic sentence to interpret; we have paragraphs that are expressed in clearer terms and that are given even more vivid meaning by our unique and relatively recent history. The citizens of Utah know, perhaps better than those of any other state, what evils can befall people, communities, and government when religious strife is pervasive.

In contrast to the Utah Supreme Court, other states have continued to apply the test from *Lemon* while recognizing that the US Supreme Court itself appears unwilling to follow it. For example, the Illinois Supreme Court in *People* v. *Falbe* declares *Lemon* to be "both applicable and useful in lieu of a viable, structured alternative analysis."40 Other courts have taken this even farther, continuing to apply *Lemon* even when they feel that it is not ideal for a specific application. This is exemplified by the California Supreme Court's decision in *East Bay Asian Local Development Corporation* v. *California*, where they hold that "the *Lemon* test is ill-suited to assessing accommodating religious exemptions from neutral, generally applicable laws. Nevertheless, in the absence of further guidance from the Supreme Court as to the means by which the validity of such exemptions should be assessed, we will apply it here."41

Despite the difference in outcomes between the Utah Supreme Court on the one hand and the California and Illinois Supreme Courts on the other with regard to the usage or nonusage of *Lemon*, two things appear to be systematically influencing these decisions. First, state high courts are aware of the continued debate both among the justices of the US Supreme Court and beyond as to whether *Lemon* remains a valid test for Establishment Clause cases, thus empowering them with greater flexibility to use it or not use it as they desire. Second, this flexibility is enhanced when the case is brought under a state constitutional provision that is textually different from the Establishment Clause in the US Constitution. In addition to the Utah Supreme Court's decision in *Society of Separationists*, several other cases

---

39 *Society of Separationists, supra* note 34, at n.36.
40 727 N.E.2d 200, 207 (Ill. 2000).
41 13 P.3d 1122, 1133 (Cal. 2000).

in our dataset show state high courts carefully noting the significant textual differences between their own constitutions and the federal one.[42]

In these and other cases, we also see the importance of the specific issue involved in the case affecting whether and how the state court would apply *Lemon*. Theoretically, we expect this to be most clearly visible in the case of civil suits involving a church that would cause a court to have to involve itself in the interpretation of church laws or doctrine. Massachusetts exemplifies this. As Table 6.1 shows, the Massachusetts Supreme Judicial Court has ignored *Lemon* in seventeen cases dealing with religious establishment questions. Yet, nine of those seventeen were cases involving civil suits against a church where *Lemon* is arguably least relevant even assuming the most generous interpretation of its relevance. At the same time, the flexibility of state high courts to use precedent works in both directions. Two out of the eight times the Minnesota Supreme Court has positively treated *Lemon* have been in these types of cases. In doing so, the Court specifically observes that "no US Supreme Court case applying the ecclesiastical abstention doctrine has used the *Lemon* test."[43] Thus, it is clear that while *Lemon*'s status as good law is questioned by some – including some of the justices on the US Supreme Court – many state high courts continue to apply it even while explicitly acknowledging this fact. Moreover, the Minnesota Supreme Court has even gone one step farther and has expanded *Lemon* to areas where the US Supreme Court itself appears never to have meant for it to apply.

While ecclesiastical abstention doctrine cases are a minor part of the universe of religious establishment cases, these examples highlight the importance of the specific issue in a case on state high court decisions on whether and how to use *Lemon*. The zombification of *Lemon* through the development of other tests and standards provides state high courts with doctrinally sound justifications to either ignore *Lemon* altogether or simply cite it in passing. This is especially true when a state high court is resolving a specific Establishment Clause question that mirrors one of the cases where the US Supreme Court applied an alternative standard. One such area would be cases involving government-mandated participation in a religious activity where the coercion standard from *Lee* v. *Weisman* provides a means of avoiding *Lemon*. For example, both the New York Court of Appeals and the Tennessee

[42] See, e.g., *Kentucky State Board for Elementary and Secondary Education* v. *Rudasill*, 589 S.W. 2d 877 (Ky. 1979), *Witters* v. *Commission for the Blind*, 771 P.2d 1119 (Wash. 1989).

[43] *Pfeil* v. *St. Matthews Evangelical Lutheran Church of the Unaltered Augsburg Confession of Worthington*, 877 N.W.2d 528, 537 (Minn. 2016). See also *Odenthal* v. *Minnesota Conference of Seventh-Day Adventists*, 649 N.W. 2d 426 (Minn. 2002).

TABLE 6.1. *Treatment patterns by state high court of* Lemon

State	Positive treatment	Negative treatment	Cited	Ignored
Alabama	2	0	0	4
Alaska	2	0	1	3
Arizona	1	0	0	2
Arkansas	1	0	1	3
California	4	0	4	5
Colorado	6	0	2	6
Connecticut	1	0	2	4
Delaware	0	0	2	1
Florida	1	0	0	1
Georgia	0	0	0	4
Hawaii	1	0	0	0
Idaho	1	0	2	1
Illinois	3	0	2	0
Indiana	0	0	0	3
Iowa	0	0	2	3
Kansas	0	0	0	2
Kentucky	1	0	1	7
Louisiana	0	0	0	1
Maine	1	0	2	3
Maryland	1	0	2	8
Massachusetts	3	0	10	17
Michigan	1	0	4	1
Minnesota	8	0	2	2
Mississippi	1	0	1	7
Missouri	2	1	2	4
Montana	3	0	1	2
Nebraska	1	1	4	1
Nevada	0	0	0	1
New Hampshire	1	0	0	5
New Jersey	5	2	5	5
New Mexico	1	0	1	2
New York	5	0	3	6
North Carolina	4	0	1	2
North Dakota	2	0	3	1
Ohio	1	3	1	2
Oklahoma	2	1	1	10
Oregon	1	0	1	8
Pennsylvania	3	0	2	5
Rhode Island	0	1	1	1
South Carolina	1	1	1	5
South Dakota	0	0	1	5
Tennessee	1	0	1	5
Texas	2	1	2	2
Utah	2	1	0	6
Vermont	2	0	1	2
Virginia	0	0	5	4
Washington	4	0	5	8
West Virginia	0	0	3	5
Wisconsin	3	1	5	5
Wyoming	0	0	0	0

Supreme Court have expressly applied the coercion standard in cases involving mandatory participation in religious-themed alcohol-treatment programs. In *Griffin* v. *Coughlin*,[44] the New York Court of Appeals quoted directly from *Lee* v. *Weisman* in holding "that the Shawangunk Correctional Facility may not constitutionally require petitioner to forfeit his benefits [eligibility for the Family Reunion Program] as the price of resisting conformance to state-sponsored religious practice."[45] Similarly, the Tennessee Supreme Court found that making parole conditional on participation in a religious-themed alcohol-treatment program violates the Establishment Clause.[46]

Much like the use of the coercion standard by the high courts of New York and Tennessee, some state courts have also relied upon the endorsement test to address Establishment Clause issues. For example, the Ohio Supreme Court applied the endorsement test to find that a teacher keeping a personal copy of the Bible in his desk did not represent state endorsement of religion.[47] Alternatively, this lack of a single standard on which a majority of US Supreme Court justices can agree could lead more state high courts to follow the lead of the Wisconsin Supreme Court in *King* v. *Village of Waunakee*.[48] Rather than applying a specific standard, the Wisconsin Supreme Court simply speculated about how individual US Supreme Court justices would feel about a specific display given their individual dissents and concurrences in cases involving similar displays.

6.4 APPLICATION OF OUR GENERAL THEORY TO *LEMON*

Despite the US Supreme Court's mixed signals regarding whether *Lemon* is still its preferred Establishment Clause test – short of being formally overruled by the Court – it remains binding on lower federal courts and state courts applying the US Constitution. Thus, during the same period that Justice Scalia was referring to the decision with imagery from a horror film, all of the US Courts of Appeals and most state courts were continuing to rely on *Lemon* in their decisions (McConnell 1997).

This makes *Lemon* an ideal case for our study due to the contrast with *Atkins*. Whereas the Supreme Court's decision in *Atkins* laid out a hard rule (no execution of the intellectually disabled) combined with a relatively vague standard, *Lemon* provided only a vague standard in the form of its three-prong test. This distinction is an important one. With the lack of a clear rule and

---

[44] 673 N.E.2d 98 (N.Y. 1996).
[45] Id. at 106 (quoting *Lee* v. *Weisman, supra* note 22, at 596) (internal quotation marks omitted).
[46] *Arnold* v. *Tennessee Board of Paroles*, 956 S.W.2d 478 (Tenn. 1997).
[47] *Freshwater* v. *Mt. Vernon City School District*, 1 N.E.3d 335 (2013).
[48] 517 N.W.2d 671 (Wis. 1994).

the Supreme Court's own use of alternative standards post-*Lemon*, state high courts facing Establishment Clause cases have enhanced flexibility not only in terms of how to interpret this precedent but in determining whether to apply it at all.

Additionally, like most civil liberties issues, Establishment Clause cases are important and highly salient. Most state high courts deal with significantly larger dockets than the US Supreme Court. Yet, these courts still devote substantial time and attention to salient cases (Vining Jr and Wilhelm 2011). Combining this with the significant lack of clarity in this area of the law – due to competing and conflicting US Supreme Court precedents – it is highly likely that state high courts will attempt to provide clear guidelines for the rest of the judges in their state.

The application of our general theory of state high court usage of US Supreme Court precedent to *Lemon* is rather straightforward. As *Lemon* provides only a vague standard for guidance in Establishment Clause cases, it provides state high courts with significant flexibility regarding its application in individual cases. This could lead to two conflicting predictions regarding general trends. As Fix, Kingsland, and Montgomery (2017) show in their examination of *Miller* v. *California*, precedents containing vague standards might be more likely to be followed by state high courts as they offer a mechanism to claim compliance with the precedent while reaching their desired policy outcome. Conversely, it may be the case that state high courts may see such a vague standard – combined with the Supreme Court's own ambivalence towards it – as a reason to ignore the precedent altogether or simply cite it with minimal engagement. As our theory states, these general predictions are likely of little value at the micro-level. Rather, a state high court's decision regarding how to deal with a relevant US Supreme Court precedent is a function of an array of factors at the time of a given case.

We first turn to the legal factors that our theory predicts should assert a strong influence on state high court decisions regarding whether and how to use US Supreme Court precedents. Fix, Kingsland, and Montgomery (2017) provide evidence that how states treated a precedent in the past is a strong predictor of how they will treat it in the future. Because an array of legal mechanisms provide state high court judges with substantial freedom to interpret precedents in the manner they see as optimal without fear of interference by the US Supreme Court (Kassow, Songer, and Fix 2012), what a state high court has done in the past should have an especially large influence on its future behavior. Magnifying this effect is the notion that as state high courts interpret precedents over time, the meaning of those precedents evolve within that state (Black and Spriggs 2013; Fix, Kingsland, and Montgomery 2017; Hansford and Spriggs 2006; Landes and Posner 1976; Merryman 1953).

Simply put, whether and how a state high court first uses a precedent will impact how they interpret and use that precedent in the future. From this we derive our first hypothesis:

H_1:   If a state high court positively treated *Lemon* in the past, then it is more likely to treat *Lemon* positively and less likely to ignore *Lemon*.

As noted in the prior chapter, existing research shows that case-specific facts influence a variety of aspects of judicial decision-making. In legal areas as varied as the death penalty (Brace and Hall 1995; 1997), obscenity (Fix, Kingsland, and Montgomery 2017), and abortion (Caldarone, Canes-Wrone, and Clark 2009), prior work has consistently shown that these factors play a significant role in decision-making in state high courts. We expect this to be the case here as well. Specifically, we expect two sets of case facts to have a major influence on high court court decisions regarding whether and how to use *Lemon*. First, cases dealing with civil suits against churches should represent an area where *Lemon* will be of minimal use to state high courts in resolving Establishment Clause issues. Both federal and state courts in the United States have long relied on the ecclesiastical abstention doctrine holding that the First Amendment prohibits civil courts from deciding questions that would require "inquiring into religious doctrine, belief, discipline, or faith in order to resolve disputes over church property, church policy, or church administration" (Wellford 1994, 194). This doctrine dates back at least to the late 1880s with the US Supreme Court's decision in *Watson v. Jones*,[49] and continues to be the primary guidance for courts deciding cases involving such issues today. In fact, even in those instances where *Lemon* is used in such cases, there is an accompanying recognition that the US Supreme Court has never applied the *Lemon* test in a case involving the ecclesiastical abstention doctrine.[50] This is the area of Establishment Clause law where state courts are the least likely to consider *Lemon* relevant. However, the ambiguity over when the *Lemon* test applies leads to the possibility that some state high courts may seize the opportunity to use *Lemon* more expansively than the US Supreme Court intended. Thus, while we expect that *Lemon* is quite likely to be ignored in any case involving a civil suit against a church, we feel it necessary to include these cases in our analysis. This leads to our second hypothesis:

H_2:   If a case involves a civil suit against a church, the probability of a state high court ignoring *Lemon* will increase.

---

[49] 80 U.S. 679 (1872).
[50] See, e.g., *Kedroff v. Saint Nicholas Cathedral of the Russian Orthodox Church in North America*, 344 U.S. 94 (1952); *Hosanna-Tabor Evangelical Lutheran Church and School v. Equal Employment Opportunity Commission*, 132 S.Ct. 694 (2012).

In contrast to cases involving questions pertaining to the ecclesiastical abstention doctrine, when state high courts decide cases involving questions of public funds being directly or indirectly used to benefit religious schools they ought to be more likely to use *Lemon*. As the *Lemon* case itself dealt with a scenario where public funds were paid to private schools to cover the costs of teacher salaries, the precedent will be most clearly relevant in cases dealing with factually similar issues. As such, it will be more difficult for state high courts to legitimately avoid applying *Lemon* in these cases, as compared to cases dealing with other types of Establishment Clause issues. Moreover, even those courts that may doubt whether *Lemon* continues to enjoy its status as the dominant standard in Establishment Clause jurisprudence are likely to view it as a binding precedent with respect to the narrow question of public funding for religious schools. Therefore, our third hypothesis states:

H_3:   If a case involves a challenge to the use of public funds for religious schools, the probability of a state high court ignoring *Lemon* will decrease and the probability of a state high court positively treating *Lemon* will increase.

In addition to legal factors, our theory asserts that the political environment in which a state high court operates may influence its use of precedents. Evidence suggests that state high courts are constrained in their ability to act on their own preferences due to concerns about retention. Thus, if a state constituency is extremely conservative, then ideologically divergent judges are likely to be constrained (Langer 2002). Applying this general finding in the literature to the application of precedent, we argue that more liberal precedents ought to be eschewed by state high courts in conservative states regardless of the judges' individual preferences. With respect to *Lemon*, we argue that a state high court in a conservative political environment ought to be more likely to negatively treat *Lemon* or to ignore the decision altogether. This leads to our fourth hypothesis:

H_4:   State high courts in relatively conservative states will be more likely to ignore or negatively treat *Lemon*, compared with state high courts in more liberal states.

Finally, our theory argues that institutional factors will influence state court decisions on whether and how to use US Supreme Court precedents. While these factors are likely to assert systematic influences on a wide array of state high court behaviors, we have no specific a priori expectations regarding the way in which the method of retention used in a state would impact whether and how the state's high court would use *Lemon*.

6.5 DATA AND METHODS

In order to test our theoretical predictions regarding the impact of various legal, political, contextual, and institutional factors on state high court usage or nonusage of *Lemon*, we collected an original dataset of all state high court cases decided between 1972 and 2016 where *Lemon* was relevant (regardless of whether it was actually cited). To collect the universe of cases, we followed a three-step process. First, we located all cases that were decided by a state high court that cited *Lemon* during our time frame using the *Shepard's* Report feature in LexisNexis. As this first step would miss any cases where the state court could have, but did not, cite *Lemon* as a relevant precedent, we conducted a second search to capture these missing cases using the following Boolean search criterion in LexisNexis: "Establishment Clause" OR "Establishment of Religion." Finally, we manually searched through the cases to remove any duplicate cases and any that had been included in our search results but which did not actually belong in our study (e.g., Free Speech cases where the entire First Amendment was quoted). This yielded a total of 366 cases.

Our dependent variable measures the type of treatment given *Lemon* in a state high court decision. We treat this as a nominal variable coded "4" for decisions where the court follows or otherwise positively treats *Lemon*, "3" for decisions where the court simply cites or neutrally treats *Lemon*, "2" for decisions where the court ignores *Lemon* and no mention of it is made in the decision, and "1" for decisions where the court distinguishes or otherwise negatively treats *Lemon*. As *Shepard's Citations* coding of state high court treatments of US Supreme Court decisions is not reliable prior to the late 1990s (Kassow, Songer, and Fix 2012), we were required to manually code treatments. However, our coding of our dependent variable followed *Shepard's* coding rules. Descriptively, about half of the cases in our dataset represented instances where the state high court ignored *Lemon* in a case where it was relevant.[51] Of the remaining cases, most were divided between cases where *Lemon* was just cited (23.77 percent) and those where it was followed or otherwise positively treated (22.48 percent). Only 3.36 percent of the cases involved a negative treatment. Table 6.1 in the previous section breaks this down by state high court.

To measure the factors we theoretically expect to influence whether and how state high courts use *Lemon*, we include a series of relevant independent variables. First, to test Hypothesis 1, we include a measure of how a given state high court has treated *Lemon* in its prior decisions. This variable, *State-Specific*

---

[51] Of these, 47.7 percent were cases involving a civil suit involving a church.

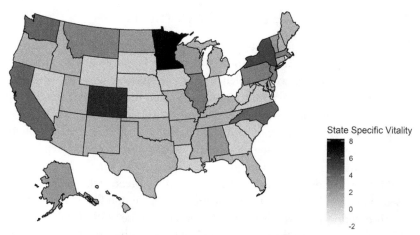

FIGURE 6.2. Variation in state-specific vitality for *Lemon* (2017)

Vitality, mirrors the coding of Fix, Kingsland, and Montgomery (2017) as a sum of all prior positive treatments minus all prior negative treatments. Building from work by Hansford and Spriggs (2006) examining how the vitality of a US Supreme Court precedent varies over time depending on whether or not the Court continues to support the precedent, Fix, Kingsland, and Montgomery (2017) observe that how a given state high court treats a US Supreme Court precedent is a stronger predictor of future state high court treatments than the Supreme Court's treatment of its own precedents. In theory this variable can range from negative infinity to positive infinity, but in our data the actual range is -2 (Ohio 1992, New Jersey 1981–1982) to 7 (Minnesota 2016). The variation in state-specific vitality is illustrated in Figure 6.2.

The next two independent variables capture the key case-specific facts we argue in Hypothesis 2 and 3 should influence how state high courts deal with *Lemon*. First, we include a simple dichotomous indicator of whether the case involved a *Civil Suit against a Church*. This variable is coded "1" if the case involves a civil suit brought against a church such that it is likely that the ecclesiastical abstention doctrine will be relied upon by the state high court. If no such issue is involved, this variable is coded "0." Second, to capture factual similarity to *Lemon*, we include another dichotomous variable indicating whether the case involved a dispute over the use of public funds in a way that benefits a religious school. This variable, *Public Funding*, is coded "1" if the case involves a factual dispute of this nature, and "0" otherwise.

To test our fourth hypothesis, we need a measure of the political environment faced by the state high court. For this, we use the updated

Berry et al. (1998; Berry et al. 2010) measure of state ideology. Consistent with the theoretical reason for including a measure of state ideology, we use their elite ideology measure for those states that use elite reappointment to retain their judges and their mass ideology score for states that retain judges via elections.

Finally, we include a series of dummy variables indicating the type of retention mechanism used by the state deciding a given case. As noted above, we expect that high courts in states with competitive, popular elections might be systematically different than their neighbors in states with elite retention mechanisms or Missouri Plan-style retention elections in terms of how they respond to the *Lemon* precedent. Thus, we include one variable that denotes all states that use a partisan election for their retention mechanism and a second variable denotes states that use a nonpartisan election as their retention mechanism (with states using retention elections or elite appointment excluded as a baseline category). We also include a measure of the *Age of Lemon* (in years) to account for the tendency of positive treatments of precedents to decline over time (Black and Spriggs 2013; Boyd and Spriggs 2009; Hansford, Spriggs, and Stenger 2013; Westerland et al. 2010).

6.6 RESULTS AND DISCUSSION

As our dependent variable is nominal in nature, we estimate a multinomial logit model to test our theoretical predictions.[52] Table 6.2 shows the estimates from our model, where each of the possible options (negatively treat, ignore, and positively treat) are compared against a baseline category of citation without treatment. Overall, the results show support for our broad theoretical argument that the decision by state high courts regarding whether and how to use a relevant US Supreme Court precedent is a complex one. This justifies our theoretical argument that the choice set available to these courts is not a neatly ordered array of options. Rather, these results broadly show that an array of specific factors influence the choice between different options in unique ways.

---

[52] As in Chapter 5, we estimated two alternative models. First, to ensure the robustness of our results, we estimated an identically specified multinomial probit model. The results of that model were substantively identical to those presented in Table 6.2. Second, as an additional test of our assumption that the choice of whether to ignore a precedent is made simultaneous with other treatment types, we specified a selection model mirroring the one discussed in Chapter 5. Again, we found no statistically significant evidence of a selection effect, thus supporting our assumption regarding the nature of the decision-making process.

TABLE 6.2. *Determinants of treatment types for* Lemon

	Negative	Ignored	Positive
State-Specific Vitality	−0.080	−0.066	0.055
	(0.237)	(0.132)	(0.150)
Civil Suit vs Church	0.536	1.056*	−0.969*
	(0.798)	(0.321)	(0.446)
Public Funding	−0.602	−0.648*	−0.167
	(1.038)	(0.351)	(0.358)
State Ideology	−0.034	−0.017*	−0.002
	(0.023)	(0.009)	(0.009)
Partisan Elections	0.591	−0.635	0.498
	(0.705)	(0.509)	(0.515)
Nonpartisan Elections	−1.692*	−0.366	0.163
	(1.007)	(0.304)	(0.342)
Age of *Lemon*	0.025	0.022*	0.026*
	(0.027)	(0.013)	(0.014)
Constant	0.490	1.210*	−0.359
	(1.373)	(0.543)	(0.619)
Observations		366	
X^2		60.03*	

Estimates are from a multinomial logit model comparing each outcome to a baseline of just cited or neutral treatment. Robust standard errors in parentheses.
* $p < 0.1$

While we see no support for our first hypothesis, as state-specific vitality does not appear to influence the likelihood of any of the outcomes being selected versus the baseline category, case-specific fact patterns tend to strongly predict the treatment decision consistent with our second and third hypotheses. In cases involving a civil suit against a church, where the ecclesiastical abstention doctrine is likely to form the primary legal basis for the state court decision, these courts are significantly more likely to ignore *Lemon* than to cite it and significantly less likely to follow it than to simply cite it.[53] Similarly, in cases

---

[53] As a robustness check we estimated an alternative model with all cases involving a civil suit against a church removed. We feel it is necessary to include these cases based on our theoretically determined search criteria, yet we recognize that these cases represent a disproportionate number of the cases where *Lemon* was ignored. Specifically, *Lemon* was ignored in 93 of the 128 cases involving a civil suit against a church (72.66 percent), but only 99 out of the 256 cases (38.67 percent) not involving a civil suit against a church. The results of this alternative model largely conform with the results in Table 6.2. All statistically significant coefficient estimates in the original model retain significance in the alternative

involving public funds being used to benefit religious schools – the factual scenario in *Lemon* itself – state high courts are significantly less likely to ignore *Lemon* than they are to cite it. However, contrary to our predictions, there is no statistically significant difference between the likelihood a court will positively treat *Lemon* when this issue is present and the likelihood it will just cite it. In part, this might be explained by the number of states with a constitutional provision directly prohibiting the use of public funds for religious organization.

Examining the baseline probabilities holding all variables constant at their means (for continuous variables) or medians (for discrete variables) shows that ignoring *Lemon* is the most likely outcome, all else being equal. The baseline probability a court will ignore *Lemon* is 0.466, consistent with our earlier discussion regarding the tremendous flexibility that the precedent affords state courts and the strategic advantage of ignoring distasteful precedents rather than directly criticizing them. This is made even more apparent when considering that the baseline probability for negative treatments is a mere 0.038. The baseline probability of positively treating *Lemon* or just citing it fall almost perfectly in between these two extremes with probabilities of 0.259 and 0.237, respectively.

Additionally, the substantive impact of our two case fact variables is quite strong. When a case involves a question of state funding for religious schools, the probability a court will ignore *Lemon* decreases from 0.465 to 0.343. While this is a significant substantive effect, the impact of whether a case involves a civil suit against a church is even larger. Looking at Figure 6.3, we see that when a case involves a civil suit against a church, the likelihood the state high court will ignore *Lemon* increases to 0.771 from 0.468, holding all other variables constant. Simultaneously, the likelihood of a positive treatment goes down from near its baseline probability at 0.252 to only 0.060.

Turning to our other variables, we see partial support for our fourth hypothesis. While state ideology appears to have no impact on the likelihood of a positive (or negative) treatment, it does appear to impact the probability the court will ignore *Lemon* rather than simply citing it. Specifically, the negative coefficient implies that as the relevant population of a state becomes more liberal, the high court of that state is less likely to ignore *Lemon*, all

model and are signed in the same direction with the single exception of the Age of *Lemon* in the positive treatment versus citation condition. This coefficient fails to achieve statistical significance ($p = 0.104$) in the alternative model. What is perhaps most interesting about this alternative model is that even without the cases involving a civil suit against a church, the estimated baseline probability a court will ignore *Lemon* does not decrease, but actually increases slightly to 0.471 compared to 0.466 in our primary model. Thus, we are confident that our results are not merely an artifact of this case selection decision.

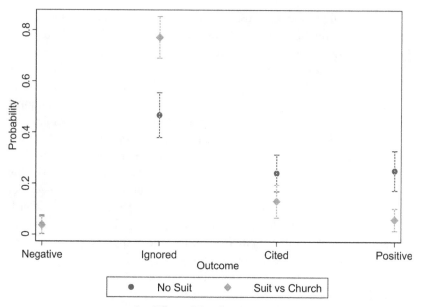

FIGURE 6.3. Effects of church suit on treatment type
Predicted margins calculated holding all continuous variables at their mean and dichotomous variables at their mode. Points represent probability estimates, error bars are a 95 percent confidence interval.

else being equal. Substantively, this effect is quite strong. A high court in the most conservative state in our sample (by this measure) would have a 0.569 probability of ignoring *Lemon*, but this probability drops to 0.453 for a state at the mean ideology level, and to 0.315 for the most liberal state in our sample.

Finally, one of the more unusual findings in our analysis relates to the impact of time. While the probability of ignoring *Lemon* increases over time consistent with what we would expect from prior work, the probability of *Lemon* being positively treated also appears to increase over time. Both of these effects are relatively small, with the former representing about a 0.07 increase in the probability of *Lemon* being ignored and the latter just under a 0.107 increase in the probability of a positive treatment. However, the latter is still an interesting anomaly given the general trend of precedents getting fewer positive treatments over time.

6.7 CONCLUDING THOUGHTS

In this chapter we presented a second test of our theoretical framework for understanding the mechanisms that drive state high court decisions on whether and how to use relevant US Supreme Court precedents. We argue that *Lemon* makes an ideal case to test our theory. It provides state high courts with extreme flexibility regarding its application due to the fact that it offers a vague standard rather than a strict rule and deals with a salient substantive topic. Additionally, the fact that *Lemon* has been harshly criticized by some members of the US Supreme Court to the point that many scholars view it as dead or dying makes it an important case to understand due to its implications for other such cases. Little work has been done on what happens to these zombie precedents once the US Supreme Court has chopped off their heads and buried them. Yet, we know that in a few important areas they have been resurrected into state constitutional law.

To test our theory, we analyze a unique dataset containing all state high court decisions from 1972 to 2016 where the court either cited or should have been reasonably expected to cite *Lemon* v. *Kurtzman* due to the issue in the case. Our results show support for our theory broadly with respect to our central argument that state high court decisions regarding whether and how to use a relevant US Supreme Court precedent is multifaceted and the available choice set is more nuanced than previously treated in the literature. This last point is clear simply from the descriptive examination of our dependent variable. In approximately half of the state high court Establishment Clause cases decided since 1972, there is no mention at all of *Lemon*. This fact alone is both normatively important as it shows the willingness of state high courts to completely ignore the existence of a relevant US Supreme Court precedent, and empirically supportive of our theoretical assertion that a failure to account for instances when state high courts ignore relevant precedents represents an important oversight in the compliance literature.

Shifting away from the general level, the results also support several of our specific expectations. The strongest systematic effects relate to the relationship between the presence of certain specific facts in a case and the likelihood that a state high court will ignore *Lemon* (and in one case positively treat *Lemon*) compared to a baseline behavior of simply citing the precedent without positive or negative treatment. This is an important finding in terms of our theoretical interest and also for the broader implications it has for our understanding of the influence of traditional legal considerations in the crafting of opinions by state high courts. Finally, our findings in this chapter with respect to *Lemon* can add to our understanding of zombie precedents more generally. We strongly encourage future empirical and doctrinal study on this specific topic.

In the next chapter, we turn to a pair of precedents that fall between *Atkins* and *Lemon* in terms of discretion. In *District of Columbia* v. *Heller* and

McDonald v. *City of Chicago*, the US Supreme Court held that the Second Amendment protects an individual right to keep and bear arms, but that such a right was subject to "reasonable restrictions." However, in neither *Heller* nor *McDonald* did the Court provide any guidance as to the standard for determining what constituted a reasonable restriction. Thus, while the two cases mirror *Atkins* to some degree, the total lack of a standard in *Heller* and *McDonald* provides even greater levels of flexibility. At the same time, the US Supreme Court has not questioned the validity of either precedent implicitly or explicitly, thus – unlike *Lemon* – it is clear that both are still good law.

7

State High Court Usage of *District of Columbia* v. *Heller* and *McDonald* v. *City of Chicago*

Moderate Degrees of Flexibility

As noted in the previous two chapters, we focused on examining cases where state high courts have at least some flexibility to interpret the specific precedent discussed in each chapter. This chapter and its focus on recent US Supreme Court Second Amendment decisions is no exception. When it comes to how state high courts interpret *District of Columbia* v. *Heller*[1] and *McDonald* v. *City of Chicago*,[2] the degree of discretion that lower courts have to interpret these precedents is intermediate relative to the cases in the two previous chapters, with *Atkins* being the clearest and *Lemon* the vaguest. Specifically, we argue that while there was not a clear rule created in *Heller* or *McDonald*, and the standard that they create is rather flexible, unlike *Lemon*, there is no doubt as to the legal validity of these precedents. Additionally, the issue of Second Amendment rights and how they apply to individuals is an area that has become highly salient politically, with Republicans tending to have a strong position on the issue of Second Amendment rights, and Democrats having a position that is in opposition. In real-world terms, this means that state high court justices may either be heavily reliant on the political environment in a state or may be able to act rather freely when interpreting relevant Supreme Court precedents in Second Amendment cases that appear on their dockets.

This chapter explores how state high courts responded to recent Second Amendment precedents via case studies examining three states. Similar to previous chapters, we expect to find that the relatively loose standard from *Heller* will allow state high courts to rely on and follow *McDonald* and/or *Heller*, while reaching decisional outcomes across the ideological spectrum. This should manifest in several ways. First, we expect to find that state-specific precedent vitality (Fix, Kingsland, and Montgomery 2017)

[1] 554 U.S. 570 (2008).
[2] 561 U.S. 742 (2010).

will potentially affect how state high courts treat *Heller* and *McDonald*. The cases we examine show some potential evidence of this. Additionally, given that we are using a case study approach, we are able to examine differences in legal doctrine among several states that have interpreted Second Amendment jurisprudence post-*McDonald*. Given the ideological influences that are pervasive on the issue, we believe that differences based on ideology may emerge in terms of how each state addresses Second Amendment-related concerns, even though state high court ideology itself may not affect how state high courts treat *McDonald*.[3] We also find *possible* evidence that the manner in which elections take place (district versus at-large) may also affect treatments of these cases, in the case of the Illinois and Louisiana Supreme Courts.[4]

7.1 *HELLER* AND *MCDONALD*: ESTABLISHING A SECOND AMENDMENT CONSTITUTIONAL "FLOOR"

As we have done in our previous two chapters, we begin with a brief discussion of why these precedents are useful for understanding state high court reactions to US Supreme Court precedent. The Supreme Court's decisions in *Heller* and *McDonald* forced state high courts to respond to a new legal policy. This allowed state high courts to act opportunistically, especially in the immediate aftermath of *Heller*, when it was unclear whether the Second Amendment directly applied to the states in the two years between *Heller* (2008) and *McDonald* (2010).[5]

In terms of the precedent itself from *Heller*, there is a large degree of ambiguity found in Justice Scalia's majority opinion. Specifically, as we discuss in more detail below, the opinion states that Second Amendment rights are fundamental, but are subject to reasonable restrictions. In fact, the opinion only bans one specific type of restriction as relates to firearms, if interpreted as

---

3 Of course, plenty of political science research illustrates the importance of ideology in state high court decision-making (see, e.g., Brace and Boyea 2008; Brace, Langer, and Hall 2000; Canes-Wrone, Clark, and Kelly 2014; Hoekstra 2005). But the evidence on ideology directly impacting how state high courts treat US Supreme Court precedent is less compelling (Comparato and McClurg 2007; Kassow, Songer, and Fix 2012).

4 The idea that having individual districts might affect judicial behavior originates in a piece authored by Hall (1995) and is discussed in more detail in a later publication (Hall 2014).

5 In fact, *McDonald* itself did not create any new rights, but applied rights that were created from the *Heller* decision directly to the states, rather than leaving ambiguity that was in place immediately post-*Heller*. So perhaps the best way to think of *McDonald* is that it was used as a signal by the justices to the states that *Heller* is binding precedent (rather than being treated as persuasive precedent) on the states.

narrowly as possible. That is, making an absolute ban on keeping a handgun, or other firearms primarily used for lawful purposes, available for use in one's home for the purpose of self-defense.[6] Yet, it provides an opportunity for state high courts to easily engage in policy-making if they so choose, and can be interpreted rather flexibly by state high court justices, allowing them to follow it faithfully while reaching (almost) any substantive outcome they may desire.

The flexibility and highly symbolic nature of the opinions in both *Heller* and *McDonald* should make it especially easy for state high courts to be able to discuss the two precedents when they deal with Second Amendment-related cases, in whichever direction they desire. There should be relatively little reason for any state high court to attack these opinions given the immense degree of flexibility that the US Supreme Court has given state high courts in interpreting the decision. In one of the cases we discuss later in the chapter, the Massachusetts Supreme Judicial Court interpreted *McDonald* and *Heller* as allowing states to ban weapons, such as stun guns, given that they were not in existence in 1789. The most interesting part of this opinion was that the Massachusetts Supreme Court explicitly stated that it was making this decision given that it had received no further guidance from the US Supreme Court. The Massachusetts Supreme Court also went on to invite the US Supreme Court to reverse the decision if it disagreed with that interpretation of *McDonald*.[7]

7.2 A BRIEF HISTORY OF SECOND AMENDMENT CASE LAW

We now continue with a brief exploration of Second Amendment legal doctrine, beginning with a discussion of *United States* v. *Cruikshank*[8] and *Presser* v. *Illinois*.[9] In both of these cases, the US Supreme Court ruled

---

[6] *Heller* does not even mandate that states make concealed carry permits available if interpreted narrowly, although one state high court (the Illinois Supreme Court) used *Heller* expansively to do exactly this in *People* v. *Aguilar*, 2 N.E.3d 321 (Ill. 2011).

[7] This argument is also interesting in that it directly contravenes a theoretical argument that suggests that lower court judges may have a fear of being reversed by the US Supreme Court (see, e.g., Songer, Segal, and Cameron 1994), in that the Massachusetts Supreme Court is explicitly asking the US Supreme Court to reverse it if they believe this decision was in error, in the name of providing more guidance as to how states should interpret Second Amendment precedent. See *Commonwealth* v. *Caetano*, 26 N.E.3d 688 (Mass. 2015). While it is impossible to prove, one has to wonder whether the Massachusetts Supreme Court put this language in intentionally to encourage the US Supreme Court to grant certiorari in the name of giving further guidance to the states in a relatively low-stakes case.

[8] 92 U.S. 542 (1876).

[9] 116 U.S. 252 (1886).

that the Second Amendment did not apply to the states, despite the ratification of the Fourteenth Amendment in 1868. *Cruikshank* dealt with the Colfax Massacre, where a white militia massacred approximately 150 African Americans at a courthouse in Colfax, Louisiana following the contentious gubernatorial election in Louisiana in 1872. The US government charged three members of the militia with violating the Enforcement Act of 1870, which was designed to allow the federal government to stop violence by the Ku Klux Klan and to enforce the constitutional rights of recently freed slaves in the South. Ultimately, the US Supreme Court ruled that the Enforcement Act was unconstitutional because the Fourteenth Amendment only applied to direct state actions and not to the actions of individuals within those states. Additionally, they interpreted the Second Amendment in such a way that it only acted as a preventative against Congress infringing on the rights of gun ownership (i.e., it did not apply to the states).

In *Presser*, the US Supreme Court dealt with an Illinois statute that banned individuals from parading with arms in groups, except for individuals parading as part of a state militia. Mr. Presser led armed members of a fraternity in a parade and challenged the constitutionality of this statute under the Second and Fourteenth Amendments. The US Supreme Court went further in this opinion than in *Cruikshank* and explicitly held that the Second Amendment only applied to the federal government. However, the Court opinion specifically notes that state governments could not disarm their populations as that would interfere with the federal government's ability to raise a militia in time of war. Given the complicated legal doctrine that emerged from this case and the long period of time since this case was decided, it is rather unclear as to how well this particular case applies to Second Amendment jurisprudence today.

The most well-known US Supreme Court decision dealing with the Second Amendment prior to *Heller* was *United States* v. *Miller*.[10] In this case, however, the US Supreme Court did not deal with the Second Amendment directly. Rather, the Court stated that a federal registration requirement for sawed-off shotguns was constitutional under the Interstate Commerce Clause. Given that the facts of this case dealt solely with the federal government, there was no reason for the Court to address the possible incorporation of the Second Amendment. However, the US Supreme Court ultimately ducked this larger question by stating that sawed-off shotguns were not protected by the Second Amendment given their finding that this would not be related to a "well regulated militia." As is fairly well known, this decision was cited

[10] 307 U.S. 174 (1939).

quite infrequently, which is not surprising given the limited applicability of this opinion to other factual issues.[11]

Cruiskshank, Presser, and *Miller,* however, were not the first court cases in the United States to make a ruling related to the Second Amendment. In a much earlier case, *Nunn v. State,*[12] the Georgia Supreme Court stated that the Georgia legislature could not ban the open carrying of handguns, because to do so would violate the Second Amendment. Interestingly, according to Ruben and Cornell (2015), it was only in former slave states that a general right to carry firearms existed, for two reasons. First, carrying a firearm openly was considered to be essential for protection against slaves at this time. The second reason related to duels, which were still common in the South even into the 1840s, and where a gun might be seen as essential for being able to have an honorable duel (Hildreth 1854). A particularly interesting aspect of this is that this view was not shared universally in the South. In fact, one can track the idea of prohibiting the carrying of firearms to the English Statute of Northampton (1328) which banned armed travel through crowded areas.[13] While there was debate as to when this type of statute would apply,[14] William Blackstone stated in the 1760s that being openly armed would make a *prima facie* case of terrorizing the public. This means that carrying firearms in crowded areas could be banned in any circumstance. Similar laws banning the carrying of firearms in crowded areas existed in several states, including both New Jersey and North Carolina (Ewing 1805; Martin 1792).

We find from early United States and English colonial history that the Second Amendment would not have had a clear legal understanding from the perspective of an originalist. How one viewed this would likely have been dependent on how one viewed these early English statutes and similar ones in the thirteen colonies. In fact, Ruben and Cornell (2015) argue that it was only in Southern states that there was extensive jurisprudence relating to Second Amendment rights. They argue that it is questionable whether this regional link substantially harms the generalizability of relying on these states for a national understanding of the Second Amendment from this time. Ultimately, and *perhaps* more relevant for our discussion of *McDonald,* the US Supreme Court heard no cases directly related to the Second Amendment following *United States* v. *Miller* for almost seventy years.

[11] It had a very clear legal rule, but did not make for easy applicability to factual situations not directly related to those in *Miller.*

[12] 1 Ga. 243 (Ga. 1846).

[13] Statute of Northampton, 2 Edw. 3, c. 3 (1328).

[14] Some state statutes with a similar law used a phrase such as "to the fear or terror of the good citizens."

Yet, events in the 1990s increased the salience of Second Amendment-related concerns. The largest, most salience concern for conservatives in the 1990s was the passage of the Brady Handgun Violence Prevention Act in 1993. The Brady Act mandated federal background checks for individuals who had purchased firearms,[15] and placed a mandatory five-day waiting period to purchase a firearm until instant background checks became available in 1998 (the National Rifle Association had been heavily involved in winning the instant background check concession).[16] Additionally, salience of the issue increased after a series of publicized school shootings, starting with the Jonesboro school shooting in 1998 and the Columbine school shooting in 1999.[17]

7.3 *HELLER* AND *MCDONALD*: CASES AND IMMEDIATE AFTERMATH

Ultimately, the Supreme Court ended up granting certiorari in *Heller* in 2007, to review a split panel decision from the DC Circuit Court of Appeals.[18] Eventually, as is implied from discussion above, the DC Circuit's decision was affirmed by the US Supreme Court in a 5–4 majority opinion written by Justice Scalia. Both Justice Scalia and Justice Breyer – who authored the dissent – used "original meaning" approaches, but came to opposite conclusions. This fact is not particularly surprising given the apparent split early on with regard to the extent that individuals have a right to possess firearms. In the majority opinion, the Court also noted that "reasonable regulations" of gun control did not violate the Second Amendment. In dicta, the court provided examples of reasonable regulations, including restrictions on violent criminals from having firearms. The opinion also noted that restrictions on firearms that have historically been used primarily for unlawful purposes, such as the sawed-off shotgun at issue in *United States* v. *Miller*, would not violate the Second Amendment. However, several potential issues with the opinion (even if following the dicta) remain in terms of compliance. These include the lack of a defined legal standard for determining what constitutes a "reasonable regulation," as well as the lack of one for dealing with regulations that are not "reasonable." Another issue with the opinion that may have affected

---

[15] In *Printz* v. *United States*, 521 U.S. 898 (1997), a portion of the Brady Act was held unconstitutional for violating the anticommandeering doctrine, and thus the Tenth Amendment. However, *Printz* did not involve the Second Amendment.

[16] For more information about the NRA's endorsement of background checks, see Price and Norris (2008).

[17] See discussion of this issue in Plouffe (2000).

[18] 478 F.3d 370 (D.C. Cir. 2007).

compliance relates to the fact that *Heller* itself could not be applied directly to the states, so another ruling was needed. While the Court's decision in *McDonald* settled this question, it did not address any of the others.

In *McDonald*, the US Supreme Court incorporated the Second Amendment to the states, holding that an individual has a fundamental right to keep a firearm for lawful purposes, such as keeping a handgun "for the core lawful purpose of self-defense," which at a minimum applies in the home. The facts involved in this case were quite similar to those of *Heller*. In this case, McDonald had an interest in having a handgun in his home for self-defense, but was unable to do so due to a Chicago ordinance that had two requirements. First, it required that anyone who wished to legally possess a firearm in Chicago city limits would be required to have a registration certificate for said firearm. Second, it banned the registration of most handguns, making it a de facto ban on handguns within Chicago city limits. While McDonald owned handguns that he kept outside of city limits, he argued that he was threatened with violence by drug dealers in the neighborhood where he lived. Therefore, he would be better able to protect his life if he was able to legally have a handgun in his home.

While the core holdings of *McDonald* and *Heller* were similar, the two differed significantly beyond that. In dicta in the *Heller* opinion, the Court discussed types of regulations that might be seen as reasonable in substantial detail, but references to reasonable regulations in *McDonald* were substantially limited by comparison.[19] Essentially, the core of the *McDonald* opinion simply served to apply *Heller* to the states using a combination of the Second Amendment and the Due Process Clause of the Fourteenth Amendment.[20] The opinion, when interpreted narrowly, could be read to only apply to keeping a handgun in the home, thus providing lower federal courts and state high courts with substantial flexibility to give a narrow reading to the decision or to expand the applicability of *McDonald* and *Heller* to other areas.

Examining Second Amendment decisions in the lower federal courts post-*McDonald* (of which there have been approximately 200), show it to be very rare for a law to be struck down as unconstitutional on the basis of violating

[19] The only specific reference to "reasonable regulation" in the *McDonald* opinion is a favorable reference to an *amicus curiae* brief filed by Texas and 37 other states asserting that "reasonable firearms regulations" would still be allowed if the Second Amendment was incorporated to the states. *McDonald, supra* note 2, at 785.

[20] Ironically, the method of incorporation is actually a plurality opinion here because only four justices signed on to this part of the opinion. Justice Thomas, argued that the Court should instead use the Privileges and Immunities Clause of the Fourteenth Amendment to effectively accomplish the same thing.

the Second Amendment. This suggests two possibilities. First, the standard espoused in *Heller* and *McDonald* is rather flexible and gives lower federal courts the ability to interpret the "reasonable regulations" dicta in the way that they generally desire. The second possibility is these courts felt no need to address *Heller* and *McDonald* at all, given that they did not really provide a legal standard as to how to deal with future Second Amendment cases. Thus, state and federal courts were given essentially no guidance as to how to address future Second Amendment cases that may differ in factual details from *Heller* or *McDonald*. The lack of clarity regarding legal standards from *Heller* continued after *McDonald*, as that opinion did nothing to clarify what level of scrutiny or legal test a lower court should use in dealing with various types of firearm regulations. Moreover, the US Supreme Court has issued only one opinion discussing the Second Amendment in the nine years following *McDonald*.

7.4 RESEARCH DESIGN AND METHOD

For this chapter, we provide a partially descriptive and partially doctrinal discussion of how state high courts responded to *Heller* and *McDonald*. The focus of the descriptive section is on general trends in how state high courts have treated these precedents using *Shepards' Citations*. The doctrinal sections involves an in-depth discussion of how three specific state high courts dealt with the precedent: the Massachusetts Supreme Judicial Court, the Illinois Supreme Court, and the Louisiana Supreme Court. These states were chosen because they vary on several important dimensions. In the case of Massachusetts and Illinois, both are relatively liberal states in terms of their electorate. By contrast, the Louisiana Supreme Court is in a much more conservative state and, as we outline below, is a relatively conservative state high court as well.

7.4.1 *General Trends in State Court Responses to* Heller *and* McDonald

Examining state high court patterns of treatments (and potential treatments) of both *Heller* and *McDonald*, several interesting patterns emerge. First is the strong lack of negative treatments of *Heller* or *McDonald* with a total of only eight negative treatments out of 181 total potential treatments (approximately 4.4 percent). This pattern is not especially surprising based on our theory and is quite similar to *Lemon*. Given the large degree of flexibility that is featured in these precedents, there should be a low number of cases that one or both would unquestionably apply to directly. On the other hand, a state high court wanting to apply *Heller* or *McDonald* could do so easily, with little strategic fear of being reversed by the US Supreme Court. The second thing that stands out from this descriptive account is the extremely high rate of state high courts ignoring *Heller* and *McDonald* in cases involving questions about the right to bear arms (roughly 30 percent for *Heller* and almost 40 percent for *McDonald*). We find this relatively high proportion of cases ignoring these precedents in cases where they are relevant to be surprising given the degree of flexibility that is innate in the two precedents.

Yet, we believe it is instructive to examine *which* states were most commonly ignoring the two precedents. What we find is that in a relative sense (compared to the number of citations and positive treatments of the two precedents) it is largely conservative states that are ignoring *McDonald* and *Heller*. The reason for this becomes clearer when one examines the specific cases that conservative state high courts hear that relate to Second Amendment cases, and we believe that much of this difference relates to the interaction between state laws and the cases making up individual state high court dockets. Specifically, the vast majority of Second Amendment-related cases that conservative state high courts receive relate to criminals who claimed that restrictions on felons having firearms violated the Second Amendment, despite the fact that *Heller* explicitly allowed for this.[21]

In terms of the types of cases that state high courts examined relating to Second Amendment rights, broadly defined, substantial heterogeneity exists (this is especially the case in more liberal states). A few states in particular found interesting ways to use *Heller* (Illinois, Washington, and Delaware) to expand Second Amendment rights. These typically include cases that deal with a general right to possess or carry firearms. One instance of this was in the case of the Washington Supreme Court where the Court ruled that *Heller* should be incorporated to the states, prior to the ruling in *McDonald* where the US Supreme Court decided this nationally.[22]

Table 7.1 includes a list of each state high court that has treated *Heller* along with the number of positive treatments, negative treatments, citations, and incidences of it being ignored. The states with the most positive treatments of *Heller* include Massachusetts (4), Illinois (3), and Washington (3). The states with the largest number of negative treatments of *Heller* are Massachusetts (3),

---

[21] We admittedly still find it a bit odd that conservative state high courts were reluctant to cite *Heller* and *McDonald* in these case, even if in a perfunctory way.

[22] *State v. Sieyes*, 225 P.3d 995 (Wash. 2010). The Washington Supreme Court's decision was made in close proximity to *McDonald*, so perhaps they were just reading the tea leaves and strategically anticipating this decision.

TABLE 7.1. *Treatment patterns by state high court of* Heller

State	Positive treatment	Negative treatment	Cited	Ignored
Alabama	0	0	0	0
Alaska	1	1	1	0
Arizona	0	0	1	0
Arkansas	0	0	0	1
California	0	0	1	0
Colorado	0	0	0	2
Connecticut	1	0	1	1
Delaware	2	0	0	3
Florida	0	0	0	0
Georgia	2	0	3	0
Hawaii	0	0	0	0
Idaho	0	0	0	1
Illinois	3	1	5	0
Indiana	0	0	1	0
Iowa	0	0	1	0
Kansas	0	0	0	0
Kentucky	0	0	0	1
Louisiana	0	0	3	1
Maine	0	0	1	1
Maryland	0	1	0	0
Massachusetts	4	3	9	0
Michigan	0	0	0	0
Minnesota	1	1	0	1
Mississippi	0	0	0	2
Missouri	1	0	4	3
Montana	1	0	0	0
Nebraska	0	0	0	0
Nevada	1	0	0	0
New Hampshire	0	0	2	0
New Jersey	0	0	2	0
New Mexico	0	0	0	0
New York	0	0	1	0
North Carolina	0	0	1	1
North Dakota	0	0	1	0
Ohio	0	0	0	1
Oklahoma	0	0	0	0
Oregon	0	0	1	1
Pennsylvania	0	0	0	0
Rhode Island	0	0	0	1
South Carolina	0	0	1	1
South Dakota	0	0	0	0
Tennessee	0	0	0	0
Texas	0	0	0	0
Utah	0	0	0	2
Vermont	0	0	0	0
Virginia	0	0	1	0
Washington	3	0	1	3
West Virginia	0	0	0	0
Wisconsin	0	0	1	2
Wyoming	0	0	1	0

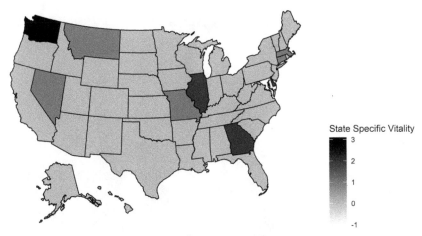

FIGURE 7.1. Variation in state-specific vitality for *Heller* (2018)

followed by Alaska, Illinois, Maryland, and Minnesota with one each. In terms of citations, Massachusetts had the greatest number of citations of *Heller* with nine. Finally, when examining the number of times a state ignored *Heller*, Delaware, Missouri, and Washington each have three cases in our dataset where their state high courts ignored *Heller*.

Figure 7.1 includes a map of all fifty states in the United States with the state-specific vitality of *Heller* as of 2018. Darker shades denote a higher state-specific precedent vitality, and lighter shades denote a lower state-specific precedent vitality. This figure puts in graphical form what we discuss in tabular form in Table 7.1. In particular, combined with information from the table, one can easily see that several states have a relatively high state-specific precedent vitality score for *Heller*. These include Connecticut, Delaware, Massachusetts, Missouri, Montana, and Nevada, which all have state-specific precedent vitality scores of 2. Figure 7.1 also illustrates that a strong state-level precedent vitality of *Heller* does not seem to be concentrated within a specific geographic area, or in states that one would characterize as especially conservative or liberal.

In contrast to the spatial variation examined in Table 7.1 and Figure 7.1, Figure 7.2 plots the frequency of each possible treatment type over time. A couple of patterns are evident when examining the data. First, the number of potential treatments gradually increases for several years after the initial decision in 2008, which is as one would expect given a new opinion in a relatively uncharted area of the law. The second interesting descriptive finding that emerges from Figure 7.2 is that negative treatments of *Heller* all happened

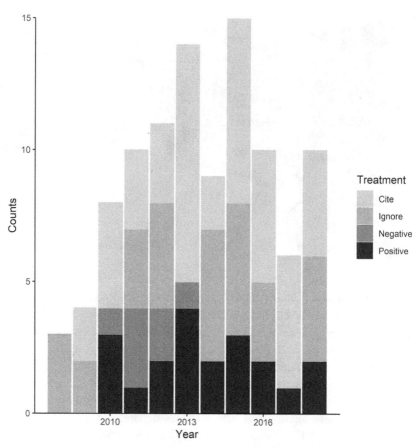

FIGURE 7.2. Variation in treatments of *Heller* over time

within the first four years after the precedent was issued. In other words, the last negative treatment of *Heller* in our data was in 2013, which was five years after the Court issued the decision. Finally, there is an interesting decrease in the pool of cases that would potentially deal with *Heller* in the last three years of the dataset. While the time period examined is too short in our view to say anything from a causal perspective, this may suggest a potential for future drop-off of the number of state high court cases dealing with the Second Amendment, at least in the absence of more decisions that implicate the Second Amendment from the US Supreme Court.

Table 7.2 shows a list of each state high court along with the number of positive treatments, negative treatments, citations, and incidences where the court ignored *McDonald*. The state high court with the greatest number of

TABLE 7.2. *Treatment patterns by state high court of* McDonald

State	Positive treatment	Negative treatment	Cited	Ignored
Alabama	0	0	0	0
Alaska	0	1	0	1
Arizona	0	0	1	0
Arkansas	0	0	0	1
California	0	0	0	0
Colorado	0	0	0	2
Connecticut	0	0	2	1
Delaware	2	0	0	2
Florida	0	0	0	0
Georgia	1	0	3	0
Hawaii	0	0	0	0
Idaho	0	0	0	1
Illinois	2	0	6	1
Indiana	0	0	0	1
Iowa	0	0	1	0
Kansas	0	0	0	0
Kentucky	0	0	0	1
Louisiana	0	0	2	2
Maine	0	0	0	2
Maryland	0	1	0	0
Massachusetts	5	1	7	0
Michigan	0	0	0	0
Minnesota	1	0	1	1
Mississippi	0	0	0	2
Missouri	0	0	4	2
Montana	0	0	0	1
Nebraska	0	0	0	0
Nevada	1	0	0	0
New Hampshire	0	0	2	0
New Jersey	0	0	1	0
New Mexico	0	0	0	0
New York	1	0	0	0
North Carolina	0	0	0	0
North Dakota	0	0	1	0
Ohio	0	0	0	0
Oklahoma	0	0	0	0
Oregon	0	0	1	1
Pennsylvania	0	0	0	0
Rhode Island	0	0	0	1
South Carolina	0	0	0	1
South Dakota	0	0	0	0
Tennessee	0	0	0	0
Texas	0	0	0	0
Utah	0	0	0	2
Vermont	0	0	0	0
Virginia	0	0	1	0
Washington	0	0	2	4
West Virginia	0	0	0	0
Wisconsin	0	0	0	2
Wyoming	0	0	0	0

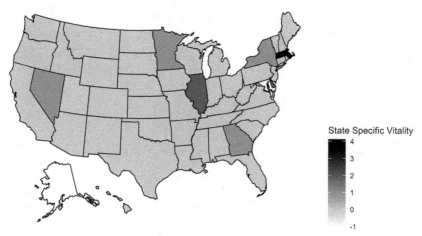

FIGURE 7.3. Variation in state-specific vitality for *McDonald* (2018)

positive treatments of *McDonald* is the Massachusetts Supreme Judicial Court (5), followed by several state high courts with two. These include the Delaware and Illinois Supreme Courts. Only three states have any negative treatments of *McDonald*, with the Alaska Supreme Court, the Maryland Court of Appeals, and the Massachusetts Supreme Judicial Court each having one negative treatment. The Massachusetts Supreme Judicial Court also has the great number of citations of *McDonald* at seven. Finally, the state high court with the greatest number of examples where *McDonald* was ignored was the Washington Supreme Court (4), followed by multiple state high courts with two.[23]

Figure 7.3 is a map of all fifty states that includes a state-specific precedent vitality score that ranges from −1 to 4. As we noted in the previous paragraph, the state with the highest state-specific precedent vitality is Massachusetts (vitality score of 4), which we discuss in more detail in the next section. Illinois has a state-specific precedent vitality score of 2, and four states have a precedent vitality score of 1 (Georgia, Minnesota, Nevada, and New York). Finally, two states have a state-specific precedent vitality score of −1, those being Alaska and Maryland. Similar to our observations about *Heller* in Figure 7.1, there does not seem to be any easily discernible pattern in state-specific precedent vitality, based on either geographic region or state ideology.

Figure 7.4 is a bar graph of state high court treatments of *McDonald* by year, from 2011 through 2018. It mirrors Figure 7.2, where the temporal variation in

[23] These include the Colorado Supreme Court, Delaware Supreme Court, Louisiana Supreme Court, Maine Supreme Judicial Court, Mississippi Supreme Court, and Missouri Supreme Court.

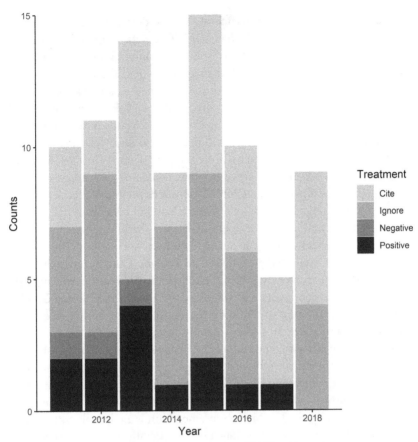

FIGURE 7.4. Variation in treatments of *McDonald* over time

state high court treatments (and potential treatments) of *Heller* was presented. Unlike *Heller*, there is not really any increase in the size of the pool of Second Amendment cases post-*McDonald*, which is perhaps mildly surprising, given what the precedent does. At the same time, we see that negative treatments are comparatively rare for *McDonald*, even compared with *Heller*. However, like *Heller*, all negative treatments occurred in the first few years after the precedent was handed down by the US Supreme Court. There is also some degree of fluctuation when examining the relative proportion of times a state high court ignored *McDonald*, with 2013 and 2017 both having no instances. Given the short time period and relatively small number of cases, we are not necessarily inferring that this is a result of anything systematic. It may simply be a function of the pool of state court Second Amendment cases in those years.

The remainder of this chapter focuses on the different reactions of three state high courts to *Heller* and *McDonald*. These state high courts include the Massachusetts Supreme Judicial Court, the Illinois Supreme Court, and the Louisiana Supreme Court. While we save much of our explanation as to why we chose these three states for the next section, a quick summary of the cases in which the state high courts treated and discussed the Second Amendment is rather illuminating. In the case of Massachusetts, the court generally attempted to use language within the *Heller* and *McDonald* opinions by praising aspects of the opinions, describing the opinions in a great level of detail, and then using them to arrive at a liberal outcome. This approach is not particularly surprising given that the Massachusetts Supreme Judicial Court is a relatively liberal state high court in a liberal state, and one where the justices hold life tenure (until mandatory retirement age). The Illinois Supreme Court provided the broadest interpretations of *Heller*. On one occasion, the Illinois Supreme Court used *Heller* to invalidate a Cook County ordinance that banned individuals from being able to obtain a concealed carry permit in Cook County (which is contiguous with Chicago).[24] The Illinois Supreme Court is somewhat of an unusual institution given that it is a relatively conservative body in a liberal state. An additional institutional feature of the court that makes it unique is that the state high court justices face elections in districts.[25] Thus, they do not represent the state at large individually, meaning that their electoral constituencies may be fundamentally different compared with state high court justices who are elected at large within states to represent the entire state. Finally, the Louisiana Supreme Court is a relatively conservative court in a relatively conservative state, but yet generally interpreted *Heller* and *McDonald* in a relatively "liberal" way.[26] Like Illinois, the Louisiana Supreme Court also uses district-based elections for its state high court justices, but unlike the Illinois Supreme Court it uses a partisan election system to retain (not only to initially select) state high court justices.

7.5 CASE STUDIES IN STATE HIGH COURT REACTIONS TO *HELLER* AND *MCDONALD*

One of the complicating factors with regard to state high court usage of both *Heller* and *McDonald* is that relatively few conservative states have had Second

---

[24] *People v. Aguilar, supra* note 6.

[25] Apart from the Illinois and Louisiana Supreme Courts, only two other states that select their high court judges via contestable elections do so in districts (Kentucky and Mississippi).

[26] This is largely due to the types of cases that the Louisiana Supreme Court received on its docket, as we discuss later in the chapter.

Amendment cases percolate through their high court system since *McDonald*. As Tables 7.1 and 7.2 show, most states that had a large number of Second Amendment-based claims (broadly defined) were relatively liberal, with few moderate to conservative states having a relatively large pool of cases. However, this fact may not be a substantial concern in terms of our theoretical argument that most of the variation – and potential for a lack of compliance – would be occurring in liberal states where there are popular movements against a broad interpretation of the Second Amendment and where the pressure for a state high court to defy, or narrowly interpret, *Heller* and *McDonald* should be at its highest. Thus, it is primarily judges on liberal state high courts who face tension between what US Supreme Court precedents tell them to do, and what their state populace (or their own beliefs) would tell them to do. Additionally, relatively liberal states are more likely than relatively conservative ones to have restrictive gun control laws. As such, there are simply more opportunities for litigants in these states to challenge the constitutionality of laws they feel are in violation of their Second Amendment rights. Thus, it is perhaps not surprising that many of the states with relatively high numbers of Second Amendment cases are comparatively liberal.[27]

In terms of raw numbers of treatments and citations, it makes sense to include both the Massachusetts Supreme Judicial Court and the Illinois Supreme Courts by virtue of their having a significant number of potential treatments of *Heller* and *McDonald*, meaning that Second Amendment-related issues are appearing with reasonable regularity on their dockets. In the case of the Louisiana Supreme Court, it was the conservative state high court that had the greatest number of Second Amendment-related claims, and thus allows us to get leverage on how conservative state high courts react to *Heller* and *McDonald*. Among all three states, there is a large degree of variation in terms of state high court ideology,[28] state political environment, and election/retention system.

---

[27] Two conservative state high courts – Georgia and Louisiana – represent an exception to this in that they that have a fairly large number of high court cases where *Heller* and *McDonald* would potentially apply.

[28] According to the Windett, Harden, and Hall (2015) state high court ideology measure, the Massachusetts Supreme Judicial Court was the 22nd most liberal state high court in the United States in 2010, with a median state high court ideology score of −0.26. While perhaps surprising on its face, five of the seven justices on the Massachusetts Supreme Judicial Court in 2010 were appointed by Republican governors, so this result actually makes a good deal of sense. The Louisiana Supreme Court is rather conservative, as one might expect, and is the twelfth most conservative state high court, with a median score of 0.38. Finally, Illinois is also relatively close to the middle, with the Illinois Supreme Court having the 24th most liberal state high court ideology score at −0.23.

In the case of both Massachusetts and Illinois, the state high courts are in a relatively liberal state environment overall, although features of both the Massachusetts and Illinois high courts insulate them to a greater degree from statewide trends than many other states. In particular, the Massachusetts Supreme Judicial Court is one of three state high courts nationally where the state high court justices do not face any election and can only be removed via impeachment, making their tenure more or less comparable to that of federal judges. In the case of Illinois, the state high court uses a hybrid selection/retention system where a judge is initially selected in a partisan election. However, after initial election to the state high court bench, a justice on the Illinois Supreme Court must merely survive a merit retention election, making these justices relatively insulated from the electorate once they are in office. Additionally, elections for Illinois Supreme Court justices are district-based rather than at-large statewide elections, meaning that a justice's constituency is not the entire state, but one of seven districts in the state.[29]

The Louisiana Supreme Court has a somewhat different environment from the other two state high courts. In particular, the Louisiana Supreme Court is relatively conservative (although far from the most conservative) and is in a highly conservative state environment, meaning that incentives for how it would interpret the Second Amendment may be different compared with state high courts in more liberal environments. Additionally, Louisiana Supreme Court justices face partisan elections, with their party label known to voters at reelection time, meaning that there might be greater incentives for these justices to posture or take extreme positions to win a general election or primary election where partisan cues exist for these judges. Finally, like Illinois, the Louisiana Supreme Court justices are elected in district-based elections (seven of them) rather than in a statewide election, as is the case in nearly all other state high courts that use electoral systems.

7.5.1 *States' Citations and Treatments of* Heller *Prior to* McDonald

Only one of the three states we examine in the section heard a Second Amendment case between the time *Heller* and *McDonald* were decided,

---

[29] We are undecided as to whether this would promote electoral stability or instability as it probably depends on the particular circumstances of how well a justice fits in with their specific district, but we note that it likely makes the Court more evenly divided from a partisan perspective than it would be otherwise.

the Massachusetts Supreme Judicial Court. This lack of cases by the other two states that we include in this section makes it impossible to examine the potential counterfactual as to how less liberal states dealt with *Heller* prior to the release of *McDonald*, which explicitly incorporated the Second Amendment to the states. Nonetheless, because we believe it is important to show how courts may use precedent (or guidance more generally) from the Supreme Court in varying ways over time, we include the example of the Massachusetts Supreme Judicial Court, which in fact cited or treated *Heller* three times in 2010, shortly before the release of *McDonald*.

In its first Second Amendment case post-*Heller*, *Commonwealth* v. *Runyan*,[30] the Massachusetts Supreme Judicial Court distinguished *Heller* and argued that *Heller* did not apply the Second Amendment to the states. In this case, the Commonwealth of Massachusetts had appealed a state district court decision that ruling that Massachusetts' ban on keeping a firearm in an unsecured condition violated the Second Amendment. The district court found that there was no way to distinguish Massachusetts' handgun regulations from DC's. However, the Massachusetts Supreme Judicial Court noted that the Massachusetts law was distinguishable as it did not require that firearms at home be kept inoperable at all times, and it also noted that *Heller* did not apply the Second Amendment to the states. The Court also noted that *Cruikshank* stated that the Second Amendment "means no more than that [the right to bear arms] shall not be infringed by Congress. This is one of the amendments that has no other effect than to restrict the powers of the national government."[31]

The Massachusetts Supreme Judicial Court cited *Heller* two additional times prior to *McDonald* in *Commonwealth* v. *Depina*[32] and *Commonwealth* v. *Loadholt*.[33] In *Depina*, a defendant had argued that Massachusetts' firearm regulatory scheme served as a prior restraint on his fundamental Second Amendment rights. In this case, the Massachusetts Supreme Judicial Court again noted that *Heller* did not apply the Second Amendment to the states and that the Massachusetts Constitution does not recognize a right to bear arms. In *Loadholt*, the Court again noted that the Supreme Court itself stated that *Heller* did not by itself automatically apply the Second Amendment to the states, as the Fourteenth Amendment's Due Process Clause needed to be

---

[30] 922 N.E.2d 794 (2010).
[31] Id. at 797 (quoting from *Cruikshank, supra* note 8, at 553).
[32] 922 N.E.2d 778 (2010).
[33] 923 N.E.2d 1037 (2010).

used to make the Second Amendment enforceable on the states,[34] but noted in short what *Heller* had stated specifically in terms of its substantive scope.

7.5.2 *Massachusetts' Treatments of* McDonald *and* Heller *Post-*McDonald

According to *Shepards' Citations*, the Massachusetts Supreme Judicial Court has positively treated *McDonald* five times since its creation and has negatively treated *McDonald* once. It has treated *Heller* positively three times, but negatively treated *Heller* three times (sometimes while treating *McDonald* positively). In this section, we include a brief discussion of the six cases in which Massachusetts has interpreted *McDonald*. These include the following cases: *Commonwealth* v. *Powell*,[35] *Commonwealth* v. *Loadholt II*,[36] *Commonwealth* v. *McGowan*,[37] *Chardin* v. *Police Commissioner of Boston*,[38] *Commonwealth* v. *Caetano*,[39] and *Commonwealth* v. *Gouse*.[40] In the first five cases, *Shepard's* reports *McDonald* being treated positively, whereas *Gouse* was distinguished from *McDonald*.[41]

Overall, we find that Massachusetts' applications of *Heller* and *McDonald* shows a good-faith attempt to comply with the precedents, even though it is a court that has generally been quite liberal when it comes to interpreting the Second Amendment. In most of the cases in which it dealt with *McDonald* and/or *Heller* explicitly, the Massachusetts Supreme Judicial Court painstakingly tied its decisions into the language of the two opinions. Additionally, rather than trying to argue that *Heller* did not apply, the Court generally tried to use language in *Heller* or *McDonald* specifically affirming what they were doing, thus directly tying in their argumentation to the language in the conservative *Heller* and *McDonald* opinions, while reaching liberal results. Yet, it is interesting that they are the only state high court reversed by the US Supreme Court in a Second Amendment-related case post-*McDonald*. It is also interesting to note that the lone negative treatment that the Massachusetts

---

[34] The Massachusetts Supreme Judicial Court's decision in *Loadholt* received a grant, vacate, and remand order from the US Supreme Court shortly after *McDonald* was handed down. See *Loadholt* v. *Massachusetts*, 131 S.Ct. 459 (2010).

[35] 946 N.E.2d 114 (Mass. 2011).

[36] 954 N.E.2d 1128 (Mass. 2011).

[37] 982 N.E.2d 495 (Mass. 2013).

[38] 989 N.E.2d 392 (Mass. 2013).

[39] *Supra* note 7.

[40] 965 N.E.2d 774 (Mass. 2012).

[41] Several other cases were heard by the Massachusetts Supreme Judicial Court that cited *Heller* and/or *McDonald*, but due to reasons of space we have chosen to leave those out of our discussion.

Supreme Judicial Court gave to *McDonald* came in 2012. In fact, in three cases since that time, the Massachusetts Supreme Judicial Court positively treated *McDonald*, suggesting that the Court now prefers to discuss *Heller* and *McDonald* in a positive light.

The first case that the Massachusetts Supreme Judicial Court chose to substantively treat *McDonald* in was *Commonwealth* v. *Powell*. The case facts in *Commonwealth* v. *Powell* were relatively straightforward. Powell was convicted of illegally possessing a .22 caliber revolver without a license to carry the gun. Powell claimed that Massachusetts' statute requiring a license, as part of a greater licensing scheme, to carry a firearm in public was unconstitutional as it violated his Second Amendment rights, the Equal Protection Clause of the Fourteenth Amendment, as well as the Massachusetts Constitution. In its opinion, the Massachusetts Supreme Judicial Court relied heavily on *Heller* and *McDonald*, describing the opinion in great detail, and specifically noting that the Supreme Court did not decide the applicability of *Cruikshank* to the states in *Heller* given that it was not asked to do so by either party. Therefore, because of *Cruikshank* and the precedent that it set, the Massachusetts Supreme Judicial Court had refused to apply the Second Amendment prior to *McDonald*. Additionally, the opinion described both *Heller* and *McDonald* as not doing anything to disturb the presumably legal restrictions on Second Amendment rights, specifically highlighting the examples provided in *Heller*. The state court continued to note that the core of both *Heller* and *McDonald* dealt with prohibitions on having an operable firearm in the home, and that both Supreme Court opinions allowed for Massachusetts to deny classes of individuals (if there was a good reason to do so) the right to have a firearm. Thus, the Massachusetts high court attempted to strongly couch its opinion in the text of the Supreme Court's recent opinions.

The second case in which the Supreme Judicial Court of Massachusetts substantively treated *McDonald* was *Commonwealth* v. *Loadholt II*.[42] *Loadhold II* dealt with a grant, vacate, and remand (GVR) order from the US Supreme Court in light of *McDonald*. The facts in *Loadholt* were essentially identical to those of *Powell*, with Powell being arrested for illegal possession of a firearm outside of the home, as he did not go through the process of getting a firearm identification card. The defendant in *Loadholt II* made the argument on remand that *McDonald* bans any type of state licensing system of firearms if one must receive "prior approval by a government officer." As the original decision by the Massachusetts court (prior to the remand) was issued before *McDonald*, the US Supreme Court simply asked the Massachusetts

---

[42] *Supra* note 36.

high court to reconsider the case to address the new *McDonald* precedent. On remand, the Massachusetts Supreme Judicial Court noted that *McDonald* and *Heller* did not support the conclusion that all state licensing systems were unconstitutional. Instead, the Massachusetts Supreme Judicial Court noted that *Heller* and *McDonald* did not support the petitioner's conclusion because *Heller* specifically recognized that an individual right to carry arms is limited in scope, and noted that a licensing system to carry a handgun outside of the home does not violate the Constitution on its face. Additionally, the Massachusetts Supreme Judicial Court noted in *Heller* that after discussing the list of restrictions on Second Amendment rights that were presumed legal, the US Supreme Court noted: "We identify these presumptively lawful regulatory measures only as examples; our list does not purport to be exhaustive."[43]

In *Commonwealth* v. *McGowan*,[44] the Massachusetts Supreme Judicial Court addressed a question in a criminal case relating to the constitutionality of a statute that made it illegal to store a firearm without a trigger lock in an open drawer in a house.[45] While the majority opinion in *McGowan* stated that this law could constitutionally be enforced, it relied extensively on aspects of the opinion in *McDonald* and *Heller*. Specifically, the Massachusetts high court noted that longstanding exemptions that did not substantially burden the ability of an individual to use their legally owned firearm in their own home fell under the portion of *Heller* that allowed for existing firearm regulations to largely stand. Additionally, the Massachusetts Supreme Court differentiated the law in Massachusetts from those in Chicago and in Washington, DC by arguing that the Washington, DC and Chicago ordinances effectively constituted a complete ban on handgun ownership, which the US Supreme Court had concluded would fail at any level of scrutiny (including rational basis). The Massachusetts court also noted that reasonable regulations on firearms fall outside of the protection of the Second Amendment because laws are presumptively lawful if they do not rely on heightened scrutiny. Thus, while closely following the text of *McDonald*, the Massachusetts court nonetheless concluded that reasonable regulations receive only a rational basis standard of review and that this falls outside of the protection of the Second Amendment.

The majority opinion argued that the Massachusetts law that required a firearm outside of the immediate control of an individual in the home to be

---

[43] Id. at 1130 (quoting *Heller* at 626–627).
[44] *Supra* note 37.
[45] Specifically, the relevant Massachusetts statute required that a firearm must be kept in either a locked container or must contain a trigger lock, if not in the immediate control of its owner.

either equipped with a trigger lock or to be stored in a locked container differed from the laws at issue in *Heller* and *McDonald* in a couple of ways. First, the majority opinion noted that in Massachusetts, if one has a firearm within one's immediate control, that firearm need not be equipped with a safety lock if it is in one's vicinity. The court also noted specifically that in *Heller*, laws that were "regulating the storage of firearms to prevent accidents" were perfectly acceptable.[46] The Massachusetts Supreme Judicial Court also noted that if the brief delay needed to unlock a storage container for a firearm violated the Second Amendment, *Heller* would not have specifically cited the presumed constitutionality of safe storage requirements for firearms.

The fourth example of the Massachusetts high court positively treating *McDonald* came in *Chardin* v. *Police Commissioner of Boston*.[47] This case involved a challenge to a Massachusetts law banning convicted felons from possessing a firearm. Mirko Chardin had been arrested for illegally possessing a firearm without a license, as well as illegally possessing ammunition in 1995. Because he faced prison time related to this crime, by Massachusetts law he was labeled as a felon. The majority opinion specifically claimed that the Massachusetts' law preventing Chardin from obtaining a firearm was fully compliant with *Heller*, as reinforced and applied to the states in *McDonald*. In fact, the opinion also notes that while having a firearm is a fundamental right according to the US Supreme Court, *McDonald* itself states that it "does not imperil every law regulating firearms" and that there are a series of exemptions, which this law falls under.[48] Therefore, given that this law fit in effectively with the specific examples given in *Heller*, the Massachusetts Supreme Judicial Court held it to be valid to restrict the Second Amendment rights of convicted felons for life under state law.

The fifth example of Massachusetts positively treating *McDonald* came in a much simpler case involving a challenge to the constitutionality of Massachusetts' ban on possessing stun guns in public, in *Commonwealth* v. *Caetano*.[49] Here, Jaime Caetano had been arrested for possessing a stun gun in a supermarket parking lot. Upon her detention, she claimed that she felt she needed to protect herself against an abusive ex-boyfriend, and then claimed that Massachusetts' ban on the public possession of stun guns was unconstitutional. As one might predict, the Massachusetts Supreme Court's majority opinion noted that a stun gun is not protected by the Second

---

[46] *McGowan, supra* note 37, at 503 (quoting *Heller* at 632).

[47] *Supra* note 38.

[48] Id. at 323 (quoting *McDonald* at 3047).

[49] *Supra* note 7.

Amendment and stated that the Congress in 1789 could not have contemplated stun guns being protected by the Second Amendment. The Massachusetts high court additionally argued that a stun gun was not "in common use at the time of" the enactment of the Second Amendment,[50] and the stun gun was not used by Caetano to defend herself in her home. Finally, the Court stated that without additional guidance from the US Supreme Court, it would not extend the Second Amendment to cover stun guns.[51] The Massachusetts Supreme Judicial Court's use of *McDonald* was relatively limited in this case except to note that the US Supreme Court extended the right of self-defense through the Second Amendment using *McDonald*. However, the opinion relied heavily on *Heller,* and argued that Massachusetts' ban on stun guns was in compliance with both *Heller* and *McDonald.*

As with the four prior opinions we discussed, the Massachusetts Supreme Judicial Court in *Caetano* carefully used language directly from the *Heller* and *McDonald* opinions in drawing the conclusion that the Second Amendment does not give an unlimited individual right to keep and bear arms. Rather, the Massachusetts high court noted in each of these cases that under *Heller* certain types of prohibitions on those rights are presumed to be valid, including pro-hibiting weapons that were "dangerous and unusual."[52] Interestingly, despite its careful adherence to the text of *Heller* and *McDonald,* this decision was later reversed by the US Supreme Court in a *per curiam* opinion stating that the Massachusetts court had interpreted *McDonald* and *Heller* incorrectly. This was due to an overly literal reading of *Heller* by the Massachusetts Supreme Judicial Court in its holding that *Heller* and *McDonald* only applied to weapons that were "in common use at the time of enactment of the Second Amendment." The US Supreme Court questioned the Massachusetts court's interpretation of the original meaning of the Second Amendment, and its use of the phrase "in common use" to refer only to a given historical period of time. The US Supreme Court also noted that while stun guns are a modern weapon, they are not unusual, as they are commonly used by law enforcement and corrections officers.

One more interesting note regarding Massachusetts' usage of *McDonald* is worthy of mention in our view, and came in a follow-up case relating to *Caetano: Ramirez* v. *Commonwealth.*[53] Because this opinion did not explicitly

---

[50] Id. at 777.

[51] Ironically, the Massachusetts Supreme Judicial Court received additional guidance in *Caetano* v. *Massachusetts,* 136 S.Ct. 1027 (2016), where their opinion upholding the constitutionality of a stun gun ban was reversed in a *per curiam* opinion.

[52] *Caetano, supra* note 7, at 778 (quoting *Heller* at 627).

[53] 94 N.E.3d 809 (Mass. 2018).

rely on *Heller* or *McDonald*, it was not coded as treating *McDonald* or *Heller*. In *Ramirez*, there was a second case of an individual arrested for possessing a stun gun after a frisk during a traffic stop for a broken taillight. In fact, the Massachusetts law at this time explicitly prohibited the possession of a stun gun, even inside the home (he was also charged with illegal possession of a firearm). This case had occurred after the US Supreme Court reversed the Massachusetts Supreme Judicial Court's decision in *Caetano*, saying that a blanket ban on stun guns in a state violates the Second Amendment, as a stun gun is not designed to be a "dangerous" weapon and was not likely the type of weapon that would have been banned in 1789, had it existed. In *Ramirez*, the Massachusetts Supreme Judicial Court noted that it had now received guidance, which it asked for in *Caetano*, and recognized stun guns as protected by the Second Amendment as a type of "arms." The Court then concluded that the ban on stun guns violated the US Constitution and that the Commonwealth could regulate stun guns, but could not ban them outright. Finally, the Court concluded by noting that it would not step beyond its judicial boundaries and was unable to rewrite the law due to separation of powers principles, but noted that the Massachusetts legislature could come up with a regulatory scheme for stun guns that was similar to what it did for firearms.[54]

The final instance where the Massachusetts Supreme Court substantively interpreted *Heller* and *McDonald* was the one instance in which the court negatively treated *McDonald*. In *Commonwealth* v. *Gouse*,[55] the defendant was arrested for assault and battery, as well as the unlawful possession of a firearm outside of his residence. In this case, there was no argument made against the constitutionality of Massachusetts' firearm license requirement, as he had never attempted to apply for a license. Rather, he argued that the Massachusetts state law requiring a license for firearm usage outside of the home created a "presumption of criminality from constitutionally protected conduct – the possession of a firearm."[56] In this case, the Massachusetts Supreme Court's opinion stated that neither *McDonald* nor *Heller* altered the crime of unlawful possession of a firearm and how it would be prosecuted mechanistically in the state of Massachusetts. Because of this discussion of the elements of a crime being unrelated to *McDonald*, and the Court specifically stated that neither *Heller* nor *McDonald* had any effect on their handgun

---

[54] And in the summer of 2018, this is exactly what the Massachusetts legislature did.
[55] *Supra* note 40.
[56] Id. at 786.

regulatory scheme, the decision was coded as distinguishing the precedent by *Shepards' Citations*.

7.5.3 *Illinois' Treatments of* Heller *and* McDonald

The Illinois Supreme Court is an interesting case when it comes to interpreting *Heller* and *McDonald*, as two features combine to make it simultaneously moderate and polarized ideologically. These include the initial partisan election that is used to elect Illinois Supreme Court justices, as well as the fact that Illinois uses district-based elections for its state high court justices. Thus far (as of 2018), the Illinois Supreme Court has interpreted *McDonald* positively on two occasions, once in 2012 and again in 2015.[57] Overall, the Illinois Supreme Court's use of *Heller* and *McDonald* was more deferential to these precedents than the Massachusetts Supreme Judicial Court. This may partially be due to the fact that the Illinois high court has historically been less liberal than the Massachusetts Supreme Judicial Court. The two cases in which the Illinois Supreme Court treated *McDonald* positively provide evidence of the difference of its substantive treatments.

From our interpretation of how the Illinois Supreme Court acted regarding these two cases, it has also exercised its right to view *Heller* and *McDonald* through a flexible lens. Similar to Massachusetts, the Illinois Supreme Court's has generally attempted to treat *Heller* and *McDonald* in a good-faith attempt to abide by them. In fact, the Illinois Supreme Court has never ignored either of these precedents in any case where it had an opportunity to apply some combination of *Heller*, *McDonald*, or both. The Illinois Supreme Court made the distinction between laws that fall under the reasonable regulations discussion in *Heller*, and those laws that attempt to ban an entire type of weapon or general usage of weapons. Compared with Massachusetts, which had allowed a blanket ban of stun guns, the Illinois Supreme Court had effectively ruled that individuals had a fundamental right to carry a firearm outside of the home. By following the Seventh Circuit's opinion on the Second Amendment,[58] the Illinois Supreme Court effectively extended the core of *Heller* to cover the carrying of firearms outside of the home as well. Thus, while the Illinois Supreme Court is not particularly conservative, it has appeared to abide by *McDonald* in a good-faith and even somewhat expansive manner.

---

[57] *Wilson v. County of Cook*, 968 N.E.2d 641 (Ill. 2012); *People v. Burns*, 79 N.E.3d 159 (Ill. 2015).
[58] *Moore v. Madigan*, 705 F.3d 933 (7th Cir. 2012).

Wilson v. County of Cook involved an individual challenging the constitutionality of Cook County's blanket ban on "assault weapons."[59] In this case, the petitioner (Wilson) claimed that this law violated the Due Process and Equal Protection Clauses of the Fourteenth Amendment, as well as the Supreme Court's interpretation of the Second Amendment in *McDonald*, and sought to receive pre-enforcement action from the Illinois Supreme Court. The Illinois Supreme Court held that this ordinance did not violate the Due Process or Equal Protection Clauses of the Fourteenth Amendment, but remanded the case to a trial court to have additional proceedings about whether the assault weapons ban violated the Second Amendment.[60] While the Illinois Supreme Court did not *strongly* rely on *McDonald* for its decision, it did note that *McDonald* provided a threshold question that state courts needed to consider when dealing with Second Amendment issues. The Illinois Supreme Court noted:

> The threshold question we must consider is whether the challenged law imposes a burden on conduct falling within the scope of the Second Amendment guarantee. That inquiry involves a textual and historical inquiry to determine whether the conduct was understood to be within the scope of the right at the time of ratification.[61]

The Illinois Supreme Court's decision in *People v. Burns* provided a lengthier discussion and interpretation of *Heller* and *McDonald* compared with *Wilson*. In this case, Burns was charged with violating an Illinois statute that criminalized aggravated unlawful use of a weapon (AUUW), which made it illegal (Class 4 felony) to carry a firearm outside of the home, and was partially overruled in an earlier case.[62] However, what made this case particularly complicated was that Burns was charged with a Class 2 felony, based on having two previous felony convictions which essentially treated his criminal past as an aggravator for a longer sentence. In this case, from a substantive perspective, the Illinois Supreme Court declared the sentence heightener to be unconstitutional as it had previously declared the underlying offense (aggravated unlawful use of a weapon) to be unconstitutional. Thus, the

---

[59] *Supra* note 57.
[60] This case was originally heard in trial court prior to the ruling in *McDonald*. The Illinois Supreme Court had previously issued a GVR (grant, vacate, and remand) order to the trial court asking that it reconsider the constitutionality of Cook County's assault weapons ban post-*McDonald*. The trial court reinstated the original decision, throwing out Wilson's Second Amendment challenge, so this was the second time that the Illinois Supreme Court heard this case and remanded it back to the trial court for additional deliberation.
[61] *Wilson, supra* note 57, at 41.
[62] *People v. Aguilar, supra* note 6.

Illinois Supreme Court is one of the few state high courts to have used *Heller* and *McDonald* to declare a state law unconstitutional under the Second Amendment.[63]

In this opinion, the Illinois Supreme Court noted that the AUUW statute is unconstitutional as it "operates as an absolute ban on an individual's right to possess a gun for self-defense outside the home."[64] The Illinois high court grounded this decision in part in a Seventh Circuit Court of Appeals case.[65] This opinion by the Illinois Supreme Court noted that *McDonald* and *Heller* applied not only inside the home, but outside of the home (the Illinois Supreme Court agreed with the Seventh Circuit's interpretation of *Heller* and *McDonald*). A concurring opinion in *Burns* also noted that the Illinois Supreme Court upheld restrictions on Second Amendment rights based on the text in *Heller* that provides a potential list of regulation types that would presumably be valid under the *McDonald* and *Heller* precedents.

In addition to *Wilson* and *Burns*, the Illinois Supreme Court had a few other opportunities to react to *Heller* and/or *McDonald*. It treated the two precedents differently on several of these occasions, including simply citing both cases the last three times it dealt with either of them.[66] In *People* v. *McFadden*, the court upheld a criminal charge of unlawful use of a weapon by a felon (UUW) as constitutional, even though McFadden was previously sentenced as a felon for the AUUW charge (which was later made unconstitutional). The basic argument by the Illinois Supreme Court was that he did not clear his felon status before obtaining a firearm (this was not overriden in *Aguilar*). Additionally, the plea bargain which *McFadden* agreed to did not make it clear whether his plea bargain was implicated by *Aguilar* or not.

Two years later, in *In re N.G.*, the Illinois Supreme Court partially overruled *McFadden*, essentially arguing that if a statute is held as facially unconstitutional and it was clear that a *specific* provision that was held as unconstitutional was the predicate for another offense (based on that initial offense), then the second conviction must fall due to the unconstitutionality of the first one. Finally, in *People* v. *Chairez*, the Illinois Supreme Court noted that another portion of the UUW statute is unconstitutional, in particular a portion that

---

[63] The Massachusetts Supreme Judicial Court had effectively done this in *Caetano II*, but only after having its initial decision reversed by the US Supreme Court. So in the Massachusetts case it was not entirely "voluntary."

[64] *Burns, supra* note 57, at 21.

[65] *Moore* v. *Madigan, supra* note 58.

[66] See *People* v. *McFadden*, 61 N.E.3d 74 (Ill. 2016); *In re N.G.*, 115 N.E.3d 102 (Ill. 2018); *People* v. *Chairez*, 104 N.E.3d 1158 (Ill. 2018).

banned individuals from possessing a firearm within 1,000 feet of a public park. The argument here was that a park is not considered a "sensitive place" where restrictions on Second Amendment rights would be presumed as constitutional.[67] Additionally, the Illinois high court further relied on dicta from *Heller* to hold that even reasonable restrictions on possession of firearms in sensitive places must only be applied to the immediate location of a sensitive place, not a substantial distance away.

7.5.4 *The Louisiana Supreme Court's Discussion of* Heller *and* McDonald

The Louisiana Supreme Court had four Second Amendment-related cases between 2008 and the end of 2018. In the four cases, it cited *Heller* three times and ignored it once, and cited *McDonald* two times and ignored it twice. In this section, we discuss the individual cases (all from 2013 onward) where the Louisiana Supreme Court had an opportunity to discuss *Heller* and/or *McDonald* chronologically. In the case of Louisiana, unlike Massachusetts or Illinois, the state legislature directly responded to the US Supreme Court's decision shortly after *Heller* by beginning the process of amending the Louisiana Constitution. This amendment accomplished two things: one merely symbolic and one that had substantive implications for the Louisiana Supreme Court. By getting involved very early in the process, the Louisiana state legislature was able to effectively control how courts in Louisiana would deal with Second Amendment related cases.[68]

Unlike most state constitutions, the Louisiana Constitution explicitly gives a right to bear arms to individual residents in the state. Specifically, Article 1, Section 11 of the Louisiana Constitution states that: "The right of each citizen to keep and bear arms shall not be abridged, but this provision shall not prevent the passage of laws to prohibit the carrying of weapons concealed on the person." This constitutional provision specifically allowed the state legislature to pass laws as needed dealing with concealed carrying of firearms, but somewhat limited the state legislature's ability to pass other types of restrictions on firearms.[69] After *Heller* and *McDonald*, the Louisiana legislature became concerned with the possible erosion of the right to bear

---

[67] The court states that schools and government buildings would be examples of such sensitive places, specifically quoting dicta from *Heller*. Id. at 1168.

[68] The Louisiana Supreme Court discusses the history of this process in extensive detail in *State v. Draughter*, 130 So.3d 855 (La. 2013).

[69] Importantly, though, this older provision of the Louisiana Constitution did not state a legal standard to be used for determining when this right would be abridged, although it seems to imply some sort of heightened scrutiny.

arms in Louisiana by future state legislatures or by state courts in Louisiana. The Louisiana legislature specifically noted that both *Heller* and *McDonald* were decided by bare majorities of conservative justices voting in favor of the Second Amendment, and with liberal justices voting against the Second Amendment in both cases.

Thus, in 2012 the state legislature submitted a proposed state constitutional amendment to the electorate, which passed with more than 70 percent of the vote. Article 1, Section 11, was amended to state the following: "The right of each citizen to keep and bear arms is fundamental and shall not be infringed. Any restriction of this right shall be subject to strict scrutiny." We view such a state constitutional change as a conservative policy shift by the state legislature and electorate, designed to ensure that judges would use strict scrutiny (rather than intermediate scrutiny or rational basis) in cases involving the right to bear arms.[70] As a result of these state constitutional changes, one would expect there to be a decent number of cases that relate to the right to bear arms.[71] Interestingly, all of the cases that the Louisiana Supreme Court decided dealing with the right to bear arms related to criminal activity, primarily by convicted felons who desired a right to bear arms, but were denied that right under Louisiana statutory law.

The first case we discuss is *State* v. *Draughter*.[72] In *Draughter*, the Louisiana Supreme Court addressed an appeal from a convicted felon who was under state supervision. The individual claimed that a criminal statute banning felons under state supervision from possessing firearms violated the Louisiana Constitution. The Louisiana Supreme Court specifically noted that *Draughter* did not discuss Second Amendment rights as expounded in *Heller* and *McDonald*, but noted that the Louisiana legislature had amended the state constitution while observing that *Heller* was decided by a mere 5–4 majority.[73] The state constitutional amendment specifically notes that all alleged

---

[70] This specification of a standard of scrutiny in the amended Louisiana Constitution, while seemingly minute, is actually a rational thing for a conservative state legislature and electorate to do. This is the case, given that neither *Heller* nor *McDonald* gave an explicit federal standard of review for cases that implicated the Second Amendment. As we have seen in the prior subsection on the Massachusetts Supreme Judicial Court's reaction to *Heller* and *McDonald*, this ambiguity leaves room for state courts to apply a rational basis standard in at least some cases while still following the US Supreme Court's precedents.

[71] In fact, this might be why Louisiana is one of the few relatively conservative states to get a series of cases that implicate the right to bear arms following *Heller* and *McDonald*.

[72] *Supra* note 68.

[73] In other words, the main impetus for Louisiana amending its state constitution was to protect Second Amendment rights should *Heller* be overruled by the Supreme Court in the future under a more liberal majority. The Louisiana Supreme Court also noted that only a bare

violations of the right to bear arms under the Louisiana Constitution must survive strict scrutiny. However, the Louisiana high court interpreted the amendment to note that public safety is a compelling interest. The Louisiana Supreme Court then applied strict scrutiny to Draughter's claim and came to the conclusion that the state law banning him from having firearms – given that he was still under supervision by the state and serving part of his sentence – survived strict scrutiny.

The second case that Louisiana dealt with in this area was *State* v. *Eberhardt*.[74] The facts of this case were fairly similar to that of *Draughter*, although there were a few differences that made it potentially important for the Louisiana Supreme Court to address. Like *Draughter*, this case again involved felons who were challenging Louisiana's prohibition against convicted felons owning firearms based on the Louisiana Constitution. Unlike in *Draughter*, Eberhardt had already completed his sentence and period of state supervision, yet Louisiana law still banned him from owning firearms for ten years after the completion of his sentence and parole. The Louisiana Supreme Court used identical grounds and arguments to declare this particular provision of Louisiana statutory law constitutional, as it did in *Draughter*.

The third right to bear arms case from Louisiana in this period was *State* v. *Webb*.[75] In this decision, the Louisiana Supreme Court ignored both *Heller* and *McDonald*. Instead, it relied on *Smith* v. *U.S.*,[76] where the US Supreme Court had upheld the constitutionality of of a federal law that made possession of a firearm a sentence enhancer for drug-related crimes. In our view, this makes sense given that the Louisiana law challenged was specifically a sentence enhancer for illegal drug possession. The Louisiana Supreme Court also noted that having a right to possess a firearm while possessing illegal drugs was not essential to ordered liberty, and thus did not fall under the protection of either the Second Amendment or the Louisiana Constitution.

The Louisiana Supreme Court heard one more case that related to the Second Amendment and the associated provision of the Louisiana Constitution. In *State ex rel. J.M.*,[77] a lower court found that a Louisiana statute that banned minors from carrying concealed weapons was unconstitutional, given that it was fully duplicated by a related provision that banned minors from possessing

---

majority of the US Supreme Court recognized that the Second Amendment applied to "use arms in defense of hearth and home." Id. at 861.

[74] 145 So.3d 377 (La. 2014).

[75] 144 So.3d 971 (La. 2014).

[76] 508 U.S. 223 (1993).

[77] 144 So.3d 853 (La. 2014).

handguns – with several exceptions – in Louisiana.[78] Additionally, the juvenile court stated that the four exceptions relating to parental permission needed to be removed from the statute as they were overly restrictive (e.g., requiring written permission from a parent if off-property, or being on one's private property with a parent on the premises), and the juvenile court severed these exceptions from the rest of the law. The Louisiana Supreme Court stated that these exceptions should not have been severed and also noted that the separate charge of illegally carrying a concealed weapon for minors was constitutional (the juvenile court had declared this as violating the Louisiana Constitution). In this case, the court cited *Heller* in a perfunctory manner to simply note that Louisiana's interpretation of the Second Amendment and the US Supreme Court's were comparable. However, *McDonald* was not mentioned at all in the Louisiana Supreme Court's decision.

Examining all of the information that we have on citations and treatments of *Heller* and *McDonald*, we find several apparent trends. First, given the descriptive statistics on how frequently state high courts cited these two cases, it seems that most of these courts simply did not deal with the Second Amendment much following *Heller* and *McDonald*. Further, of those state high courts that did see these issues on their dockets frequently, most were in relatively liberal state political environments, with the exceptions of the Georgia and Louisiana Supreme Courts. Based on the three case studies that we included in this chapter, it seems that how *Heller* and *McDonald* get used substantively varies dramatically. As we discussed earlier in this section, the Massachusetts Supreme Judicial Court was very careful to use language from *Heller* and *McDonald* to interpret the Second Amendment while still reaching liberal outcomes. However, it never acted in a way that seemed to be outwardly defiant, going so far in *Caetano* as to essentially beg the US Supreme Court for further guidance. Of the three state high courts we examine in depth, the Illinois Supreme Court was arguably the most expansive in its use of *Heller* and *McDonald*, using these precedents to invalidate state laws for violating the Second Amendment. This came most notably with respect to the state's AAUW statute, which criminalized the possession of guns outside of the home for purposes of self-defense.

Finally, in the case of the Louisiana Supreme Court, it had relatively little discretion in terms of determining what standard of review it used to adjudicate Second Amendment-related claims given the previous action of the Louisiana

---

[78] The handgun ban specifically provided exemptions in the law for hunting, trapping, and gun-safety courses. Additionally, it provided four exceptions for which having written permission from a parent was sufficient.

legislature. As the Louisiana Constitution required a higher level of protection for individuals' right to bear arms in the state, the Louisiana Supreme Court relied more on the state constitution than the Second Amendment. Interestingly, the Louisiana high court ruled for the state in all four cases concerning the right to bear arms it has decided since *McDonald*, allowing restrictions on the right to bear arms in each and citing *Heller* as evidence to do so. This seeming inconsistency is largely due to the nature of the cases in front of the Louisiana Supreme Court, compared with Massachusetts and Illinois, as the specifics of the cases in Louisiana differed. Specifically, in Louisiana, all of the cases that related to the Second Amendment dealt with either convicted felons who desired to have their Second Amendment rights restored or whether juveniles should be allowed to carry handguns outside of the home. In any case, most of the cases that the Louisiana Supreme Court heard fell squarely under "reasonable regulations" as were defined in dicta in the US Supreme Court's opinions in *Heller* and *McDonald*.

7.6 CONCLUSION

If one had to boil down the findings of this chapter into one word, the one we would use is *ambiguity*. State high courts clearly seemed to respond to *Heller* and *McDonald* as though the specific message given by the US Supreme Court about how to interpret the Second Amendment was absent altogether. In fact, conservative state high courts that could have potentially latched on to *Heller* and *McDonald* failed to do so. This could be for one of a few reasons. First, conservative state high courts had relatively few challenges that pertained to Second Amendment rights, although both the Georgia and Louisiana Supreme Courts had a few opportunities. However, most of these cases involved specific issues that clearly fell under the "reasonable regulations" language from both *Heller* and *McDonald*. Second, there just may not have been much of a need for conservative courts to use *Heller* and *McDonald* due to the minimal restrictions placed on the use and possession of firearms under state law. The bulk of gun control laws that might be challenged as overly restrictive under the Second Amendment are generally not common in conservative states. Louisiana is a bit of an exception to this general principle, given the amendment to the Louisiana Constitution that occurred shortly after the release of *McDonald*. As a part of this constitutional amendment, state courts in Louisiana received a mandated legal standard to use for all cases that implicated the right to bear or keep arms. Even if conservative states did not feel a need to change their state laws or constitutions post-*McDonald* (i.e., they did not act similarly to the Louisiana legislature), it still seems rather unlikely that conservative states would have received many challenges relating to the right to bear arms, given that *Heller* and *McDonald* would likely have a minimal effect on their state laws.

Similar to what we find in the previous chapters examining state high court responses to US Supreme Court precedent, state high courts exhibited substantial flexibility to faithfully comply with US Supreme Court precedents, while interpreting them in a manner that would shape state legal policy consistent with their preferences. In the case of *McDonald* and *Heller*, one feature that made it especially easy for state high courts to interpret these opinions was the lack of a clear standard from either. Also, the unwillingness of the US Supreme Court to review any major Second Amendment cases post-*McDonald* meant that as long as states were minimally compliant with the Court's Second Amendment jurisprudence, they had little strategic reason to fear reversal. Essentially, the US Supreme Court had made it clear that there were no actual expectations as to how state high courts ruled on Second Amendment decisions in areas that deviated from the case facts shown in *Heller* or *McDonald*.[79] Yet on at least one occasion, in a relatively liberal state, the Illinois Supreme Court was willing to go beyond the minimum requirements of complying with *McDonald* and apply at least a slightly expansive direction to the US Supreme Court's Second Amendment jurisprudence.

Perhaps the biggest takeaway from the chapter is a reinforcement of the central theoretical finding of this book. Given the goal of state high courts to craft legal policy in line with their ideal preferences, they will take advantage of the flexibility afforded them by ambiguous precedents to do exactly that. As with *Atkins* and *Lemon*, we find here that specific case facts appear to be the strongest determinant of how state high courts will treat relevant precedents. The fact patterns in both *Heller* and *McDonald* represented somewhat extreme restrictions of Second Amendment rights and thus were unique. None of the cases we examined involved laws that mirrored those struck down in *Heller* and *McDonald*. This has allowed state high courts to exercise substantial flexibility in interpreting both decisions. Thus, beyond the primary purpose of this chapter, it may help us better understand how state high courts react to precedents in a completely new area of law, as far as interpretation of the US Constitution is concerned. We speculate that as the Supreme Court gets more involved in time with a particular issue area and is able to give more specificity

---

[79] The one exception to this was reversing the Massachusetts Supreme Judicial Court's decision upholding a complete ban on stun guns in *Caetano* v. *Massachusetts, supra* note 7. This case, however, seems to have relatively little general applicability. Moreover, the Massachusetts Court had explicitly called for further guidance from the US Supreme Court in their opinion.

to lower courts, some lower courts may be more likely to take an expansive view of those precedents. We already see early evidence of this with how the Illinois Supreme Court dealt with a law in *Aguilar* that essentially banned carrying firearms outside of the home. On the other hand, the relatively conservative Louisiana Supreme Court upheld all restrictions on Second Amendment rights that were challenged.[80]

The Massachusetts Supreme Judicial Court's approach was a bit different, discussing the two cases frequently and in substantial detail, but nevertheless reaching conclusions in favor of a narrow interpretation of the Second Amendment. In fact, the Massachusetts Supreme Judicial Court is the only state thus far to have Second Amendment decision reversed by the US Supreme Court post-*McDonald*. Yet, on reading the opinion and its explicit request to the US Supreme Court to give more guidance regarding Second Amendment interpretation to the states, it is not especially surprising that this case was the one to be reversed by the US Supreme Court.[81] So these highly varying responses by state high courts to a seemingly unclear US Supreme Court precedent may be typical in that it illustrates the flexibility that state high courts have and the "give and take" that goes on between state high courts – and likely federal Courts of Appeals – and the US Supreme Court.

---

[80] To be fair, the statutes in Louisiana that were challenged were different in many cases compared with that of Illinois and Massachusetts, so it is a bit of an apples to oranges comparison given the difference in docket composition among the three states.

[81] Unfortunately, the Massachusetts Supreme Judicial Court was not given much additional guidance on how to interpret Second Amendment claims as requested. Rather, their decision was reversed on extremely narrow grounds, substantially limiting the applicability of the US Supreme Court's opinion.

8

Concluding Thoughts and Future Extensions

In this chapter we briefly summarize the findings of the three previous empirical chapters, and tie the empirical results back to our central theory. We also discuss important lessons for future research in the area of judicial implementation and impact. Finally, we chart out a course for future research directions that we believe are derived directly from the theory and results found earlier in the book. As we expand upon below, we believe that future work analyzing how lower courts respond to US Supreme Court precedents should consider all possible ways that lower courts can respond to precedent. This includes the possibility of ignoring US Supreme Court precedent. In this vein, we also argue that future work examining how lower courts explicitly respond to precedents should use a nominal-based measure to best examine the full range of responses that a lower court can use to respond to relevant precedents.

8.1 PURPOSE AND GENERAL FINDINGS OF THE BOOK

As readers may recall, the purpose of this book is threefold. First, we develop a new theory regarding how state high courts can choose to respond to US Supreme Court precedent.[1] As a part of developing this theory, we argue that state high courts are in a unique position due to the fact that they are both superior courts for state-related issues *and* inferior courts (to the US Supreme Court) for federal issues. This particular position gives state high courts an

---

[1] This theory is generalizable, in basic principle, to any court that is at least partially an "inferior court" and that is part of a judicial hierarchy. Thus, it does not apply to the US Supreme Court, but would apply to all other courts dealing with US Supreme Court precedent. However, as an important caveat, we believe that any effects and ability for lower courts to act "independently" will be somewhat reduced when it exists in a purely vertical relationship. Such would be true of the US Courts of Appeals, in particular.

immense degree of both discretion and power when determining how, and when, to use US Supreme Court precedents. Second, we use a simple and highly replicable measurement strategy to determine most appropriately how state high courts actually deal with US Supreme Court precedents. This represents a departure from most previous work examining how lower courts treat US Supreme Court precedent in two ways: the examination of cases where state high courts ignore a relevant precedent and the use of a nominal measure.[2] In the measurement chapter, we made a strong argument that using a nominal measure to understand treatment is more appropriate compared with an ordinal (or dichotomous) one. We believe that our measurement strategy more accurately reflects how inferior courts would potentially deal with US Supreme Court precedents. Third, we empirically tested our new theory and measurement approach across a broad range of substantive legal areas. To accomplish this, we examined state high court reactions to US Supreme Court precedents from a death penalty case, an Establishment Clause case, and two interlinked Second Amendment cases. Examining the results from the cases in these three areas, we find compelling evidence in favor of the idea that state high courts enjoy enormous degrees of discretion when it comes to how they deal with precedents from the US Supreme Court, in line with the expectations of our new theoretical framework.

We leverage different research strategies to provide additional insight as to the scope of the questions that we are examining, and to allow us to look at our key questions in new and fascinating ways. This is especially the case in Chapter 2, which provides a historical analysis of the history of precedent as a legal concept. Chapter 2 also provides historical context for our general understanding of how courts deal with precedent from the time that it is created into the future, with particular insights on reasons why state high courts occupy this unique position in the judicial hierarchy. Chapters 5 and 6 use statistical analyses to examine how state high courts have responded to two US Supreme Court precedents: *Atkins* v. *Virginia* and *Lemon* v. *Kurtzman*. Finally, Chapter 7 uses a qualitative case study-based approach to examine how three state high courts have used *District of Columbia* v. *Heller* and *McDonald* v. *City of Chicago* in different ways.[3]

---

[2] While we are the first to introduce both of these innovations in an analysis of state high court reactions to US Supreme Court precedent, Hinkle (2015) has previously introduced the use of a nominal measure in her study of the US Courts of Appeals. However, Hinkle did not include ignored cases in her study.

[3] The three state high courts are the Massachusetts Supreme Judicial Court, the Illinois Supreme Court, and the Louisiana Supreme Court.

Cumulatively, based on the results of all three empirical chapters, we find several general themes. The first theme is probably the least novel, and is that direct attacks (or other forms of outright defiance) by state high courts on US Supreme Court precedents are rather uncommon. State high court opinions acting in an openly defiant manner to the US Supreme Court represent aberrations (Hansford and Spriggs 2006; Johnson 1979; 1987). This is largely the case even with the most controversial and least clear precedent that we examine, *Lemon*. Second, explicit reliance on US Supreme Court precedent is fairly common and occurs in a variety of forms. As scholars have noted in the past, positively treating a precedent does not necessarily mean that a court will decide a case outcome in the same *ideological direction* as the original precedent (Comparato and McClurg 2007; Fix, Kingsland, and Montgomery 2017). In fact, one of the interesting attributes of precedents is that they lay down ground rules for lower court judges to use. Depending on the particular factual circumstances of a case, the same case could promote either liberal or conservative outcomes. Interestingly, it is easy to argue that using a precedent to arrive at either a liberal or conservative outcome can in fact be wholly consistent with what a precedent actually does. For the purpose of our analyses, this distinction between treating precedent and using precedent to reach a *particular* ideological outcome is important for defining the scope of our project, given that we almost exclusively focus on treatment type in this book.[4]

The third general finding is the most important and novel one in our view. We find substantial evidence that state high courts easily can, and do, ignore US Supreme Court precedents, even in cases that are at times fairly similar to the Court precedent itself. We find in our examination of *Atkins* – the clearest of the three sets of precedents we examine – that state high courts ignored *Atkins* roughly 11 percent of the time. Therefore, it should provide the least discretion for state high court justices on how to interpret it, as the basic legal principle from *Atkins* is fairly clear. Additionally, the core of *Atkins* was not strongly challenged, even if the specific implementation instructions to lower

---

4 One reason for this is that there are relatively few occasions where state high courts deal with a case that is incredibly similar to US Supreme Court precedent. Rather, most of the state high court cases that we examine are moderately similar in a factual sense to particular US Supreme Court precedents. According to Braman's (2009) account of analogical reasoning, judges have the most discretion over how to engage in analogical reasoning with cases that are moderately similar to a hypothetical precedent. If cases are quite similar factually to a hypothetical precedent, the precedent is easy to apply. If case are divergent then it is quite easy (objectively) to say that a precedent does not apply. This argument is in line with theories of motivated reasoning from a vast experimental psychology literature.

courts were not incredibly clear. This is magnified significantly with respect to the precedent we examine that affords the most flexibility. *Lemon* has the highest proportion of potential treatments where the precedent was ignored, at approximately 50 percent. In fact, the modal category of treatment of *Lemon* was ignoring it. From a theoretical perspective, this is not especially surprising given that *Lemon* was rather unclear when it was first announced, the US Supreme Court questioned the applicability of *Lemon* on multiple occasions, and various judges and scholars questioned the philosophical viability of such a test over time. Finally, *Heller* and *McDonald* occupy an intermediate position with regard to how often these precedents are ignored (about 34 percent of the time for *Heller* and about 42 percent of the time for *McDonald*). This was the case in our view for a couple of reasons. First, *McDonald* itself really just applies *Heller* to the states, and it would in fact be theoretically possible for state high courts to incorporate it on their own. In the case of *Heller*, many of the cases potentially dealing with it relied on state constitutional provisions as well as state statutes rather than the federal constitution, opening the door for state high courts to decide cases under the adequate and independent state grounds doctrine. We now continue with a brief discussion of notes regarding case selection – including a descriptive examination of state high court treatments of *Alden* v. *Maine*[5] – to address potential case selection concerns in the book. We then conclude with brief summaries of the results from each of the empirical chapters, an examination of the implications that derive from our theory and findings, and discussion of future lines of research that naturally extend from the book.

8.2 CASE SELECTION CONCERNS

We consider this book to be primarily a study of first impression. We believe this study serves in this role and we are hopeful that it will inspire future work to examine more questions related to how lower courts respond to US Supreme Court precedents, as well as examining relationships within judicial hierarchies more broadly. One area of potential limitation as to the generalizability of our study comes from the overall selection of the cases that we use for our empirical examinations in the book. Namely, that we base our empirical analyses of the judicial hierarchy on three specific lines of precedent: one relating to the death penalty, one relating to the Establishment Clause, and one relating to the Second Amendment. One common denominator

---

[5] 527 U.S. 706 (1999).

among all of these general issue areas, and among the specific cases that we use for our analyses, is that they are all relatively salient and are important to the public (Collins and Cooper 2012; Epstein and Segal 2000; Vining Jr and Wilhelm 2011). In Chapter 3 we discussed the assumption that our theory will be most pronounced in explaining state high court decision-making with respect to salient precedents. While we are confident that our theory will hold even in the face of a relaxation of this assumption – albeit potentially in a weaker form – it is important to offer a brief examination of how our theory performs when examining state high court responses to a nonsalient precedent.

8.2.1 *Additional Notes on Case Selection:* Alden v. Maine

One potential concern that comes with the particular case studies we chose to focus on with this book is the concern of generalizability. In particular, the fact that there may be selection bias embedded in our results due to the fact that we chose three cases that were of relatively high interest to the public, and possibly to the US Supreme Court justices themselves. The worry with this concern arises if state high courts systematically treat lower-salience cases differently. In particular, state high courts may *never* choose to ignore US Supreme Court precedents when it comes to treating and discussing less salient US Supreme Court precedents. On the other hand, an argument could also be made that they would *always* ignore nonsalient US Supreme Court precedents given that they might have no compelling need to address them from a legal or strategic perspective. If either of these is the case, then our theory could have limited generalizability. While a detailed analysis of this assumption is beyond the scope of the book for reasons of brevity, we do include descriptive statistics regarding a less salient precedent: *Alden* v. *Maine*.[6]

Alden v. *Maine* is an Eleventh Amendment sovereign immunity case addressing when Congress could use its Article I powers to strip state sovereign immunity. In particular, the US Supreme Court was asked to decide if the Congress could abrogate sovereign immunity when it came to enforcing the Fair Labor Standards Act (FLSA). In this divided 5–4 decision, the US Supreme Court ultimately stated that Congress could not abrogate sovereign immunity to allow residents of a state to sue a nonconsenting state in its own state courts to achieve financial damages based on violations of federal law.[7]

---

[6] 527 U.S. 706 (1999).
[7] The Court has uphold some limited circumstances under which Congress can abrogate sovereign immunity. See, e.g., *Fitzpatrick* v. *Bitzer*, 427 U.S. 445 (1976) (allowing abrogation

For our descriptive analysis, we adopted a procedure mirroring that used in Chapters 5–7 to locate the universe of relevant cases. Specifically, we executed a LexisNexis search on the phrase "state sovereign immunity." After locating all state high court cases between 1999 and 2018, we then manually culled cases that did not relate to attempted Congressional abrogations of state sovereign immunity. We were left with an *n* of 142 state high court cases that did (or could have plausibly) cited *Alden*. Of the 142, we found 1 state high court case that negatively treated *Alden* (less than 1 percent), 78 that ignored *Alden* (about 55 percent), 45 that cited *Alden* (about 32 percent), and 16 that treated *Alden* positively (about 11 percent). In fact, what these basic descriptive statistics suggest is that at least for this one low-salience case, the most common treatment type by state high courts is simply to ignore it. Yet, it is nowhere near all instances where state high courts actually ignored *Alden*. In fact, when comparing the descriptive statistics of *Alden* to that of the three cases that we include, it seems most similar to that of *Lemon*. Given the lack of a clear standard for applying *Alden* to broader questions related to the abrogation of state sovereign immunity, this does not appear to present any evidence of significant difference in treatment based on the salience of the issue alone.

What this finding based on *Alden* suggests is that cases involving low-salience issues may be similar to *Lemon* in terms of how they are treated, and there is a relatively large percentage of incidences where state high courts ignore the precedent. Yet, we want to be careful based on this analysis not to assume too much about other low-salience cases, as they cover a wide variety of issues. In other cases, it may be that state high courts in fact cite or rely on said Supreme Court precedent much more regularly. Most importantly for our analysis, we find no evidence based on this example that cases that are of lower salience are treated systematically differently compared with those that are more salient.

8.3 SUMMARY OF SPECIFIC FINDINGS FROM OUR APPLICATIONS

This section details the empirical findings from each of our application chapters. While certain specific elements of our findings vary across the empirical chapters in the book, one common theme is the fact that state high courts consistently ignore relevant US Supreme Court precedent for

---

of sovereign immunity under the Fourteenth Amendment); *Central Virginia Community College* v. *Katz*, 546 U.S. 356 (2006) (allowing abrogation of sovereign immunity based on the Bankruptcy Clause of Article 1).

systematic reasons. Additionally, we find that specific fact patterns in instant cases consistently exert the strongest impact on how state high courts deal with US Supreme Court precedents. Taken as a whole, we find strong evidence suggesting that both ideological and legal factors systematically affect how state high courts use US Supreme Court precedent.

8.3.1 *Summary of Findings from* Atkins *Chapter*

Our first empirical chapter analyzes and discusses how state high courts have treated and discussed *Atkins* since 2002. In this chapter, we theorize that the state high court environment, the manner in which state high courts have treated *Atkins* in the past, electoral retention mechanisms, and specific facts that relate to the *Atkins* precedent will all help to explain how, and why, state high courts treat (or do not treat) *Atkins*. In this chapter, we show evidence that suggests state high courts vary rather dramatically in how they have dealt with *Atkins*. To get at this point, we provide brief doctrinal analyses of multiple decisions from a few state high courts that show differences in the application of *Atkins* across states and over time.

Our statistical analysis shows that several factors strongly influence how state high courts use and treat *Atkins*. First, we find that the way in which state high courts have treated *Atkins* in the past strongly influences future treatments of the precedent. In particular, state high courts that have tended to rely on *Atkins* in the past become less likely to ignore potential uses of *Atkins* in the future. On the other hand, if a state high court has been less likely to rely on *Atkins* in the past (even if still citing or mentioning the precedent in their opinions), the probability of that state high court ignoring *Atkins* in the future increases.

Unlike the other two sets of precedents that we examine in the book, the fundamental legal rule from *Atkins* is rather clear. Simply put, individuals who are intellectually disabled cannot be given the death penalty. Where *Atkins* is a bit less clear is in terms of how the legal rules are applied to the states. This is the case because *Atkins* itself does not mandate a particular legal test to be used for determining which individuals are intellectually disabled. Rather, it leaves that decision up to the states.[8] In our theory, we argue that a case such as *Atkins*, which couples both a clear legal rule and a flexible application standard, makes it especially easy for state high courts to follow while still

---

[8]   There is a "suggested" model that states can use for determining who is intellectually disabled in the opinion itself, but this specific legal test is not *mandated* by the *Atkins* decision. Rather, state legislatures and state high courts are largely free to develop their own specific tests for determining who is intellectually disabled.

reaching their preferred outcome. In fact, we find that of the three sets of cases in the book, *Atkins* has by far the lowest percentage of instances where state high court opinions ignored the precedent.

8.3.2 *Summary of Findings from* Lemon *Chapter*

Our second empirical chapter examines how state high courts have used *Lemon* since 1973. Similar to the *Atkins* chapter, we theorize that the state environment that a court is in, how a state court has dealt with *Lemon* in the past, and specific case facts that relate to *Lemon* will help to explain when and how state high courts address or ignore *Lemon* in their opinions. This chapter provides several interesting findings. Perhaps the largest single finding is descriptive, that state high courts have ignored *Lemon* quite a bit since its genesis in 1973 (approximately 50 percent of the time it was relevant). In a sense, this is not surprising given that the *Lemon* test covers a wide variety of potential issues within the Establishment Clause, and that there has been substantial disagreement about when *Lemon* should apply in the US Supreme Court itself. State high courts have noted this disagreement on multiple occasions, and have themselves dealt with *Lemon* in divergent ways over time. However, the growing disagreement on the US Supreme Court over the continued validity of *Lemon* is not sufficient by itself to explain this. Where that the case, then we would expect the instances of state high courts ignoring *Lemon* would be growing over time as this criticism increased. However, Figure 6.1 shows that this is not the case as the frequency with which state high courts have ignored *Lemon* has fluctuated over time.

When it comes to specific results regarding *Lemon*, we find at least partial support for several of our hypotheses in the chapter. First, we find that state high courts are much more likely to ignore *Lemon* and less likely to positively treat *Lemon* in cases involving civil suits against churches or religious institutions. While this finding is perhaps not surprising given the ecclesiastical abstention doctrine, we still find cases where state high courts have relied on *Lemon* despite the general trend in this area.[9] Additionally, we find in cases that involve public funds to benefit religious schools (the specific issue in *Lemon*), state high courts were substantially less likely to ignore *Lemon* than otherwise. Finally, we also find partial support for the role of ideology. As the political environment in which a state high court operates becomes more liberal, it is less likely to ignore *Lemon* compared with its counterparts in more

9   See, e.g., *Pfeil v. St. Matthews Evangelical Lutheran Church of the Unaltered St. Augsburg Confession of Worthington*, 877 N.W.2d 538 at 537 (Minn. 2016).

conservative state environments. Finally, we find that the probability of *Lemon* receiving a positive treatment over time increases, which is somewhat counter to what we would expect to find.

8.3.3 *Summary of Findings from Second Amendment Chapter*

The third empirical chapter of our book analyzes state high court responses to *Heller* and *McDonald*. Unlike the previous two chapters, we use a qualitative case study approach to examine how state high courts use these two precedents. We made this decision for two reasons. First, the relatively small number of cases where state courts have had the opportunity to respond to *Heller* and *McDonald* precludes any statistical approaches that would be consistent with both our theoretical and measurement innovations. Second, we believe that it is useful to provide more in-depth insight into how individual states responded to the Supreme Court's Second Amendment decisions. Specifically, while we provide descriptive statistics about the high courts of all fifty states and how they dealt with *Heller* and *McDonald*, our primary focus in this chapter was an examination of the decisions of three state high courts: the Massachusetts Supreme Judicial Court, the Illinois Supreme Court, and the Louisiana Supreme Court. We find that there were substantial differences in the courts' dockets that led to partially divergent results. However, the Massachusetts Supreme Judicial Court and Illinois Supreme Court had somewhat different reactions to *Heller* and *McDonald* despite having Second Amendment-related dockets that were reasonably similar to one another. The descriptive statistics show that in over 30 percent of relevant cases state high courts ignored *Heller* and in roughly 40 percent of relevant cases state high courts ignored *McDonald*, which is an intermediate rate when compared with *Atkins* and *Lemon*. In fact, for a relatively new precedent that the Supreme Court has validated on multiple occasions, we believe that this rate of ignoring *Heller* and *McDonald* is quite high. In fact, even this finding by itself seems noteworthy.

Importantly, the qualitative approach that we take for this chapter reaps several benefits for the book as a whole. We discuss how the three state high courts dealt with *Heller* and *McDonald* over a roughly ten-year period of time. In the case of the Massachusetts Supreme Judicial Court, we find that they tend to discuss both *Heller* and *McDonald* rather extensively, but typically used both precedents to reach liberal conclusions in terms of policy. Depending on the Massachusetts Supreme Judicial Court's specific rulings, using *Heller* to arrive at a liberal outcome may be wholly consistent with appropriate uses of precedent. In the case of the Illinois Supreme Court, the court also interpreted *Heller* and *McDonald* rather positively in general. However, unlike the Massachusetts Supreme Judicial Court, the Illinois Supreme Court used both *Heller* and *McDonald* to invalidate state laws that it found in violation of the Second Amendment. Finally, in the case of the Louisiana Supreme Court, the Court largely used *Heller* and *McDonald* to reinforce state law that actually restricted Second Amendment rights for certain classes of citizens, most notably convicted felons. However, given the fact that *Heller* presumes that certain types of firearm regulations are likely to be constitutional, we believe that upholding this sort of restriction is in tune with the intent of *Heller*, despite the fact that it would arguably result in a liberal decision.[10]

8.4 IMPLICATIONS OF OUR BOOK

Much of the existing literature asserts – theoretically and empirically – that judges use precedent as if treatments fit on an ordinal scale. This ordinal scale typically has three choices: negatively treating precedent, neutrally treating precedent, or positively treating precedent. While work by Hinkle (2015) argues that judges use precedent in a nominal way, Hinkle's work (2015) focuses on the US Courts of Appeal specifically, so the nominal ordering used in this work does not directly translate into findings for state high courts.[11] Our book is also the first to examine state high court treatments of US Supreme Court precedents within a realistic empirical framework that allows for state high court opinions to ignore potentially appropriate uses of precedent, in addition to the conventional positive, neutral, and negative treatment types that many works have used (Corley 2009; Fix, Kingsland, and Montgomery 2017; Hansford and Spriggs 2006; Hansford, Spriggs, and Stenger 2013; Hinkle 2015; Kassow, Songer, and Fix 2012; Spriggs and Hansford 2002).

By making the specific research design and theory choices that we made, we are able to reach several key findings noted above, which have direct implications on a variety of questions that relate to the interplay of law and politics in the study of judicial decision-making. First, we believe that future studies that examine how lower courts treat US Supreme Court precedents should account for the possibility that lower courts can, at least in theory,

---

[10] In any case, when dealing with Second Amendment issues, what is liberal or conservative becomes difficult to determine given the specific facts involved in each case.

[11] Additionally, an early work by Spriggs and Hansford (2002) creates a nominal measure of precedent treatment as applied to the US Supreme Court. Yet, this measure is different from ours in form, in that it does not include citations or neutral treatments. Furthermore, the choice set that they use to examine Supreme Court usage of precedent is vastly different from ours.

ignore US Supreme Court precedent. We show that the determinants of ignoring precedents are systematic, and failing to account for this option may result in varying degrees of error, which may lead to questionable inferences in such studies. Second, we believe that our study serves as a reminder to others that judges, and courts, are involved in the business of matching specific fact patterns to a series of possibly relevant precedents when they write opinions. The specific fact patterns that may emerge in a particular case may be critically important for understanding *why* majority opinons discuss precedents in systematically varying ways. Our findings also reinforce existing research on state high court decision-making, which finds that noting and incorporating specific fact-based patterns is important for understanding how state high courts make decisions.

Finally, a third key theoretical implication that comes from the results of our study relates to a larger question about the role of opinion construction when it comes to judicial implementation and impact. Several recent studies have begun to examine this question in a serious way, including work by Hitt (2016; 2019) and Wofford (2015; 2018; 2019). We believe, given our theoretical argument about the inherent degree of ambiguity in judicial opinions – illustrated by the three lines of precedents that we examine in this book – future work should examine in more detail how vagueness in judicial opinions may lead to differences in the impact of particular precedents over time.[12]

8.5 FUTURE WORK

We believe that future work can build from this book in several ways. First, studies that examine how state high courts deal with one another could be an interesting area of study. While there has been recent work on this subject that finds interesting and important results regarding how state high courts use each others' precedents (Hinkle and Nelson 2016), future work could examine this topic in more detail. One interesting future analysis could focus on whether precedents from state high courts affect how other state high courts respond to US Supreme Court precedents. This could involve an exploration

---

[12] We are not assigning a value judgment as to whether vague opinions are bad (in fact, they arguably have some merits), but merely that precedents that are relatively vague may be used differently by courts compared with precedents that are relatively clear. In fact, earlier work by Fix, Kingsland, and Montgomery (2017) observes this in the case of *Miller v. California*, 413 U.S. 15 (1973). They conclude that the relative vagueness of the precedent may have helped with its acceptance over time. This is the case because precedents that are vague can potentially be interpreted in multiple ways, leading to doctrinal confusion in terms of substantive interpretations, but may also yield a greater degree of acceptance of those exact same precedents due to the inherent flexibility afforded lower courts with respect to their application.

of whether states use precedents from other state high courts that ignore or otherwise avoid direct compliance with new US Supreme Court precedents to help them construct their own legal standards and tests distinct from those handed down by the US Supreme Court. As the anecdotal examination of *Greenwood* in the introduction showed, the New Jersey Supreme Court in its *Hempele* decision was not alone in using its state constitution to grant its citizens greater protection from warrantless search and seizure. Moreover, in line with this potential line of future research, a later case from the Oregon Supreme Court used the New Jersey case as a persuasive precedent in holding that a similar protection existed under its own state constitution.[13]

A second interesting application of the theory espoused in the book would be to examine how the US Courts of Appeals respond to US Supreme Court precedent.[14] The relationship between the Courts of Appeal and the US Supreme Court is somewhat different from that between state high courts and the US Supreme Court. However, we expect that several of the same theoretical arguments that we make regarding state high courts may also apply to US Courts of Appeal. In fact, a future study examining the degree to which the federal courts of appeal ignore US Supreme Court precedent would be of theoretical importance to see if the results are generalizable to other courts where the degree of independence is reduced. Other studies could include additional hierarchical relationships in judiciaries, including the relationship between state high courts and state intermediate appellate courts, as well as examining hierarchical court relationships in other common law countries. Doing so, and focusing on the possibility that lower courts might ignore superior court precedents, would be helpful for generating additional theory and helping both political scientists and legal scholars to think about future research on hierarchical relationships within the judicial branch.

Finally, we believe that additional examinations of lower salience cases would be quite useful for further expansion and testing of the theory that we propose in this book. As we note above, while we believe that including lower-salience cases likely would not dramatically change the results we have seen here, it will only be able to be tested with any degree of certainty through additional future work. Even if the results for lower-salience cases diverge dramatically from what we have seen thus far, we believe this too would be interesting to note for future research.

---

[13] *State v. Lien*, 441 P.3d 185, 191–194 (Or. 2019) ("We are not the first such court to conclude that our state constitution imposes more stringent constraints than the federal constitution, as our references to *Hempele* make clear").

[14] Building from Klein's (2002) book would be a good place to start, at least in terms of how he examines diffusion among the circuits.

Bibliography

Adler, Matthew D. 2001. "State Sovereignty and the Anti-commandeering Cases." *Annals of the American Academy of Political and Social Science* 574(1): 158–172.

Almand, Bond. 1943. "The Supreme Court of Georgia: An Account of Its Delayed Birth." *Georgia Bar Journal* 6: 95.

Alvarez, R Michael, and Jonathan Nagler. 1998. "When Politics and Models Collide: Estimating Models of Multiparty Elections." *American Journal of Political Science* 42(1): 56–96.

Banks, Christopher P. 1991. "The Supreme Court and Precedent: An Analysis of Natural Courts and Reversal Trends." *Judicature* 75(5): 262–268.

Baum, Lawrence. 1978. "Lower-Court Response to Supreme Court Decisions: Reconsidering a Negative Picture." *Justice System Journal* 3(3): 208–219.

Baum, Lawrence. 1997. *The Puzzle of Judicial Behavior*. Ann Arbor, MI: University of Michigan Press.

Baum, Lawrence. 2009. *Judges and Their Audiences: A Perspective on Judicial Behavior*. Princeton, NJ: Princeton University Press.

Beatty, Jerry K. 1971. "State Court Evasion of United States Supreme Court Mandates during the Last Decade of the Warren Court." *Valparaiso University Law Review* 6(3): 260–285.

Benesh, Sara C, and Wendy L Martinek. 2002. "State Supreme Court Decision Making in Confession Cases." *Justice System Journal* 23(1): 109–133.

Benesh, Sara C, and Malia Reddick. 2002. "Overruled: An Event History Analysis of Lower Court Reaction to Supreme Court Alteration of Precedent." *Journal of Politics* 64(2): 534–550.

Berry, William D, Evan J Ringquist, Richard C Fording, and Russell L Hanson. 1998. "Measuring Citizen and Government Ideology in the American States, 1960–93." *American Journal of Political Science* 23(1): 327–348.

Berry, William D, Richard C Fording, Evan J Ringquist, Russell L Hanson, and Carl E Klamer. 2010. "Measuring Citizen and Government Ideology in the U.S. States: A Re-appraisal." *State Politics & Policy Quarterly* 10(2): 117–135.

Bierce, Ambrose. [1911] 2015. The Devil's Dictionary. Project Gutenberg eBook. www .gutenberg.org/files/972/972-h/972-h.htm

Black, Ryan C, and James F Spriggs. 2013. "The Citation and Depreciation of US Supreme Court Precedent." *Journal of Empirical Legal Studies* 10(2): 325–358.

Black, Ryan C, Ryan J Owens, Justin Wedeking, and Patrick C Wohlfarth. 2016. *US Supreme Court Opinions and Their Audiences*. Cambridge: Cambridge University Press.

Blume, John H, Sheri Lynn Johnson, Paul Marcus, and Emily Paavola. 2014. "A Tale of Two (and Possibly Three) *Atkins*: Intellectual Disability and Capital Punishment Twelve Years after the Supreme Court's Creation of a Categorical Bar." *William & Mary Bill of Rights Journal* 23(2): 393–414.

Bonneau, Chris W, and Damon M Cann. 2015. *Voters' Verdicts: Citizens, Campaigns, and Institutions in State Supreme Court Elections*. Charlottesville: University of Virginia Press.

Bonneau, Chris W, and Melinda Gann Hall. 2003. "Predicting Challengers in State Supreme Court Elections: Context and the Politics of Institutional Design." *Political Research Quarterly* 56(3): 337–349.

Bonneau, Chris W, and Melinda Gann Hall. 2009. *In Defense of Judicial Elections*. Abingdon: Routledge.

Boyd, Christina L, and James F Spriggs. 2009. "An Examination of Strategic Anticipation of Appellate Court Preferences by Federal District Court Judges." *Washington University Journal of Law & Policy* 29(1): 37–82.

Brace, Paul, and Brent D Boyea. 2008. "State Public Opinion, the Death Penalty, and the Practice of Electing Judges." *American Journal of Political Science* 52(2): 360–372.

Brace, Paul, and Melinda Gann Hall. 1990. "Neo-institutionalism and Dissent in State Supreme Courts." *Journal of Politics* 52(1): 54–70.

Brace, Paul, and Melinda Gann Hall. 1993. "Integrated Models of Judicial Dissent." *Journal of Politics* 55(4): 914–935.

Brace, Paul, and Melinda Gann Hall. 1995. "Studying Courts Comparatively: The View from the American States." *Political Research Quarterly* 48(1): 5–29.

Brace, Paul R, and Melinda Gann Hall. 1997. "The Interplay of Preferences, Case Facts, Context, and Rules in the Politics of Judicial Choice." *Journal of Politics* 59(4): 1206–1231.

Brace, Paul, and Melinda Gann Hall. 2001. "'Haves' versus 'Have Nots' in State Supreme Courts: Allocating Docket Space and Wins in Power Asymmetric Cases." *Law & Society Review* 35(2): 393–417.

Brace, Paul, Laura Langer, and Melinda Gann Hall. 2000. "Measuring the Preferences of State Supreme Court Judges." *Journal of Politics* 59(4): 387–413.

Braman, Eileen. 2009. *Law, Politics, and Perception: How Policy Preferences Influence Legal Reasoning*. Charlottesville: University of Virginia Press.

Braman, Eileen. 2012. "Embracing Complexity in Law Courts: A Psychological Approach." *Law & Courts Newsletter* 22(3): 18–23.

Brennan Jr, William J. 1977. "State Constitutions and the Protection of Individual Rights." *Harvard Law Review* 90(3): 489–504.

Brunner, Heinrich. 1907. "The Sources of English Law." In *Select Essays in Anglo-American Legal History*, Vol. 2, ed. Committee of the Association of American Law Schools, 7–52. Boston, MA: Little, Brown.

Bueno de Mesquita, Ethan, and Matthew Stephenson. 2002. "Informative Precedent and Intrajudicial Communication." *American Political Science Review* 96(4): 755–766.

Caldarone, Richard P, Brandice Canes-Wrone, and Tom S Clark. 2009. "Partisan Labels and Democratic Accountability: An Analysis of State Supreme Court Abortion Decisions." *Journal of Politics* 71(2): 560–573.

Caminker, Evan H. 1994. "Why Must Inferior Courts Obey Superior Court Precedents?" *Stanford Law Review* 46(4): 817–873.

Canes-Wrone, Brandice, Tom S Clark, and Jason P Kelly. 2014. "Judicial Selection and Death Penalty Decisions." *American Political Science Review* 108(1): 23–39.

Canon, Bradley C. 1973. "Reactions of State Supreme Courts to a US Supreme Court Civil Liberties Decision." *Law & Society Review* 8(1): 109–134.

Canon, Bradley C, and Charles A Johnson. 1999. *Judicial Policies: Implementation and Impact.* Washington, DC: CQ Press.

Canon, Bradley C, and Kenneth Kolson. 1970. "Rural Compliance with Gault: Kentucky, a Case Study." *Journal of Family Law* 10(3): 300–326.

Choper, Jesse H. 2002. "The Endorsement Test: Its Status and Desirability." *Journal of Law & Politics* 18(2): 499–536.

Collins, Todd A, and Christopher A Cooper. 2012. "Case Salience and Media Coverage of Supreme Court Decisions: Toward a New Measure." *Political Research Quarterly* 65(2): 396–407.

Collins, Todd A, and Christopher A Cooper. 2016. "The Case Salience Index, Public Opinion, and Decision Making on the US Supreme Court." *Justice System Journal* 37(3): 232–245.

Comparato, Scott A, and Scott D McClurg. 2007. "A Neo-institutional Explanation of State Supreme Court Responses in Search and Seizure Cases." *American Politics Research* 35(5): 726–754.

Corley, Pamela C. 2009. "Uncertain Precedent: Circuit Court Responses to Supreme Court Plurality Opinions." *American Politics Research* 37(1): 30–49.

Corwin, Edward S. 1949. "The Supreme Court as National School Board." *Law & Contemporary Problems* 14(1): 3–22.

Curry, Todd A, and Michael P Fix. 2019. "May It Please the Twitterverse: The Use of Twitter by State High Court Judges." *Journal of Information Technology & Politics* 16(4): 379–393.

Dahl, Robert A. 1957. "Decision-making in a Democracy: The Supreme Court as a National Policy-Maker." *Journal of Public Law* 6(2): 279–297.

Dear, Jake, and Edward W. Jessen. 2007. "'Followed Rates' and Leading State Cases, 1940–2005." *UC Davis Law Review* 41: 683–711.

Dow, Jay K, and James W Endersby. 2004. "Multinomial Probit and Multinomial Logit: A Comparison of Choice Models for Voting Research." *Electoral Studies* 23(1): 107–122.

Drakeman, Donald L. 2004. "*Reynolds* v. *United States*: The Historical Construction of Constitutional Reality." *Constitutional Commentary* 21(3): 697–726.

Epstein, Lee, and Jeffrey A Segal. 2000. "Measuring Issue Salience." *American Journal of Political Science* 44(1): 66–83.

Ewing, James. 1805. *A Treatise on the Office and Duty of a Justice of the Peace, Sheriff, Coroner, Constable, and of Executors, Administrators, and Guardians: In which Is*

Particularly Laid Down, the Rules for Conducting an Action in the Court for the Trial of Small Causes. Printed, for the author, by James Oram.

Feeley, Malcolm M. 1992. "Hollow Hopes, Flypaper, and Metaphors." *Law & Social Inquiry* 17(4): 745–760.

Feldman, Noah. 2002. "The Intellectual Origins of the Establishment Clause." *New York University Law Review* 77(2): 346–428.

Fix, Michael P. 2014. "Does Deference Depend on Distinction? Issue Salience and Judicial Decision-Making in Administrative Law Cases." *Justice System Journal* 35(2): 122–138.

Fix, Michael P. 2016a. "The Evolution of Obscenity Standards in the Common Law World." *Journal of Comparative Law* 11(2): 75–99.

Fix, Michael P. 2016b. "A Universal Standard for Obscenity? The Importance of Context and Other Considerations." *Justice System Journal* 37(1): 72–88.

Fix, Michael P. 2018. "Understanding the Mechanisms Driving the Evolution of Obscenity Law in Five Common Law Countries." *Journal of Comparative Law* 13(2): 147–163.

Fix, Michael P, Justin T Kingsland, and Matthew D Montgomery. 2017. "The Complexities of State Court Compliance with US Supreme Court Precedent." *Justice System Journal* 38(2): 149–163.

Fountaine, Cynthia L. 1998. "Article III and the Adequate and Independent State Grounds Doctrine." *American University Law Review* 48(5): 1053–1100.

Frank, Jerome. 1945. "The Cult of the Robe." *Saturday Review of Literature* 28: 12–13.

Frost, Amanda. 2015. "Inferiority Complex: Should State Courts Follow Lower Federal Court Precedent on the Meaning of Federal Law." *Vanderbilt Law Review* 68(1): 53–103.

Gerhardt, Michael J. 2005. "Super Precedent." *Minnesota Law Review* 90(5): 1204–1231.

Gerhardt, Michael J. 2011. *The Power of Precedent.* Oxford: Oxford University Press.

Gey, Steven G. 2006. "Reconciling the Supreme Court's Four Establishment Clauses." *University of Pennsylvania Journal of Constitutional Law* 8(4): 725–800.

Gibson, James L, and Michael J Nelson. 2017. "Reconsidering Positivity Theory: What Roles Do Politicization, Ideological Disagreement, and Legal Realism Play in Shaping US Supreme Court Legitimacy?" *Journal of Empirical Legal Studies* 14(3): 592–617.

Gillman, Howard, and Cornell W Clayton. 1999. "Beyond Judicial Attitudes: Institutional Approaches to Supreme Court Decision-Making." In *Supreme Court Decision-Making: New Institutionalist Approaches,* ed. Cornell W Clayton and Howard Gillman, 1–12. Chicago, IL: University of Chicago Press.

Goelzhauser, Greg. 2016. *Choosing State Supreme Court Justices: Merit Selection and the Consequences of Institutional Reform.* Philadelphia, PA: Temple University Press.

Goodhart, Arthur L. 1930. "Case Law in England and America." *Cornell Law Quarterly* 15(2): 173–193.

Hall, Matthew EK. 2010. *The Nature of Supreme Court Power.* Cambridge: Cambridge University Press.

Hall, Matthew EK. 2014. "The Semiconstrained Court: Public Opinion, the Separation of Powers, and the US Supreme Court's Fear of Nonimplementation." *American Journal of Political Science* 58(2): 352–366.

Hall, Melinda Gann. 1987. "Constituent Influence in State Supreme Courts: Conceptual Notes and a Case Study." *Journal of Politics* 49(4): 1117–1124.

Hall, Melinda Gann. 1995. "Justices as Representatives: Elections and Judicial Politics in the American States." *American Politics Quarterly* 23(4): 485–503.

Hall, Melinda Gann. 2001. "State Supreme Courts in American Democracy: Probing the Myths of Judicial Reform." *American Political Science Review* 95(2): 315–330.

Hall, Melinda Gann. 2014. "Representation in State Supreme Courts: Evidence from the Terminal Term." *Political Research Quarterly* 67(2): 335–346.

Hall, Melinda Gann, and Paul Brace. 1989. "Order in the Courts: A Neo-institutional Approach to Judicial Consensus." *Western Political Quarterly* 42(3): 391–407.

Hall, Melinda Gann, and Paul Brace. 1992. "Toward an Integrated Model of Judicial Voting Behavior." *American Politics Quarterly* 20(2): 147–168.

Hall, Melinda Gann, and Paul Brace. 1994. "The Vicissitudes of Death by Decree: Forces Influencing Capital Punishment Decision Making in State Supreme Courts." *Social Science Quarterly* 75(1): 136–155.

Hall, Melinda Gann, and Paul Brace. 1996. "Justices' Responses to Case Facts: An Interactive Model." *American Politics Quarterly* 24(2): 237–261.

Hamilton, Charles V. 1973. *The Bench and the Ballot: Southern Federal Judges and Black Voters*. Oxford: Oxford University Press.

Hansford, Thomas G, and James F Spriggs. 2006. *The Politics of Precedent on the US Supreme Court*. Princeton, NJ: Princeton University Press.

Hansford, Thomas G, James F Spriggs, and Anthony A Stenger. 2013. "The Information Dynamics of Vertical Stare Decisis." *Journal of Politics* 75(4): 894–906.

Healy, Thomas. 2001. "Stare Decisis as a Constitutional Requirement." *West Virginia Law Review* 104(1): 43–121.

Hildreth, Richard. 1854. *Despotism in America: An Inquiry into the Nature, Results, and Legal Basis of the Slave-Holding System*. Boston, MA: J. P. Jewett.

Hinkle, Rachael K. 2015. "Legal Constraint in the US Courts of Appeals." *Journal of Politics* 77(3): 721–735.

Hinkle, Rachael K, and Michael J Nelson. 2016. "The Transmission of Legal Precedent among State Supreme Courts in the Twenty-First Century." *State Politics & Policy Quarterly* 16(4): 391–410.

Hitt, Matthew P. 2016. "Measuring Precedent in a Judicial Hierarchy." *Law & Society Review* 50(1): 57–81.

Hitt, Matthew P. 2019. *Inconsistency and Indecision in the United States Supreme Court*. Ann Arbor: University of Michigan Press.

Hoekstra, Valerie. 2005. "Competing Constraints: State Court Responses to Supreme Court Decisions and Legislation on Wages and Hours." *Political Research Quarterly* 58(2): 317–328.

Holdsworth, William Searle. 1907. "The Year Books." In *Select Essays in Anglo-American Legal History, Vol. 2*, ed. Committee of the Association of American Law Schools, 96–122. Boston, MA: Little, Brown.

Horowitz, Donald L. 1977. *Courts and Social Policy*. Washington, DC: Brookings Institution Press.

Hughes, David A. 2020 "Does Local Journalism Stimulate Voter Participation in State Supreme Court Elections?" *Journal of Law and Courts* 8(1): 95–126.

Jacobi, Tonja, and Emerson H Tiller. 2007. "Legal Doctrine and Political Control." *Journal of Law, Economics, & Organization* 23(2): 326–345.

Johnson, Charles A. 1979. "Lower Court Reactions to Supreme Court Decisions: A Quantitative Examination." *American Journal of Political Science* 23(4): 792–804.

Johnson, Charles A. 1987. "Law, Politics, and Judicial Decision Making: Lower Federal Court Uses of Supreme Court Decisions." *Law & Society Review* 21(2): 325–340.

Joyce, Craig. 1985. "The Rise of the Supreme Court Reporter: An Institutional Perspective on Marshall Court Ascendancy." *Michigan Law Review* 83(5): 1291–1391.

Kassow, Benjamin, Donald R Songer, and Michael P Fix. 2012. "The Influence of Precedent on State Supreme Courts." *Political Research Quarterly* 65(2): 372–384.

Kastellec, Jonathan P. 2018. "How Courts Structure State-Level Representation." *State Politics & Policy Quarterly* 18(1): 27–60.

Kempin, Frederick G. 1959. "Precedent and Stare Decisis: The Critical Years, 1800 to 1850." *American Journal of Legal History* 3(1): 28–54.

Klein, David E. 2002. *Making Law in the United States Courts of Appeals.* Cambridge: Cambridge University Press.

Kropko, Jonathan. 2007. "Choosing· between Multinomial Logit and Multinomial Probit Models for Analysis of Unordered Choice Data." PhD diss. University of North Carolina at Chapel Hill.

Kurland, Philip B. 1979. "The Irrelevance of the Constitution: The Religion Clauses of the First Amendment and the Supreme Court." *Villanova Law Review* 24(1): 3–27.

Kurland, Philip B. 1985. "The Origins of the Religion Clauses of the Constitution." *William and Mary Law Review* 27(5): 839–862.

Landes, William M, and Richard A Posner. 1976. "Legal Precedent: A Theoretical and Empirical Analysis." *Journal of Law and Economics* 19(2): 249–307.

Langer, Laura. 2002. *Judicial Review in State Supreme Courts: A Comparative Study.* New York: SUNY Press.

Leach, W Barton. 1967. "Revisionism in the House of Lords: The Bastion of Rigid Stare Decisis Falls." *Harvard Law Review* 80(4): 797–803.

Lee, Thomas R. 1999. "Stare Decisis in Historical Perspective: From the Founding Era to the Rehnquist Court." *Vanderbilt Law Review* 52(3): 645–735.

Leonard, Meghan E. 2016. "State Legislatures, State High Courts, and Judicial Independence: An Examination of Court-Curbing Legislation in the States." *Justice System Journal* 37(1): 53–62.

Levy, Leonard W. 2017. *The Establishment Clause: Religion and the First Amendment.* Chapel Hill: University of North Carolina Press.

Lewis, James M, and Michael L Vild. 1989. "Controversial Twist of Lemon: The Endorsement Test as the New Establishment Clause Standard." *Notre Dame Law Review* 65(4): 671–698.

Lewis, T Ellis. 1930a. "The History of Judicial Precedent I." *Law Quarterly Review* 46(2): 207–224.

Lewis, T Ellis. 1930b. "The History of Judicial Precedent II." *Law Quarterly Review* 46(3): 341–360.

Lewis, T Ellis. 1931. "The History of Judicial Precedent III." *Law Quarterly Review* 47(3): 411–427.

Lewis, T Ellis. 1932. "The History of Judicial Precedent IV." *Law Quarterly Review* 48(2): 230–246.

Maitland, Frederic William. 1907. "Materials for the History of English Law." In *Select Essays in Anglo-American Legal History, Vol. 2*, ed. Committee of the Association of American Law Schools, 53–96. Boston, MA: Little, Brown.

Mangels, Aurelie T. 2017. "Should Individuals with Severe Mental Illness Continue to be Eligible for the Death Penalty?" *Criminal Justice* 32(3): 9–14.

Manwaring, David R. 1968. "The Impact of *Mapp v. Ohio.*" In *The Supreme Court as a Policy Maker*, ed. David Everson. Carbondale, IL: Public Affairs Bureau of Southern Illinois University.

Martin, Francois Xavier. 1792. *A Collection of Statutes of the Parliament of England in Force in the State of North Carolina.* New Bern: Editor's Press.

Masood, Ali S, and Monica E Lineberger. in press. "United Kingdom, United Courts? Hierarchical Interactions and Attention to Precedent in the British Judiciary." *Political Research Quarterly:* https://doi.org/10.1177/1065912919853368.

Masood, Ali S, Benjamin J Kassow, and Donald R Songer. 2017. "Supreme Court Precedent in a Judicial Hierarchy." *American Politics Research* 45(3): 403–434.

McCann, Michael W. 1992. "Reform Litigation on Trial." *Law & Social Inquiry* 17(4): 715–743.

McConnell, Michael W. 1992. "Religious Participation in Public Programs – Religious Freedom at a Crossroads." *University of Chicago Law Review* 59(1): 115–194.

McConnell, Michael W. 1997. "Stuck with a Lemon." *ABA Journal* 83(2): 46–47.

McKenzie, Mark Jonathan, and Michael A Unger. 2011. "'New Style' Campaigning, Citizen Knowledge, and Sources of Legitimacy for State Courts: A Case Study in Texas." *Politics & Policy* 39(5): 813–834.

Merryman, John Henry. 1953. "The Authority of Authority: What the California Supreme Court Cited in 1950." *Stanford Law Review* 6(4): 613–673.

Murphy, Walter F. 1959. "Lower Court Checks on Supreme Court Power." *American Political Science Review* 53(4): 1017–1031.

Nelson, Caleb. 2001. "Stare Decisis and Demonstrably Erroneous Precedents." *Virginia Law Review* 87(1): 1–84.

Pacelle Jr, Richard L, and Lawrence Baum. 1992. "Supreme Court Authority in the Judiciary: A Study of Remands." *American Politics Quarterly* 20(2): 169–191.

Parker, Tom. 2006. "Alabama Justices Surrender to Judicial Activism." *Birmingham News*, January 1.

Paulsen, Michael A. 1986. "Religion, Equality, and the Constitution: An Equal Protection Approach to Establishment Clause Adjudication." *Notre Dame Law Review* 61(3): 311–371.

Paulsen, Michael Stokes. 1992. "*Lemon* Is Dead." *Case Western Reserve Law Review* 43(3): 795–864.

Paulsen, Michael Stokes. 2007. "Does the Supreme Court's Current Doctrine of Stare Decisis Require Adherence to the Supreme Court's Current Doctrine of Stare Decisis." *North Carolina Law Review* 86(5): 1165–1212.

Peltason, Jack Walter. 1971. *Fifty-Eight Lonely Men: Southern Federal Judges and School Desegregation.* Champaign: University of Illinois Press.

Plouffe, William C., Jr. 2000. "'A Federal Court Holds the Second Amendment Is an Fundamental Right: Jeffersonian Utopia or Apocalypse Now." *University of Memphis Law Review* 30(1): 55–130.

Plucknett, Theodore Frank Thomas. 1929. *A Concise History of the Common Law.* Rochester, NY: Lawyers' Cooperative Publishing Company.

Plucknett, Theodore Frank Thomas. 1932. "The Place of the Legal Professions in the History of English Law." *Law Quarterly Review* 48(3): 328–340.

Pongrace, Paul Earl III. 1993. "Justice Kennedy and the Establishment Clause: The Supreme Court Tries the Coercion Test." *University of Florida Journal of Law & Public Policy* 6(2): 217–230.

Posner, Richard A. 2008. "How Judges Think." Cambridge, MA: Harvard University Press.

Price, Marilyn, and Donna M Norris. 2008. "National Instant Criminal Background Check Improvement Act: Implications for Persons with Mental Illness." *Journal of the American Academy of Psychiatry and the Law* 36(1): 123–130.

Reinsch, Paul Samuel. 1907. "The English Common Law in the Early American Colonies." In *Select Essays in Anglo-American Legal History, Vol. 1*, ed. Committee of the Association of American Law Schools, 367–415. Boston, MA: Little, Brown.

Richardson, Henry Gerald. 1922. "Year Books and Plea Rolls as Sources of Historical Information." *Transactions of the Royal Historical Society* 5: 28–70.

Robinson, Rob. 2013. "Punctuated Equilibrium and the Supreme Court." *Policy Studies Journal* 41(4): 654–681.

Romano, Michael K, and Todd A Curry. 2019. *Creating the Law: State Supreme Court Opinions and the Effect of Audiences.* Abingdon: Routledge.

Romans, Neil T. 1974. "The Role of State Supreme Courts in Judicial Policy Making: *Escobedo, Miranda* and the Use of Judicial Impact Analysis." *Western Political Quarterly* 27(1): 38–59.

Rosenberg, Gerald N. 1991. *The Hollow Hope: Can Courts Bring about Social Change?* Chicago: University of Chicago Press.

Ruben, Eric M., and Saul Cornell. 2015. "Firearm Regionalism and Public Carry: Placing Southern Antebellum Case Law in Context." *Yale Law Journal Forum* 125: 121–135.

Schmidhauser, John R. 1961. "Judicial Behavior and the Sectional Crisis of 1837–1860." *Journal of Politics* 23(4): 615–640.

Scott, Joseph E, David J Eitle, and Sandra Evans Skovron. 1990. "Obscenity and the Law." *Law and Human Behavior* 14(2): 139–150.

Segal, Jeffrey A, and Harold J Spaeth. 2002. *The Supreme Court and the Attitudinal Model Revisited.* Cambridge University Press.

Segall, Eric J. 2012. *Supreme Myths: Why the Supreme Court Is Not a Court and Its Justices Are Not Judges.* Santa Barbara, CA: Praeger.

Songer, Donald R. 1988. "Alternative Approaches to the Study of Judicial Impact: *Miranda* in Five State Courts." *American Politics Quarterly* 16(4): 425–444.

Songer, Donald R, and Reginald S Sheehan. 1990. "Supreme Court Impact on Compliance and Outcomes: *Miranda* and *New York Times* in the United States Courts of Appeals." *Western Political Quarterly* 43(2): 297–316.

Songer, Donald R, Jeffrey A Segal, and Charles M. Cameron. 1994. "The Hierarchy of Justice: Testing a Principal-Agent Model of Supreme Court-Circuit Court Interactions." *American Journal of Political Science* 38(3): 673–696.

Spriggs, James F, and Thomas G Hansford. 2000. "Measuring Legal Change: The Reliability and Validity of Shepard's Citations." *Political Research Quarterly* 53(2): 327–341.

Spriggs, James F, and Thomas G Hansford. 2002. "The US Supreme Court's Incorporation and Interpretation of Precedent." *Law & Society Review* 36(1): 139–160.

Steinman, Adam N. 2008. "What Is the Erie Doctrine? (And What Does It Mean for the Contemporary Politics of Judicial Federalism)." *Notre Dame Law Review* 84(1): 245–330.

Tarr, G Alan. 1977. *Judicial Impact and State Supreme Courts*. Lexington, MA: Lexington Books.

Tarr, G Alan. 2012. *Without Fear or Favor: Judicial Independence and Judicial Accountability in the States*. Stanford, CA: Stanford University Press.

Unah, Isaac, and Ange-Marie Hancock. 2006. "US Supreme Court Decision Making, Case Salience, and the Attitudinal Model." *Law & Policy* 28(3): 295–320.

Veeder, Van Vechten. 1907a. "A Century of English Judicature, 1800–1900." In *Select Essays in Anglo-American Legal History, Vol. 1*, ed. Committee of the Association of American Law Schools, 730–837. Boston, MA: Little, Brown.

Veeder, Van Vechten. 1907b. "The English Reports, 1537–1865." In *Select Essays in Anglo-American Legal History, Vol. 2*, ed. Committee of the Association of American Law Schools, 123–155. Boston, MA: Little, Brown.

Vining Jr, Richard L, and Teena Wilhelm. 2011. "Measuring Case Salience in State Courts of Last Resort." *Political Research Quarterly* 64(3): 559–572.

Wallace, J Clifford. 2001. "The Framers' Establishment Clause: How High the Wall." *Brigham Young University Law Review* 2001(2): 755–772.

Wellford, Shea Sisk. 1994. "Tort Actions against Churches – What Protections Does the First Amendment Provide." *University of Memphis Law Review* 25(1): 193–234.

Westerland, Chad, Jeffrey A Segal, Lee Epstein, Charles M Cameron, and Scott Comparato. 2010. "Strategic Defiance and Compliance in the US Courts of Appeals." *American Journal of Political Science* 54(4): 891–905.

Wilkes Jr, Donald E. 1973. "The New Federalism in Criminal Procedure: State Court Evasion of the Burger Court." *Kentucky Law Journal* 62(2): 421–451.

Williams, EK. 1926. "Stare Decisis." *Canadian Bar Review* 4(5): 289–301.

Windett, Jason H, Jeffrey J Harden, and Matthew EK Hall. 2015. "Estimating Dynamic Ideal Points for State Supreme Courts." *Political Analysis* 23(3): 461–469.

Wise, Edward M. 1974. "The Doctrine of Stare Decisis." *Wayne Law Review* 21(4): 1043–1060.

Wofford, Claire B. 2015. "Assessing the Anecdotes: Amicus Curiae, Legal Rules, and the US Supreme Court." *Justice System Journal* 36(3): 274–294.

Wofford, Claire B. 2018. "Says Who? Case Participants and Legal Doctrine in the US Supreme Court." *Journal of Political Science* 46: 35–65.

Wofford, Claire B. 2019. "The Structure of Legal Doctrine in a Judicial Hierarchy." *Journal of Law and Courts* 7(2): 263–280.

Zane, John Maxcy. 1907. "The Five Ages of the Bench and Bar in England." In *Select Essays in Anglo-American Legal History, Vol. 1*, ed. Committee of the Association of American Law Schools, 625–739. Boston, MA: Little, Brown.

Index

CPSIA information can be obtained
at www.ICGtesting.com
Printed in the USA
LVHW080228050920
665117LV00016B/385